D0325868

3/02

If We're So in Love, Why Aren't We Happy?

*Using Spiritual Principles
to Solve Real Problems
and Restore Your Passion*

Also by Susan Page

*Using Spiritual
Principles to
Solve Real
Problems and
Restore Your
Passion*

Susan
Page

HARMONY BOOKS
NEW YORK

If
We're
So
in Love,

Why
Aren't
We
Happy?

Published by Harmony Books, New York, New York.
Member of the Crown Publishing Group, a division of
Random House, Inc.
www.randomhouse.com

HARMONY BOOKS is a registered trademark and the Harmony
Books colophon is a trademark of Random House, Inc.

Printed in the United States of America

Design by Jennifer Ann Daddio

Library of Congress Cataloging-in-Publication Data
Page, Susan.
    If we're so in love, why aren't we happy? : using spiritual
principles to solve real problems and restore your passion / by
Susan Page.
        p. cm.
    Includes bibliographical references.
    1. Married people—Psychology. 2. Marital conflict. 3. Spiritual
life. I. Title.
HQ734.P16 2002
291.4'41—dc21   2001039694

ISBN 0-609-60696-4

10 9 8 7 6 5 4 3 2 1

First Edition

For Nicole and Luke,
Beau and Travis,
Gabriel and Rachel,
Noah, Gibson, Eloise,
and Calista

May their times be
even more spiritually
informed than ours.

*"Slight shifts in imagination
have more impact on living
than major efforts at change."*
THOMAS MOORE

Contents

✍ Part II: The Five Sacred Acts of Spiritual Partnership

✍ Part III: Deepening Spiritual Partnership

If We're So in Love, Why Aren't We Happy?

Using Spiritual Principles to Solve Real Problems and Restore Your Passion

Introduction

Why Aren't We Happy?

Why is it difficult for many couples to sustain the love that brought them together in the first place?

There are numerous answers to this question. The one on which we will focus in this book is that we are unhappy because we don't know enough about how to love.

In this era of self-help books and workshops, many of us have mastered better ways to communicate and negotiate. We have learned the importance of standing up for ourselves and of being fair and reasonable with each other. These are important skills, but, I submit, they are not enough. What's missing is compassion, acceptance, tolerance, appreciation—in short, love.

If we were to divide modern relationships into three historic stages, with stage one being the classic fifties model of homemaker and breadwinner, the second stage would be our rebellion against the inadequacies of that model. In stage two we struggled to achieve equality between the sexes and a broader range of acceptable relationship lifestyles. For decades now we have focused a great deal of attention on equality and fairness in our relationships, on better communication and conflict resolution techniques. Although not every individual marriage has achieved these ideals, the model of equality and fairness in relationships is widely accepted and practiced.

I believe that we are ready now for stage three, when we will build upon the equality and fairness that we achieved in stage two and move beyond it. In stage three the emphasis will be on love.

When my husband taught ceramics, he used to draw on the blackboard a figure that looked like an hourglass. The bottom half of the hourglass, he would say, is learning the basics. You follow all the rules carefully to achieve competence at designing, throwing, glazing, and firing a pot. Then he would point to the middle of the hourglass and say, "This is the pinnacle of mediocrity." Your ceramic pots are competent, but they are not imaginative, individual, magical; they don't yet transcend the ordinary. However, it is only when you have mastered fundamental skills and achieved this "pinnacle of mediocrity" that you can burst through to levels beyond that to express your true individual creativity.

In relationship theory today, we hover at the center of the hourglass, the pinnacle of "equal, fair, open, honest relationships." These are important values, but if we stop with them, we risk limiting our relationships to the "ordinary."

Times have changed dramatically since the ideal of romantic love planted itself firmly in our collective psyche. As spiritual writer Gary Zukav observed, "When the evolutionary archetype of marriage was created for our species, the dynamic of conscious spiritual growth was far too mature a concept to be included." Now that human endeavor has advanced to a time in which spiritual consciousness is rising, we understand that love is not limited to passion and good communication, but that it includes a spiritual dimension as well. It is that spiritual dimension that we will explore in depth in this book, and it is for that reason that I have chosen to call stage three couples "Spiritual Partners."

Spiritual Partnership is *not* simply a bigger and better version of the fair and equal relationships we have valued for years. Spiritual Partnership is qualitatively different. You are about to discover some methods and techniques for resolving differences that, I strongly suspect, you have never tried before. You will not be invited to sit down with your partner and talk things out. In fact, spiritual problem solving methods do not involve communication at all! They involve finding out what it means to love, and putting that love into action. Love for yourself, and love for your partner.

And they work! As one man said to me, "We were on the verge of divorce until we began to practice Spiritual Partnership. It was so much easier than we ever dreamed it could be. And now, when I tell my wife I love her, the words truly seem inadequate for how I feel."

No matter where you are now in your journey of love, may this book open your eyes to new ways of being together and bring you all the love you seek.

Part I

Using Spiritual Principles to Solve Real Problems

ONE

Spiritual Partnership: An Overview

The Promise of Extraordinary Change in Your Relationship

Spiritual Partnership is a radically different approach to relationships. It is based on the simple idea that if you focus on behaving in a spiritual way *yourself,* rather than on fixing your relationship or your partner, then you, your partner, and your relationship will be happier and stronger. In addition, you will be furthering your own spiritual growth every day, right where it matters most—in your relationship. We might think of Spiritual Partnership as "applied spirituality." (We will have to use the word "spiritual" here in Chapter One before we have fully defined it, but Chapter Two will fill in that gap.)

For decades we have been operating in accord with the fundamental misunderstanding that the skills we use in the marketplace—like negotiating, bargaining, and reaching agreements—will work in love relationships. They won't. The purpose of the marketplace is to gain advantage; the purpose of love is to love. They are two different universes.

Spiritual Partnership allows you to move beyond conventional wisdom about how to improve relationships. For example, one common axiom is that couples must have good communication. This statement is not false, but it is limited. Even if you can achieve good communication, which is not easy, communication will take you only so far. Because communication is a limited tool, it brings about limited results. Spiritual Partnership teaches you to use "Sacred Actions," *instead of* communication, to resolve your conflicts and reignite your love. Effective communication does not create a spiritual bond but rather flows from it.

Also, most relationship techniques center on helping couples solve their problems. Spiritual Partnership helps couples not to *solve* their problems, but to achieve a new perspective that will allow them to *outgrow* their problems. As we will see, not only is problem solving a limited approach, it often moves a couple in precisely the wrong direction, for they become focused on their problems. Spiritual Partnership suggests a softer, more effective style.

Unlike traditional approaches to relationships, Spiritual Partnership works fast. It does not depend on the development of skills that take months to learn. Nor does it require in-depth exploration of one's past. Instead, Spiritual Partnership fosters a dramatic inner shift on the part of one or both partners. It is impossible to practice Spiritual Partnership seriously and not see changes in your relationship.

"I was blind, but now I see," said Sarah, after three weeks in a Spiritual Partnership group.

"In my wildest fantasy, I couldn't imagine feeling as warm and loving toward Anne as I do now," said Phillip, whose wife was relentlessly critical. He had been in a group for just two weeks.

In my Spiritual Partnership groups, I invite couples to meet once a week for ten weeks. Each week, every person in the group is invited to experiment with one or more Sacred Actions and then to report the results the following week.

"We were ready to divorce," wrote Geneen after completing a ten-week group:

> I couldn't imagine I would ever say this, but Spiritual Partnership saved our marriage. I was extremely skeptical, but I was willing to try a few experiments. What shifted for me is that I stopped expecting Greg to change. I saw for the first time some changes I could make. I didn't resent making them, because I saw that they were a spiritual choice for me, they were making me into more the person I wanted to be; I just didn't know how before. Learning Spiritual Partnership did more for us than three years of therapy, where all we did was keep rehashing the same old problems.

In this chapter I will:

- Explain how Spiritual Partnership goes beyond conventional wisdom about relationships, and why it works
- Introduce the concept of relationship as a spiritual practice
- Address the doubts people often have when they first encounter Spiritual Partnership
- Describe the origins and evolution of Spiritual Partnership and place it in context
- Clarify the idea of "experiments" I will use throughout the book

How Spiritual Partnership Goes Beyond
Conventional Relationship Strategies

Conventional Wisdom

Carole and Kit had been fighting for eight years about his spending too much time on the golf course and neglecting his family. Carole repeatedly used the only tools she knew of: she negotiated with Kit, appealed to his sense of fair play, communicated her own needs. Her ultimate goal was to persuade Kit to change. Kit made small concessions, but Carole always felt that she was losing, that her only choice was to give up and give in. She felt defeated, and powerless.

Spiritual Partnership

Then Carole came to a Spiritual Partnership group. She learned to stop seeing the situation as "right" vs. "wrong," to experiment with showing a spirit of goodwill, to create good family times that did not interfere with golf games, and to understand and accept the hole that golf helped fill in her husband's life.

We were not encouraging Carole to give up her needs or to give in to her husband. Quite the opposite—extending love and goodwill to Kit *empowered* her. By acting in accord with spiritual values, Carole was no longer at the mercy of Kit and his desires and needs. She found she could support him and support herself at the same time. The more she actively extended love to Kit, the more she was her own agent, and the happier and stronger she felt.

Carole was being loving, not as a strategy, not as an emotional bargain—I'll be nice to you, now you better be nice to me back!—but as an expression of her spiritual beliefs. When she removed the rules of negotiation and the expectation of fairness from their relationship, she experienced unmitigated love for Kit. This surge of emotion surprised her.

Kit responded warmly to Carole's changed attitude. He adored her for giving up her resentment, and he showed his appreciation. Their love life took on new sparkle. They became romantic again. They planned family outings. Eventually, Kit did cut back on his golf, because he preferred going camping with the family as his children grew older.

LOVE VS. NEGOTIATION

Our culture has not taught us to love openly and freely, and as a result the idea seems bizarre, frightening, and, well, unfair. It seems naive. Because most of us were parented imperfectly and have been through painful "love" experiences in our adult lives, we have few models for spiritually informed love. Instead, as writer Jane Smiley points out in "Why Do We Marry?", an article in *Harper's* magazine, we bring into marriage the models we have learned so well in the capitalist marketplace.

> We are often advised to become good negotiators in our relationships—that is, to communicate specifically and explicitly, to be fair in divvying up responsibilities, and to understand that relationships are like contracts. . . . But bargaining . . . implies a zero-sum situation in which domestic life is a life of limits and real or potential deprivation. Bargaining in the home shares the limitation of bargaining in the marketplace. Advantage can be gained by being dishonest or secretive, or by withholding a desired object. A bargain can never truly be fair, and so it focuses the minds of the bargainers on inequities and betrayals.

Since marriage is not about gaining or winning, the rules of the marketplace will never work there. Marriage and loving partnerships are for something else altogether: they are for learning how to give and receive love. That's all. Restraint, conscious choice, self-responsibility, acceptance, and compassion—the Five Sacred Acts of Love—are not bargaining chips. When you offer them freely, with no strings attached, you will experience them in return, no matter what the response from other people is, because you will be experiencing your own strong and loving self.

Suppose you act lovingly and your partner does not respond in kind. You have still been loving, in accord with your spiritual practice, and your kind, loving behavior is its own reward. Does the Dalai Lama stop behaving with compassion, acceptance, and restraint because the Chinese still occupy Tibet?

To live in accord with spiritual values is to live by choice and awareness, rather than in reaction to the people around you.

Chances are, the marketplace rules of negotiating and communicating have not produced desired results in your relationship anyway. Stop and think for a minute. What is the biggest source of conflict in your relationship? How far have you come in resolving it by using communication?

It is appropriate to ask yourself, "Is this the person with whom I want to learn how to love?" If you aren't sure, experimenting with the Five Sacred Acts of Love will help you decide. But whatever the nature of your commitment with each other, if you choose to bring your spiritual practice into your relationship, your only question is, "How well can I love this person?" You are not loving as a strategy to gain certain specific results, but the "results" of love are likely to be richly rewarding.

Behaving lovingly toward your partner is not a vague concept; this book will show you exactly how to do it. Since most of us lack models of pure love in our personal lives, we need guide-lines. The guidelines in this book *don't require you to change the way you feel;* they require only that you are willing to experiment with new behavior: the Five Sacred Acts of Love. For most people, acts of love are easier to learn than complex communi-cations skills, and they have much more far-reaching and long-lasting effects.

The rewards of loving go far beyond the very best you can achieve using the old rules. The couples I studied for my second book, *Eight Essential Traits of Couples Who Thrive,* were thriving precisely because they focused on loving each other, in a spirit of goodwill, not in a spirit of "Am I getting my fair share?" While couples around them were busy negotiating with each other, these couples were learning how to love.

Focusing on love rather than on negotiation makes a stagger-ing difference. It's what Spiritual Partnership is all about, and it is a revolution in relationships, like moving from certainty that the earth is flat to the radical idea that it is round. All the assumptions change; all the rules change; all the ways of mea-suring results change. There was resistance to that new idea, and there will be resistance to this one too. I will address some of the most frequently asked questions below. But the only way to find out whether Spiritual Partnership is right for you is to try it.

Let us look at specific ways in which Spiritual Partnership is different from the models and assumptions most of us still carry around in our head. For simplicity, I will call our current wide-spread assumptions the "Old Model."

In the Old Model you make progress by talking things through together.

In Spiritual Partnership you make progress by choosing spir-itual actions—by yourself.

In the Old Model your goal is to solve your problems.

In Spiritual Partnership the goal is to outgrow problems by achieving a new level of consciousness.

In the Old Model the goal is to improve the relationship, to move from dysfunctional to functional to thriving.

In Spiritual Partnership the goal is for each partner to grow spiritually.

In the Old Model you strive to fulfill the old rules: equality and fairness.

In Spiritual Partnership you strive by yourself to achieve a balance between your own needs and those of your partner.

In the Old Model you solve problems by encouraging your partner to change.

In Spiritual Partnership you encourage yourself to change.

In the Old Model you focus on the differences between you. You ask, "How can we fix what's wrong?"

In Spiritual Partnership you look for commonality, oneness, unity. You ask, "How are we both part of the human experience? How are we the same?"

In the Old Model you rely on the mind. You figure things out, come up with strategies, make decisions, stay in control; you create a lot of noise in your head.

In Spiritual Partnership you quiet the mind. You rely on inner wisdom from your body. You stop trying to figure things out and change them, and instead you pay attention to what is.

In the Old Model your continuing search for improvement keeps you in a state of discontent; you believe you can do better.

In Spiritual Partnership the state of discontent is the problem. You begin with acceptance.

In the Old Model change is slow and incremental. Old habits die hard. Progress is gradual.

In Spiritual Partnership an inner shift may create "miraculous" change in one moment. You experience quantum leaps. "I was blind, but now I see."

In the Old Model there are limits on how happy two people can be together over many years.

In Spiritual Partnership the joy of connection is unlimited.

In the Old Model relationships are hard work.

In Spiritual Partnership spiritual growth is hard work; relationships are a pleasure.

In the Old Model you believe that you have to be married to the right person.

In Spiritual Partnership you know that more important than having the right partner is being the right partner.

In the Old Model, if you want more from your partner, you must learn to ask for what you want.

In Spiritual Partnership, if you want more, give more.

In the Old Model it is impossible to work on the relationship or make any progress unless both parties are willing to talk.

In Spiritual Partnership one partner on a spiritual journey can create significant changes in a relationship, by

> *choosing unilateral spiritual actions, by offering spiri-*
> *tual leadership, often without saying a word.*

In the Old Model you approach problems by asking, "Who's right and who's wrong? Who needs to change?"

> *In Spiritual Partnership being right doesn't matter. You*
> *approach problems by asking, "No matter who is right,*
> *what can I do to make a difference?"*

Your Relationship as a Spiritual Practice

We are not used to thinking of our relationships as a spiritual practice. When we think of a "spiritual practice," we usually mean something like meditation, prayer, religious practice, reading sacred scriptures, journal writing, dream work, or developing a connection with a spiritual teacher.

The supposition throughout this book is that you can make your relationship itself an active part of your spiritual practice. If you already have a spiritual practice, you are invited to add this to it; if not, your relationship is a fine place to begin a spiritual practice. Just as you might learn how to meditate and then engage in the "practice" of meditating for many years, in this book you will learn about "Spiritual Partnership" and be invited to practice it for many years. With meditation, Spiritual Partnership, or any spiritual practice, you will learn more about yourself and your relationship to the divine, discover your resistance to spiritual growth and move through that resistance, and ultimately become a happier and more loving person.

> *Relationship is probably the most powerful spiritual path that*
> *exists in the world today. It's the greatest tool that we have. Our*

relationships can be the fastest and the most powerful route to the deepest truth, if we know how to use them.

—SHAKTI GAWAIN

Some spiritual groups create special circumstances to help them focus their spiritual practice. For example, the San Francisco Zen Center maintains a mountain retreat center where students are invited to become part of the staff. As they clean the rooms, garden, prepare meals, and put fresh flowers everywhere, they are "practicing" being mindful and reverent. I know of a Gurdjieff study group whose members volunteer in a high-stress kitchen for long hours on "practice" weekends so that together they can pay close attention to the feelings and behavior that this stress evokes.

Spiritual Partnership is simply the act of treating your relationship as a real-life laboratory for spiritual practice. Your relationship evokes certain emotions and behavior that you can pay attention to and learn from.

The term "practice" has a dual meaning when used in the phrase "spiritual practice." It means vocation or way of life, the way a doctor "practices" medicine. But it also means learning by doing. If you "practice" being loving, nonjudgmental, accepting, and forgiving in all of your life, then when you are faced with a difficult situation, you will be more likely to respond in a spiritual way, because you will be practiced. When Gandhi was suddenly confronted by his assassins, he didn't say, "Oh damn!" The words that sprang naturally to his lips were the sacred mantra that he had used in meditation for many years.

In an ongoing love relationship, you have many opportunities to practice the spiritual principles you are learning. My guitar teacher used to tell us, "Never practice your guitar!" Of course, what he meant was, whenever you play your guitar, you are playing it, not practicing it. Just like relationships. You get to "practice" being your best spiritual self all the time.

One advantage of using your relationship as a spiritual practice is that it does not require extra time; instead, it means making small changes, one at a time, in activities that you are already doing. You won't have to set aside several hours for you and your partner to do contrived exercises. There are no long, written questionnaires, no self-tests. Except for a few experiments I will suggest from time to time that might involve meditation or journal writing, you won't need to set aside extra time every day. You will need discipline, but not the kind that takes extra time.

Spiritual Partnership can change your relationship very quickly. Most couples experience positive changes as soon as they decide to practice it in a deliberate way. The *spiritual* goals of your journey—like deep self-knowledge or an expanded capacity for compassion and forgiveness—may be achieved gradually over many months and years, but wonderful changes in your *relationship* are likely to appear right away.

Spiritual Partnership at Work:
Karen and Al

Karen and Al were in love and had a solid relationship, but a big problem was beginning to undermine it: Since Karen got a troublesome new boss, Al had been trying to convince her to quit her job.

When Karen came home at night, exasperated, wanting to tell Al the outrageous things this new boss had done, Al was critical. He told her, "You just lack the courage to make a change. Don't be so afraid. Just leave. This company doesn't own you. Take a break. Get back to the writing you're so eager to do."

Karen didn't agree that they could manage without her

income, even for a short while, and there was much that she valued about her job. At first, she and Al carefully tried to use all the communication techniques they had learned. But Karen was better at using them than Al was, although he was trying hard. She would become furious when he didn't listen, didn't accurately reflect back what she had said, interrupted her, and made "you" statements instead of "I" statements. Now they were arguing not only about the job, but also about their communication process! And they each seemed to become more deeply entrenched in their positions.

Al had been meditating for several years, and he decided to participate in one of my ongoing groups, to learn about Spiritual Partnership. When he arrived, he felt angry and stuck. He felt that he was being truly supportive of Karen and, given their impasse, had no idea how to proceed.

I suggested to Al that he experiment with the spiritual practice of using restraint, the First Sacred Act, which we will discuss in Chapter Five. In response, he made a pact with himself that for two weeks, he would refrain from making any negative, critical, or demanding comments to Karen.

One week later he returned to the group with this report:

> The atmosphere in our house changed completely overnight. At first we were just quiet. About the third day, I was struck with the realization that, while I had been blaming Karen for all of our recent problems, in fact I was the cause of all the upset. When I simply didn't say anything, the arguing disappeared. I still thought she was wrong, but we were being nice to each other again. We both loved this.

Over the next weeks, as Al began to practice several other Sacred Acts—such as "acting as if," acting alone, acceptance, and compassion—he had a second major insight: He saw that

Karen had a right to her position. He moved from thinking that she was wrong, to seeing that both of their points of view might have validity.

As Al continued to practice the Sacred Act of compassion over a period of weeks, he began to look behind Karen's position to the person Karen was. He realized Karen's father had quit a job once, catapulting the family into a period of poverty and chaos. He saw that security was an extremely high priority for her. He felt compassion for Karen, and accepted that she was doing what was right *for her.* As a deliberate act of will, he stopped making any suggestions to her about her work life.

The epilogue to this story is that, after eighteen months, Karen was promoted to take the place of the boss who caused her so much trouble. She created flextime scheduling for her whole department, allowing her to work four days instead of five, and she rented a small cabin to use as a writing studio, where she unfailingly spent that fifth day every week.

Because Al focused on his own spiritual behavior and stopped trying to solve the problem, the distance that had threatened their happiness was gone.

WHICH COMES FIRST: SPIRITUALITY OR RELATIONSHIP?

I am often asked this question: In Spiritual Partnership, which is more important: each individual's spiritual growth, or the relationship? Which comes first?

The two are so intertwined that it doesn't matter.

For example, one of the Sacred Acts we will learn is to practice restraint, as Al did. If your partner yells at you, and you can think quickly enough to be quiet and then to respond later in a nondefensive way, you will have put a spiritual value into use while at the same time making your relationship a more pleasant place to be. Your relationship gave you a chance to act spiritually, to nourish your soul; and your spirituality gave you a chance to improve your relationship. Both at the same time.

So, in your own mind, view your relationship as a way to work on your spiritual life, *or* think of your spiritual life as a way to work on your relationship, whichever works for you. In Spiritual Partnership, love and spiritual growth support each other.

WHY IS RELATIONSHIP A GOOD PLACE TO PRACTICE SPIRITUALITY?

In a rousing presentation I was fortunate to attend, the spiritual writer Iyanla Vanzant told us, "If you want to test your spirituality, fall in love. You can be as spiritual as Buddha when you are by yourself."

Relationship is an excellent place to practice spiritual values because you can be certain they will be tested there. It is in your relationship that you are most likely to feel isolated, to revert to the worst aspects of your personality, and to experience anger, fear, and confusion. So, right then and there, you will have an opportunity to work on these spiritual challenges. Close relationships tend to magnify both your strong and weak points, so you can get a really good look at yourself, if you're paying attention. And you can watch your spiritual "experiments" actually making a difference.

The problem with some spiritual practices is that they don't translate very well into everyday life. You attend a moving ritual, and then repeat the same old patterns with your partner. Spiritual growth can't occur in an isolated setting, apart from the real world, and spiritual practice is useless unless it affects your life on a day-to-day basis.

Whether one leads a spiritual life depends on whether one has been successful in bringing about that disciplined, tamed state of mind and translating that state of mind into one's daily actions . . . True spirituality is a mental attitude that you can practice at any time.

—THE DALAI LAMA

Spirituality is not more and more principles you learn; it is a quality you gradually achieve.

How Spiritual Practice Deepens Connection

If relationship provides a perfect opportunity to practice spirituality, the reverse is also true: A more spiritual "you" will be able to practice relationship at its very finest. *Your soul has the power to love far, far beyond what your personality is capable of.* The more attention you pay to your soul, the more you are motivated by your deepest inner stirrings; and the more you become your most authentic self, the more you will be able to connect with your partner at a deep level.

A woman who was a part of my women's group for several years presented us with a dramatic example of the difference between "personality" and "authentic self" and the impact it can have on relationships. (As we will see in Chapter Two, opening up to your authentic self is an important aspect of the spiritual journey.) As you read this story, consider that this book will help you to deepen your own "authentic self" through spiritual practices, so that your own relationship has a chance to deepen. For you, of course, the specific distancing behavior will be different. But this story can be a metaphor for the way spiritual practice can help you identify the habits that separate you from your authentic self—and therefore from the person or people you deeply love. If you were this woman, what would your protective behavior be?

Because she had an unusually warm demeanor, smiling and encouraging people all the time, we began to call her Florence Nightingale, in a loving way, to help her become aware of how often she rushed in to help and even rescue others in the group. Sometimes, however, her soothing comments were inappropriate because they prevented the person who was speaking from going more deeply into her problem, and thus from perhaps discovering something new about herself.

One week, "Florence" came to the group in a great deal of pain herself; her mother had been diagnosed with cancer. As we helped her express her deepest fears, we all noticed a huge transformation in her. Tears came from the deepest part of her, her face softened, and after she had cried and talked for a time, this face that had been so tightly "happy" began to shine with a radiant beauty we had never seen. Because she had become "real" with us by sharing her own deep vulnerability, an act that required enormous courage and trust on her part, we all felt connected to her and deeply touched. I can recall being overcome with love for her, while before I had found her mildly annoying. Her own experience was similar: She felt much closer to us!

After that group session, this woman spent more of her time with us as her real self. She was still warm and compassionate, but not as afraid, not as tightly wound, and as a result she did not revert to her habitual behavior out of fear. We all remarked about how much easier she was to be around and how much more trusting we felt toward her.

Several weeks later, I recall her saying something like this:

> I thought all my helpfulness would make you like me better. I didn't realize I wasn't being real or honest in some way. I don't

think I ever would have understood this until I had the *experience* of being more authentic, more my true self. I see now that you were all inviting me to be more real, but I had no concept of what you meant. That session was a turning point in my life. I feel a great blindness has been stripped away.

Often, a relationship itself brings you in touch with your authentic self. When you invest yourself in a person and pin hopes and dreams on a certain relationship, you are automatically making yourself vulnerable. It is in the nature of love that you become dependent upon your lover in certain ways. Even though a certain amount of dependency is completely healthy and normal, it can be frightening. This fear is part of the authentic you. Don't run from it because it feels strange and unpleasant; welcome it. Vulnerability always presents you with an opportunity for spiritual growth.

The you that is more real and less "conditioned" almost always feels vulnerable when it first comes out after being buried for a long time. First you feel the vulnerability, the fear, the shame, the sadness. But if you are part of any relationship in which you can experience being fully accepted and loved for the person you truly are, vulnerability and all, you will get to experience the profound pleasure of relaxing into your real, unadorned self, just as my friend "Florence" did. In that state, you are totally lovable. Others are likely to be drawn to you, to feel love for you, and to feel deeply connected.

Now, imagine having an experience like that with someone you already love.

So relationships are a good place for you to focus on your spiritual journey because they give you concrete opportunities to become more authentic. And the relationship you will create as a result of your spiritual work will be deep and genuine.

*Restoring the spiritual dimension to love means abandoning the
notion of a limited self with its limited ability to love and regain-
ing the Self with its unbounded ability to love.*

—DEEPAK CHOPRA

Common Doubts and Questions About Spiritual Partnership

Most people are skeptical when they first hear about such a
"magic" solution to deeply rooted, extremely difficult relationship problems. You may be too, as you read this. Let me address
some of the most common hesitations people have when they
first hear about Spiritual Partnership.

Q: These changes sound superficial. Will they last very long?

A: A profound inner shift to a new way of seeing is something
that never goes away. Of course, people revert to old, habitual
behaviors. But once you see that a new possibility exists, you
can never again be completely in the dark, or pretend that you
didn't once see the light.

Spiritual Partnership is not glib or simplistic. It is a way of
putting into practice centuries of wisdom from the great spiritual
traditions on this planet. We all have demons that separate us
from love; what differs is only the nature of those demons. Your
soul knows how to conquer all of yours.

Like other aspects of our spiritual journey, the growing and
learning in relationships never end. Backsliding is to be
expected.

But Spiritual Partnership helps you slip and slide up the *spiritual* path instead of some other well-meant path of relationship
techniques that will never get you to where you truly want to be.

While most strategies suggest that you make small changes within the old systems of communication and fairness, Spiritual Partnership invites you to shift to a completely new system.

Spiritual Partnership is not a destination, but a path, a journey. Just getting onto the correct path is what feels so good to so many people at the beginning. It feels "magic" because, for most people, it is something they have never tried before and it usually makes a difference quickly.

Q: Spiritual Partnership can't possibly work miracles for everyone. Aren't some partners just plain incompatible?

A: Yes. It is true that some partners will never be truly happy together.

First, relationships don't have to be "good" to be spiritual. We often learn important spiritual lessons from relationships that are difficult and don't last. If you are on a spiritual path, everything that happens presents you with an opportunity to practice and grow. It isn't what happens that makes something spiritual or not spiritual; it's what you learn from what happens that makes the difference.

Pain and difficulty can sometimes serve as the pathway to a new level of involvement. They do not necessarily mean that there is something inherently wrong with the relationship; on the contrary, relationship troubles may be a challenging initiation into intimacy.

When we look at [relationship from the soul's viewpoint], we may find positive value in failures, endings, complexities, doubts, distancing, the desire for separation and freedom, and other troubling aspects.

—THOMAS MOORE, *SOUL MATES*

Second, Spiritual Partnership helps you discover whether you are likely to do well together, and it offers you guidelines for deciding what to do about your relationship.

When you experiment with Sacred Actions, you will see fairly quickly whether your new behavior will bring about any changes, either in you or in your partner. Most likely, changes you never anticipated *will* occur. They have never happened before because *you have never tried this new behavior before*—mainly because you simply never thought of it.

If, after ten or twelve weeks of earnest experiments, no changes at all have come about, you have valuable, *new* information. For example, you may discover you don't feel good acting with loving compassion toward your partner. Or your partner may not respond at all to your loving and compassionate acts. If either or both of these occur, your spiritual response might be to separate.

(A word of caution here: You may think you know exactly what will happen when you try a Sacred Action, but you don't know whether your hypothesis is right until you actually try the experiment. *You will learn, grow, and change, not from thinking about doing a spiritual act, but by actually doing it.* Many couples who expected nothing to change when they tried Spiritual Partnership have been amazed at the positive changes that did occur.)

In the card game bridge there is a play called a "finesse," which is called for in a certain situation. Depending on which player is holding the king, the finesse may succeed or fail. Even if it fails, the finesse was the right thing to do in that situation.

In the same way, if you focus on being the most spiritually evolved partner you can be, in accord with the guidelines in this book, your efforts may preserve your relationship or help you to conclude it. Either way, you were doing the right thing, behaving in accord with your spiritual values. Part of being spiritual, as we shall see in the next chapter, is remaining open to any outcome.

Q: Why do you sometimes work with only one member of a couple? Spiritual Partnership can't possibly work unless both partners practice it, can it?

A: Most strategies for couples require the active cooperation of both partners. Together, you learn to listen, to support, to reach compromises, to resolve conflicts. In contrast, Spiritual Partnership invites you to *act on your own* by bringing your personal spiritual practice right smack into the center of your relationship. It invites you to ask, "If I were going to behave in a spiritual way right now, what would I do?"

So, in fact, Spiritual Partnership *is* something you do by yourself. Nothing I will suggest in this entire book requires the cooperation of your partner. That is precisely why Spiritual Partnership is both easier and more effective than traditional approaches based on communication.

Let's look again at Carole, who was upset by Kit's commitment to golf. When Carole was introduced to Spiritual Partnership, she began by proactively and deliberately accepting what she knew she could never change—not with a feeling of resignation, but in a spirit of love and goodwill, a fundamental spiritual principle. That one shift transformed the atmosphere in the relationship.

As long as your partner is responding positively to your spirit of goodwill and compassion, you don't *both* have to "learn" it. Don't worry, your spirit of love and goodwill will rub off! (If it doesn't rub off *at all*, you may want to reevaluate staying in the relationship.) In fact, by moving far beyond the conventional categories of right, fair, and equal, Spiritual Partnership reaps results that go far beyond those that are *merely* right, fair, and equal.

The idea of "working on your relationship" by yourself is quite radical and may not seem appealing or even possible to you. It's perfectly okay to feel some fear or anxiety about undertaking any of the experiments in this book—by yourself. After all, you may be trying something that runs counter to a lifetime of conditioning. But try not to let your fears stop you from experimenting. Gently allow yourself to try something new, even though you feel afraid. All we are suggesting in Spiritual Partnership is that you take initiative, that you provide some quiet leadership. If you find you are hesitating to experiment—because it feels strange or you're afraid of what might happen—enlist the support of a friend with whom you can talk everything over. Find one small experiment that you feel willing to do, and start with that. Don't feel that you have to change everything all at once.

For some people, being able to work alone is a singular advantage of Spiritual Partnership over other approaches, because they have never been able to move beyond the very first step of convincing their partner to cooperate. If your problem is, "My partner won't go to a counselor," or "My partner will never talk about the problem," then the suggestions in this book are perfectly suited for you; your need for that elusive "talk" is over.

If *both* you and your partner want to embark on Spiritual Partnership, you'll have an exciting time; it works well if you journey together. But if your partner isn't up for it, don't worry. Your partner has a right to be uninterested or unwilling; whatever the reason, that reason is valid for him or her. Respect it.

You can achieve progress in your own spiritual journey using Spiritual Partnership by yourself, and your relationship will reap extraordinary benefits.

Q: I'm worried that Spiritual Partnership is just a dressed-up way of telling women to back down and give in to men. Will Spiritual Partnership take women backward?

A: Let's look again at Carole and Kit. When Carole finally began to accept Kit's passion about golf, it may have looked to an outsider as if Carole finally just gave up and let Kit have his way. She lost. Once again as always, the woman wimped out and the man got his way.

But look closer. Actually, giving up is what Carole had been doing for eight years, under the old "negotiation" system. Negotiation never got her anywhere except resentful. And, in the face of her resentment, Kit never changed. Carole quite literally had no choice but to give in.

When Carole, as a conscious spiritual act and on her own initiative, gave up her fight and became gracious about Kit's golf, everything shifted. And notice, eventually Kit did change!

Carole did not become gracious as a technique to get Kit to change; she did it to experiment with putting pure love into practice. But it was only when she began to provide spiritual leadership in her relationship that genuine changes began to happen.

Did Carole lose? Did Kit get his way? In Spiritual Partnership we don't even ask these questions, which betray the old way of looking at things. Carole succeeded in behaving in accord with her spiritual values; she acted out of love—both self-love and love for Kit. And then whatever happened happened.

Each of us has a little flame deep within us. All of life is an effort to keep that flame burning brightly. Every time you interact with your intimate partner, you are either throwing sand on the flame—or breathing fresh oxygen on it to make it glow brighter. We have somehow acquired the illusion that if we throw enough sand and water on our partner's flame in the guise of being "fair," or of offering "suggestions" (usually criticisms), or of asking for compromise, we will both end up happier. We want changes, and we think "communication" is the only way to effect them.

Instead, "communication" often makes matters worse. Look at it this way: By endlessly "negotiating" with Kit to play golf less, Carole was inadvertently giving him the message, "You are a bad person; you are being unfair and inconsiderate." Kit's little flame was begging for love and support, but was receiving only criticism. It was actually *appropriate* for him to respond to her assaults by defending his behavior, by standing up for his own little flame instead of allowing Carole to squelch it. The old system sets up adversarial positions like this, and we can become trapped in them for years.

What we will see in Spiritual Partnership is that your partner is much more likely to make the changes you would like if you take the initiative to create an atmosphere of love and support, if you deliberately find ways to stoke his or her little flame and help it to burn brightly.

Spiritual Partnership may at first glance look like someone is being asked to give in, to lose, to "sacrifice." But in fact those categories don't exist in Spiritual Partnership—where your task is to find ways to balance self-love and love for your partner.

You are always in control of that balance.

In Spiritual Partnership we learn specific ways to focus more on loving than on being loved, more on understanding than on being understood. Thousands of couples have now learned that when they love more freely and openly, while still taking good care of themselves, love comes flooding back to them, often in greater abundance than they had ever dreamed.

Q: What is the relationship between Spiritual Partnership and psychology?

A: We have just come through several decades in which a psychological model dominated our understanding of relationships. We heard about how hard it is to escape early childhood programming; how we project our own unresolved issues onto our partners; how we subconsciously choose partners who will help us resolve issues with our parents; how our personality type affects our behavior; and how to understand and manage gender differences. We learned how to listen to each other and ask for what we want. We discovered the importance of viewing our families as a "system" in which each person plays an unwitting role in keeping dysfunctional patterns in place.

An important aspect of Spiritual Partnership, as we shall see, is the move toward increasing awareness. Becoming aware of how all of these psychological dynamics affect your own relationships is an important part of Spiritual Partnership. Understanding your own or your partner's personality type, early childhood programming, habitual behaviors, and "dysfunctional patterns" may be an enormous help to you in experiencing acceptance and compassion, in practicing restraint, and in acting on your own—all Sacred Acts of Love that we will learn.

Spiritual Partnership incorporates and builds upon hard-won psychological wisdom. Indeed, we wouldn't be ready now for the move to Spiritual Partnership without all this important work that has gone before.

A relationship with a competent therapist, couples counselor, or therapeutic group can be a great aid in spiritual work. When you engage fully in psychological work, you will definitely increase your awareness about yourself. You will receive help in distinguishing between your "conditioned" self and your authentic self. And, because a therapeutic relationship and therapy groups are intimate, you will experience connection, perhaps even a brand-new level or type of connection, also an aspect of spirituality, as we shall see in Chapter Two.

Traditionally, psychoanalysis was seen as different from spiritual work. Psychology helps you build a stronger ego, the belief went, while the goal of spiritual work is to transcend the ego. It's true that the final goal of some spiritual practices is in fact a loss of the experience of self as self. But at the less "advanced" levels of spiritual practice where most of us live, I believe the goals of psychology and of spiritual work are similar: to become more self-aware, more authentic, more loving, more capable of positive connections with those around us, and happier in our lives.

Buddhist teacher Jack Kornfield in his book, *The Path with Heart,* sees psychological and spiritual work as mutually supportive:

> Many serious students and teachers of the spiritual path in the West have found it necessary or useful to turn to psychotherapy for help in their spiritual life. Many others who have not done so would probably benefit by it. . . . What American [spiritual] practice has come to acknowledge is that many of the deep issues we uncover in spiritual life cannot be healed by meditation alone. . . . The best of modern therapy is much like a process of shared meditation, where therapist and client sit together, learning to pay close attention to those aspects and dimensions of the self that the client may be unable to touch on his or her own.

Alan Lew spent ten years in an intense practice of Zen Buddhism and then became a rabbi. In his autobiography, *One God Clapping,* he tells of the time when he was wracked with indecision about whether or not to leave his first wife, and found that meditation was not helping him. Finally, he decided to seek support from a therapist. In just a few sessions he was able to gain insights about early family imprinting that brought him great clarity and peace of mind.

In my own life, during an important phase of my spiritual journey, my guides were psychotherapists. The breakup of my first marriage plunged me into the dark night of despair. I was confused, without direction, and filled with self-loathing and shame. By the grace of God, I found myself in a therapy group that became so safe for me, I could share my deepest vulnerabilities. Even more important, the therapist and group members kept pointing out to me, ever so lovingly, patterns that did not serve me, lies I told myself, behavior that distanced me from others just when I was trying to become closer. They were able to see through my defenses, and each time they saw glimpses of my genuine inner strength, they nurtured it. Over and over they watched me cover up deep feelings with a smiling facade, and over and over they pointed it out, until I thought their patience would surely be wearing thin. Gradually, sustained by their love, I began to talk about painful regrets. Ever so gradually, honesty began to replace the habits I had developed over the years to protect myself. Though it was occurring in a "psychological" setting, this was most certainly spiritual work, as we shall define it in the next chapter.

The "work" we will be doing in this book is spiritual, because its goal is to develop the spiritual qualities we shall discuss. The Five Sacred Acts of Love are a spiritual practice, a discipline, an act of will. They are motivated by your desire to put your spiritual beliefs into practice, to behave in an increasingly "enlightened" way.

In short, then, we are making two observations: (1) Psychological and spiritual goals are often closely related, and (2) psychological tools can be very helpful in the journey of spiritual growth.

The Origins and Context of Spiritual Partnership

Over the past ten years or more, three separate threads in my life have been weaving themselves together into the tapestry I now call Spiritual Partnership: my marriage, my work with couples, and my spiritual journey.

From the very beginning of our relationship in 1981, I felt there was something different about Mayer and me. It wasn't that we had fewer conflicts or incompatibilities than other couples. It wasn't that we loved each other more, or that we had better communication skills or more therapy. But because of some elusive factor, we didn't allow our differences to come between us the way, it seemed to me, other couples did. We got over arguments quickly. Our mutual love and affection was virtually always apparent to both of us; it never went underground.

It was my search for the "elusive factor" that led me to write my second book, *The Eight Essential Traits of Couples Who Thrive.* I interviewed other happy couples to see if I could tease out any factors that happy couples universally share. "The factor" was not hard to find: Happy couples all approached their relationships with a spirit of goodwill. They were on each other's side; allies, not adversaries. Their spirits were open to each other. Their goodwill superseded their differences. It is a quality conspicuously absent in couples who are not doing well together.

This spirit of goodwill led to other factors I identified: Happy couples had little ambivalence about being together. They *wanted* to be happy together; they *believed* they could be happy together (this was critical; most couples buy into our culture's pervasive negativity about marriage, and don't believe true happiness is possible); and they were *committed* to being happy together. Also, they made a deliberate effort to spend time together; they shared optimism and a sense of adventure about life; they maintained a long-term perspective; and they paid attention to physical affection and sexual pleasure.

Next, I made a stunning realization: Traditional couples-work does not teach these "essential traits" at all, but instead encourages couples to examine their problems. Strategies for couples are developed by psychologists, who are trained for and interested in, not relationship health, but relationship *pathology*. They spend all of their time with couples who are experiencing high levels of dissatisfaction, and then write books about how they help those couples. Maybe this is a biased approach, I thought. Would we come up with very different strategies if we taught people what we have learned from happy couples instead of from unhappy ones?

So I began to conduct workshops for couples that deliberately bypassed problems and instead taught couples how to be happy together.

The results were extraordinary. Listen to June, a workshop participant who was interviewed on a radio talk show:

> Our problem was money. We fought all the time about it. Our therapy seemed to dig us deeper into our positions about it. Neither of us could change. We both felt in despair.
>
> Susan made us agree not to discuss money at all for three weeks. At the beginning of the three weeks, we were to plan three activities per week that would allow us to spend fun time together. They had to be activities that left us both feeling financially comfortable. We even arranged to swap child care with another couple in the group who were doing something

similar. And we thought up plenty of free and low-cost things to do: hikes, renting videos, flying a kite, playing Frisbee, taking walks, hot tubbing at a neighbor's while they were gone, going to a craft fair, driving in the country. We gave these outings more time than usual, because we made our relationship a priority for this period of time.

We were happier during that three weeks than we'd been for years. And we didn't want to let go of it. Then Susan taught us about goodwill, which we now invoke often, and about creating time for sex, which has made a big difference.

Money? Well, we've each given up the need to be "right." I spend more money on my own, without checking in with him all the time. He has let go of micromanaging me. And I respect his limits. Like right now, I've decided to drop the idea of getting a fountain in our backyard. It's beyond his limit. But I think we both know that we will get one eventually. Now that we've learned how, we drop issues instead of fighting about them. Something always works out in the end.

Being right and being fair are both booby prizes: when you get them, you don't get anything else—no love, no warmth, no fun.

The third strand of my life that makes up this book, in addition to my own marriage and my work with couples, is my spiritual journey.

My years in seminary (Union Theological in New York, and San Francisco Theological in Marin County) and in the ministry, both on college campuses and in congregations, cemented my interest in the Big Questions of life: Why are we here? What is good and evil? What is the nature of God? What is the relationship between behavior and beliefs? As I became increasingly at odds with the patriarchal and hierarchical nature of the Christian

Church, I found myself in the very center of both a burgeoning feminist spirituality movement and thriving Eastern and indigenous religious groups. I eagerly explored all of them: meditating with Buddhists, celebrating in goddess circles, studying shamanism, dancing with Sufis, and reading widely. At a Buddhist monastery, I had a deeply moving religious experience. Since I am married to a Jew, I also learned to value Jewish traditions and rituals. Though always moderately concerned about the dangers of drawing upon many religious traditions rather than settling into one, I was deeply nurtured by my spiritual explorations.

I knew that my couples-work was spiritual. But as I sought corroboration for this view in my reading, I became increasingly frustrated with the lack of specific guidelines most spiritual traditions offer to intimate partners. For example, I savored *The Art of Happiness* by the Dalai Lama, eagerly anticipating the chapter entitled "A New Model for Intimacy," not allowing myself to look ahead even though I couldn't wait to find out what it said. It turned out to be a rich chapter, but it wasn't about deep intimacy between two people. It was about "realizing the importance of compassion and cultivating it" as an antidote to loneliness; developing a healthy dependence on others (as opposed to the extreme self-sufficiency our culture tends to reinforce); and expanding our definition of intimacy "to include all the other forms [of intimacy besides just that someone special] that surround us on a daily basis." All the Dalai Lama said about a "relationship that's characterized by a deep level of intimacy between two people" was, "Yes, I believe that kind of intimacy can be seen as something positive. I think if someone is deprived of that kind of intimacy then it can lead to problems."

So it goes in spiritual literature. The Vietnamese Buddhist teacher Thich Nhat Hanh wrote a book called *Teachings on Love.* It's inspiring, and all his wisdom is useful for an intimate bond.

But it's general. It offers a rich picture of a life lived from love, but few particulars about how that love works itself out on a daily basis with a beloved partner when conflicts and dissatisfactions arise.

"Spiritual Partnership" is one attempt to spell out in detail exactly what it looks like to "cultivate compassion" with a beloved intimate partner. If you are a spiritual person, exactly how does your spiritual practice affect your relationship?

Of course, I am not alone in exploring these questions. Ondrea and Stephen Levine, John Welwood, Deepak Chopra, and other contemporary writers have discussed focusing on your intimate relationship to expand your awareness, tap into your essence, and express your loving nature. My hope here is to contribute to this conversation by suggesting a highly specific set of Sacred Actions that can become a disciplined practice to both contribute to your spiritual path and transform your relationship at the same time.

It is my belief now that a purely psychological approach to relationships has reached the limits of what it can teach us. Psychology alone, with its emphasis on pathology, simply won't carry us any further. We must turn to spirituality to uncover new levels of consciousness, to expand the reaches of what two people in love can experience together.

Over several years, as I taught couples how to be guided by spiritual principles, rather than by fairness and equality, I sought in vain for a term that would describe this dramatically different approach. One day, in a major "Eureka!" experience, the idea of "Right Relationship" came to me. This was perfect, I thought. If the Buddhist precept of "Right Livelihood" means making a living in a way that supports other people and the planet and that harms or exploits no one, then "Right Relationship" would be conducting one's relationships in a way that supports other people and harms and exploits no one. The question would always be, "How do I act in a manner that is consistent with Right Relationship?" rather than, "How can I get my needs met?" or "How can I get across to this other person what I mean, or what I want?"

In the end I decided I could not use that term, because what I am describing, while not inconsistent with Buddhism, is not strictly Buddhist. Also, the Buddhist precepts of Right Livelihood, Right Understanding, and others, are not widely known outside Buddhist circles.

Though I have been developing the ideas in this book for many years, it was in a passage in *The Seat of the Soul* by Gary Zukav that I found the name for the concepts that had been unfolding in my work:

> The archetype of marriage is no longer functional. It is being replaced with a new archetype that is designed to assist spiritual growth. This is the archetype of spiritual, or sacred, partnership.

Spiritual Partners make a sacred commitment to each other, says Zukav, to "assist each other's spiritual growth." This is the same definition Scott Peck gave us for love, way back in 1977 in *The Road Less Traveled*. "Love," said Peck, "is the will to extend one's self for the purpose of nurturing one's own or another's spiritual growth." It is what many of us have been striving to do without realizing that we were participating in the creation of a new archetype, appropriate for spiritual times.

Why Now Is the Time for the Shift to Spiritual Partnership

When the world is ready for an idea, often that idea will appear from a variety of independent sources at the same moment in time.

When I began suggesting to couples that they stop communicating and start behaving more kindly to each other, I had never heard of anyone else using this approach, with the single exception of psychologist George Pransky. Just last year, however, John Gottman, who studied couples in laboratory settings, announced that "successful conflict resolution is not what makes marriages succeed," and that couples will do better if they "nurture their admiration and fondness" and "turn toward each other instead of away." These are exactly the strategies that a spiritual approach to relationships suggests.

In a similar vein, veteran marriage therapists Andrew Christensen and the late Neil Jacobson developed an approach they call "acceptance therapy." They find that couples get along better when they work to accept each other instead of trying to change each other, also an important principle of Spiritual Partnership.

In *Relationship Rescue*, psychologist Phillip McGraw eschews "the rhetoric of traditional couples therapy" and insists that "reconnecting with your partner cannot and will not happen if you do not reconnect with yourself first." He says it is a myth to assume that you have to "straighten your partner out." These ideas, also the message of my previous book, *How One of You Can Bring the Two of You Together,* are all a radical turnaround from conventional couples-work and are at the heart of Spiritual Partnership.

In his book *Soul Mates*, Thomas Moore says, "It is my conviction that slight shifts in imagination have more impact on living than major efforts at change." This is an outrageous statement, especially when viewed in light of the elaborate strategies aimed at communication and change that psychologists developed in recent decades. But it is exactly the philosophy behind Spiritual Partnership.

An internal shift, a change of heart, a new understanding, *even on the part of just one partner,* will have a greater impact on you, your partner, and your relationship than any attempt at communication or change. This is a new idea, and its moment is *now.* Very soon, I predict, it will pervade relationship therapy and seem like an obvious idea that we have always known. Right now, however, it is still a fresh approach, out there on the cutting edge of couples-work. Most relationship strategies today are aimed at communication and persuading one or the other partner to change.

As we've seen, Spiritual Partnership does not suggest that changes don't or shouldn't occur in relationships, only that change is more likely to occur because of a "shift in imagination" than because of an "effort at change."

Without question we are moving into a time when spiritual values are gaining importance in our individual and collective lives. Our approach to relationships simply had to change to keep pace with this emerging reality. It is probably not a coincidence that the new archetype of Spiritual Partnership has appeared at the beginning of a new millennium, a symbolic opportunity for renewal and regeneration.

Divorce statistics are still high. Maybe they suggest that we have been trudging up the wrong road, trying to get our partners to communicate with us and to change!

Spiritual Partnership can transform all that.

A Word About the "Experiments" in This Book

Throughout the book, I will offer optional "experiments." It is certainly not necessary to do them in order to understand and use Spiritual Partnership in your relationship. But the experiments offer you an opportunity to work with the material you are reading. They will be useful if you are working through this material with your partner or with a friend or as part of a support group. Often, they provide a summary of the material.

If you choose to use this book as a do-it-yourself workshop, the experiments offer a structured, systematic process for integrating all the material in the book into your life.

I encourage you to buy an attractive notebook so you can keep all your experiments together. Whenever you do an experiment, date it. Part of the value of these experiments is repeating them after several months and comparing your results to earlier versions.

I deliberately use the term "experiment" because I never intend any particular outcome from any of the exercises I suggest. This aligns closely with my general philosophy of life: If you treat everything you do as an experiment, you will never fail, for your only goal is to gather data, to learn something new. No matter what the outcome of the experiment—even if you find you didn't want to or couldn't do it—you will have learned something interesting about yourself. The only requirement is that you do the experiment and then reflect, at least briefly, upon what you learned by doing it. As you will hear me say again, you learn not just by doing something new, but by doing something new and then reviewing what you did and what you learned. Without reflection, any learning is diminished, even lost.

I invite you to start your journal with the experiment on page 45.

Now let's proceed. In Chapter Two, I will establish what I mean when I use the term "spiritual." In Chapter Three, we will dive into the very heart of Spiritual Partnership by learning the fundamental principles that drive it. Then, in Section II, you will learn Five Sacred Acts that will show you *very specifically* how to put Spiritual Partnership to work in your relationship.

ℬ꙰ EXPERIMENT #1:
FIRST IMPRESSIONS

In your journal, write your answers to these questions, or discuss them with your partner or a friend:

1. After reading only this chapter, what appeals to you about Spiritual Partnership? What questions or skepticisms do you have about it? What does not appeal to you?

2. Draw a line across one page, from left to right, in the middle of the page. Above the line, list the reasons you are happy to be together with your partner, the strengths of your relationship, the qualities you love in your partner and your relationship, the things that work well. What makes you happy? Below the line, list the difficulties that are not fun, the problems, challenges, incompatibilities, areas in which you could improve, in short, anything that causes friction or unhappiness.

3. How much time do you spend above the line, and how much below the line? Write percentage figures over on the right, just above and below the line.

Give these lists careful attention, as we will make use of them later.

The Spiritual Path

What do you mean when you use the term "spiritual"?

I have long been interested in the variety of responses this question elicits, and have spent years formulating my own definition. I offer it here to encourage dialogue, and also to highlight the ways the spiritual journey and the relationship journey weave together.

I believe spirituality is a norm that one can choose to move toward or to ignore; that it is possible to be more spiritual, less spiritual, or not spiritual at all. A case can certainly be made that because we are all made up of mind, body, and spirit, everyone has a spiritual dimension, and that it is not possible to be "nonspiritual." But I have chosen to use "spiritual" to mean "being aligned with your spirit," or "choosing spiritual values." You can choose a spiritual approach to your relationship, for example, or a nonspiritual approach. So spirituality is a commitment, an act of will.

$\beta\!\!\supset$ EXPERIMENT #2:
WHAT IS SPIRITUALITY?

Answer these questions in your journal, or discuss them with your partner or a friend:

1. Before reading further, define spirituality for yourself. What do you mean when you use the term "spiritual"?
2. Do you consider yourself to be a spiritual person? Explain your answer.

Spirituality

To be spiritual, I submit, is to recognize your connection to the universe and to everyone and everything in it, *and to strive each moment for the thoughts and actions that will increase and not decrease this connection.* Your spiritual journey is your own personal journey from:

Isolation to connection: The isolation we experience is something we fabricate. We are not separate, but one with the universe and everything in it.

Your conditioned personality to your authentic self: Each of us consists of layers of beliefs and behaviors that obscure our pure, authentic self.

Fear to love: Love is a gentle, powerful force, too often overwhelmed by fear, which appears in many disguises.

Sleep to consciousness or awareness: The only true prison is the one we each create with limited consciousness.

Control to surrender: You can't control the universe; instead, be open and receptive to what it offers.

Restlessness to inner peace: As we become more connected, authentic, loving, aware, and receptive, we will experience deep inner strength and radiant joy.

If a "spiritual" person is one who is moving toward connection, authenticity, love, consciousness, receptivity, and inner peace, then a "spiritual practice" is any behavior that brings you into increasing alignment with the you who embodies these qualities. In other words, *spirituality is bringing yourself into closer and closer alignment with your highest self.*

Spiritual Communities

The components of spirituality I've mentioned above are at the heart of many specific religions, or spiritual *communities.* Each has a long history, sacred stories, rituals, practices, and scriptures that are embedded in a particular history and culture. The community is bound together by traditions that connect it to its mission and connect its members to each other.

An inherent danger of religious communities is their tendency to ossify certain "beliefs" in order to safeguard the continuing existence of the community. It is natural and important to have beliefs. But a "belief" that you buy into without questioning it first might have the effect of limiting rather than expanding your spirituality. Figuring out for yourself what you *know* to be true is exactly what the spiritual quest is. Your authentic self doesn't need to "believe" anything; it knows the truth. Great spiritual teachers guide us, not to inform us, but to transform us, to help us to discover what we know is true. Each of us must do this for ourselves.

When you *believe* something, you have to work at it. Your body may be tense, your personality rigid. You must be vigilant to keep out anything that doesn't conform with what you "believe." At some level you will be worried that some new piece of information could shatter your "belief."

Knowing has a power that comes from deep within. When you are operating from your authentic self, then your body, mind, and spirit will relax. You will never feel you have to defend yourself. Truth has the gentle strength of a giant sequoia tree that has quietly lived on this planet for many centuries.

If you are part of a religious community, it is important to respect the integrity of your spiritual tradition and to participate in it fully and with devotion, *as long as it is moving you in the direction of freeing you up, and not in the direction of limiting you or closing you down.* Remember that both Jesus and Buddha had problems with the religious communities of their time.

SPIRITUAL PRACTICE

A spiritual *practice* is a ritual, discipline, or routine that in some way connects the person doing it to his or her own spiritual path, and to the great spiritual truths.

To help seekers achieve the states of connection, authenticity, love, consciousness, receptivity, and inner peace, spiritual *communities* employ a great variety of *practices*. Jews study the sacred word. Sufis dance. Buddhists meditate. Christians pray. It is widely taught that the cultivation of a quiet mind, an inner stillness, is a great aid in the gradual acquisition of spiritual qualities, and that "attachment," "coveting," or preoccupation with desire is a deterrent to spirituality. Most traditions teach us that pain is a natural part of life and especially of spiritual growth, but that suffering comes only when we treat pain as

something that is unwelcome. Many teachings are quite specific
about the barriers to spiritual growth: apathy, fear, greed, or, as
the Dalai Lama says, "ignorance, craving, and hatred." And of
course, most traditions teach ethical behavior: the Ten Com-
mandments, the Eightfold Path of Buddhism, the Golden Rule,
the laws of Judaism. All of these teachings, rituals, practices,
and stories help to move us along the path toward the great spiritual truths, and toward a greater alignment with our highest
selves.

Of course, affiliation with a particular religious community is
not a necessary part of being spiritual. It is the rare person who
can achieve spiritual growth without support from teachers or
guides. But there are as many spiritual paths as spiritual seekers. Each one of us has a highly individualized spiritual journey
and our very own support systems and timelines for pursuing it.

Let us now explore in more detail each of the six aspects of
spirituality.

Connection

We are not separate from each other or from the universe or from
anything in it. We are each simply one form or another of being.

At one time there were no separate beings, there was only
being itself. Then, eons later, there was life as we now know it.
Then life began to manifest in different forms. Then a time came,
ever so gradually, when we became conscious that we had life,
and we began to experience our experience. And somewhere in
there, we began to experience ourselves as different from one
another.

We experience ourselves as separate now. But deep, deep in

our psyches or in our collective psyche, we know that it was not always that way.

Spirituality invites us to remember the time when there was nothing but being itself, when being was bliss because there was no separation, no division, only one unified, glorious oneness.

Spiritual practice is an attempt to remember and even to feel or sense this lost awareness of unity, of *being* itself, of the one essential nature that we all share. Mystical unity with the universe is the ultimate goal of spiritual seekers. Any attempt to put the experience into words is futile, because it will be attempting to describe something that can only be experienced. Yet all spiritual writers use words and metaphors in an attempt to describe the indescribable.

> *We do not "come into" this world; we come out of it, as leaves from a tree. As the ocean "waves," the universe "peoples." Every individual is an expression of the whole realm of nature, a unique action of the total universe.*
>
> —ALAN WATTS

> *Think of a cloudless, star-studded evening sky. Now imagine the stars as cutaways, letting light from beyond pass through them. That all-pervasive light from beyond is our essential nature, and the light that takes on the shape and form of each star is our essential self. We all share the same essential nature, that all-pervasive light, but each of us is a separate and unique manifestation of it.*
>
> —PSARIS AND LYONS

> *In Zen, a teacher may hold up two objects such as a bell and a book and ask the student, "Are these the same or different?" If*

*the student says "same," they are mistaken. If they say "differ-
ent," they are equally incorrect. . . . The appropriate reply is
often just to ring the bell or read from the book. They are what
they are! Each has the same deep essence manifest in a superfi-
cially different way. Each is Buddha-nature at a costume ball.
Each is susceptible to definition. Each is other in precisely the
same manner.*

—STEPHEN AND ONDREA LEVINE

There are definitely stages to the dawning awareness of yourself as a part of all that you see. As you practice Spiritual Partnership, you may have fleeting glimpses of the essential nature
that you share with your partner, or even experiences of mystical
unity.

CONNECTION WITH "GOD"

For many spiritual seekers, "spirituality" means, above all else,
connection with the dimension of our lives that we cannot see or
explain, the forces that create nature, the whole realm of existence that is beyond the personal, interpersonal, and material
aspects of our lives. In this area, language and concepts vary
greatly, yet with all the diversity, spiritual people everywhere are
united in their honoring of that which is beyond direct human
apprehension.

Each individual's conceptualization of the spiritual realm is
different, and most agree that attempts to reduce the conceptualization to words are inadequate. Some think of an anthropo-
morphic male figure capable of intervening in human affairs.
Many indigenous peoples pray to a whole pantheon of gods who
relate to various aspects of life like fertility, home, weather, agri-

culture, even war. Increasingly today, God is experienced as beyond gender, androgynous, or as a great creative and nurturing mother figure. Ancient goddesses from a variety of cultures are being invoked.

The language used to talk about the numinous, transcendent aspect of our lives is as varied as the concepts. "God" or "the gods" or "the Goddess" are common. A person may say, "The Universe is trying to tell you something," meaning that some intelligence or some process like "synchronicity" or "karma" is operating to help us learn our spiritual lessons. Some strive to be in connection with what they call "my higher self" or "a higher power."

Sobonfu Somé, an African woman from the Dagara tribe, left the close community of her people to share with the West the spiritual message of the Dagara people. In *The Spirit of Intimacy*, she writes:

> When indigenous people talk about spirit, they are basically referring to the life force in everything. For instance, you might refer to the spirit in an animal, that is the life force in that animal, which can help us accomplish our life purpose and maintain our connection to the spirit world.
>
> The spirit of the human being is the same way. In our tradition, each of us is seen as a spirit who has taken the form of a human in order to carry out a purpose. Spirit is the energy that helps us connect, that helps us see beyond our racially limited parameters, and also helps us in ritual and in connecting with the ancestors.

Along with spiritual seekers from many traditions, Sobonfu views the problems in our society as a direct result of our lost connection with Spirit, with community, and with each other. She is appalled at the way we live our lives separated from our families and from any connection to Spirit.

So, the first thing we mean by "spirituality" is anything that moves us toward connection: connection with each other, with the spiritual dimension of our lives, and, ultimately, with everyone and everything in the universe. Spiritual practice helps us discover that in our purest essence, we are all the same. We take on different external forms, but we all share the human experience. Separation and difference is an illusion that spiritual practice seeks to transcend.

Authenticity

The human race is a tribe of mask builders.

Take Joe as an example: When he was six years old, Joe was playing with a little kitten, and someone came along and called him a sissy. Joe felt bad, unloved, rejected. He wanted that terrible feeling to go away. So he built himself a little mask: tough guy. He found that if he wore his mask, he could fit in with the guys better. His mask covered up two parts of him: It covered up the pain of rejection, and it covered up the sweet, pure little boy who enjoyed the kitten. Think of Joe as three layers: On the outside is his tough-guy protective defense, which we might also call his "conditioned personality" or the "mask" he puts on to present himself to the world. Psychologists call it a "defense." Under that is the shame he felt at being called a sissy, the fear that he is unlovable, the reason he needs his mask. And buried deep beneath that fear is a perfect little Joe, just as he really is, adoring of kittens, playful, confident, loving, and lovable.

When Annie was growing up, her father traveled all the time, and her mother also had a career and was almost never home. Annie took over lots of household responsibilities at a young age. Her parents often criticized her but rarely praised her and almost never hugged and kissed her.

Annie longed for expressions of love from her parents. Her pain over their indifference to her was almost unbearable. Her heart ached; her body cried out to be hugged.

So Annie built a mask: self-sufficiency. Rather than having to feel the terrible pain of her parents' lack of love, she subconsciously tricked herself into believing that she did not want or need their love; she learned never to ask for or to expect it. The mask worked. Annie never had to feel the pain of longing for love and receiving nothing. Her mask covered up both her unrequited longing *and* the pure, genuine Annie inside who truly wanted love. Both her pain and her true self were hidden behind her defense, the personality she developed to protect herself from pain.

Mask building is a normal, sometimes even healthy response. Masks, or defenses, are the human organism's way of protecting itself from hostile elements in its environment. Your mask is your public self, the personality that you show to the world.

In the beginning, our masks protect us. But after a while they diminish us. Long after our defenses have outgrown their usefulness, we allow them to become mindless habits. Joe is now completely identified with tough guy; he can't cry. Annie has never been in a close relationship. Neither Joe nor Annie has any awareness of their self-built prisons.

Defenses distort our view of the world. Everything we see or hear is filtered through our habitual behavior, so that what we see is *biased*. Joe thinks that all he has achieved is a result of his ability to be tough. Annie sees everyone through her loner disguise and so becomes convinced that no one is warm and loving.

Your spiritual journey is your journey through the protective outer shell and the pain it was constructed to hide—both from yourself and from others—to the pure, authentic you, free of fear, and so comfortable with yourself that you don't need to hide.

At the center of your being you have the answer; you know who you are and you know what you want.

—LAO TSU

There is much conversation these days about soul, which, I believe, is another way of talking about authentic self. When you are identified with your public self and have lost touch with your true desires and passions, you are out of alignment with your soul. Your soul knows what is best for you and longs to bring you back to your true self. Your soul *is* your authentic self calling out to you, guiding you back home to the fullest expression of your true self.

The true you is unique in the universe and therefore vitally important. When you stay behind your mask, you look and behave like a lot of other people who have donned similar masks, instead of the fresh, shining presence that is your genuine self. Most of the world consists of masked people busily relating to other masked people, taking their masks ever so seriously, fervently caught up in doing work that is someone else's work, participating in relationships that are cluttered with defenses, and unwittingly teaching their children to build the same masks they have worn all their lives. They never embark on a spiritual quest, and they go through this entire life without ever discovering who they truly are. That is the difference between spiritual and nonspiritual people.

What is your primary personality characteristic? Are there times when you use it to cover up powerful feelings, either powerfully happy or powerfully sad? Are there times when it keeps other people from getting close to you?

Those three questions are enough to start a spiritual journey, one that can create a glorious opening up of your life. It doesn't matter how you pursue the answers; you could begin by having a conversation with a friend, by meditating, journaling, or dozens of other activities. If you have never asked these questions, expect the search to take time—and to lead to other questions, and other answers. They aren't the only entry, but those three questions are one gateway to a lifetime of spiritual growth.

> *The basis of insincerity is the idealized image we hold of ourselves and which we impose on others.*
>
> —PABLO PICASSO

YOUR AUTHENTIC SELF AND YOUR LOVE LIFE

Many of us believe that the secret to happiness is a passionate, loving connection with another person. We long to experience unmitigated joy and excitement about life and believe it will come in the form of a beloved.

But in fact that deep longing is really for your self.

When you connect with your true self, you will feel deep emotions; your longing will be satisfied. Moreover, until you do this, you won't feel satisfied connecting with another person. Your "public self" is incapable of true intimacy; it can engage only in a charade.

What you may be longing for is both: a person who can support you in reaching behind your public self to the feelings that lie hidden there. In a workshop, one participant stated this quite directly: "I long for someone who can crack open my shell. I feel like Humpty Dumpty, and I want someone to love me enough to shove me off the wall."

Though we think of intimacy as sex, or romantic walks on the beach, or close moments in front of a cozy fire, these are "intimate-style behaviors," not intimacy. Intimacy is stripping away your public self and sharing your inner life with another person. Genuine intimacy is deeply spiritual.

Remember the story of "Florence" in Chapter One? At first she hid herself behind habitual behavior: exaggerated helpfulness. It was when she shed that routine and revealed deep, authentic feelings to us that we felt love for her, and she for us. Our experience with her was both intimate and spiritual.

In much of our lives a "public self" is appropriate. But each of us must find a person with whom we feel safe enough to be real. That is a primary spiritual task. The person can be a lover, a friend, a family member, or a helping professional. And then we grow by finding more and more places in our lives where we can shed the public facade and be real, thereby inspiring others to do the same. That is why the spiritual quest sometimes leads people to leave high-powered jobs where they are laughed at or ridiculed for being authentic, or to exit relationships in which their newfound genuine self turns out to be threatening or distasteful to the other person.

So your spiritual journey to authenticity is intertwined with your journey to find true happiness with another person; they are both aspects of the same search. Spiritual Partnership is a commitment to support the search for authenticity in yourself and your partner.

All love is based on the search for spirit.

This is the first major insight to be found in romantic love—it really isn't about two people who have fallen madly for each other; it is about two people seeing spirit in each other. . . . This passage [from the Upanishads] dates from thousands of years ago:

> *Truly, it is not for the sake of the husband that the husband is dear, but for the sake of the Self.*
> *And it is not for the sake of the wife that the wife is dear, but for the sake of the Self.*

. . . Falling in love drives you to passionate merging with your beloved, but the deeper passion is for the Self, the source of all love.

—DEEPAK CHOPRA, *THE PATH TO LOVE*

Love

If spirituality is being authentic and experiencing connection, love is the manifestation of these qualities; it might be called "spiritual behavior." Love is not just the absence of conflict, but a distinctive way of being in the world. Love reaches out; it promotes the well-being of others. It seeks harmony. It creates joy, rapture, passion, and happiness.

The opposite of love is not hate, but fear. The primary fear is, "Deep down inside, I feel weak and fragile, inferior, bad. I don't want anyone to see this." Fear is the energy that contracts and closes down, or that lashes out, is manipulative and greedy. Love is the energy that expands, opens up, shares with others, seeks to heal.

SELF-LOVE

Self-love boils down, again, to being real, because to know your authentic self is to love yourself. If you have access only to your public self and don't know your real self, you will find it hard to feel self-love, for you can't love what you don't know; you can only fear it.

Most people have a major misconception about self-love. They believe that people who are self-loving are that way because they are good people to start with. They came from reasonably good families, they are smart, good-looking, successful, and in general everything they touch turns to gold. They no longer have any fears, faults, or insecurities. They are self-loving because the "package" they have is easy to love.

Wrong.

Many self-loving people had a rough time growing up, just like everyone else. They still have painful regrets, low self-esteem, insecurities, envies. But they have learned how to love the bad along with the good. Self-love is not about loving the parts of yourself that are easy to love; that's no challenge. Self-love is about loving all of yourself including the parts you don't like or don't want to look at. Self-loving people have become well-acquainted with their fears and anxieties, their bad moods, their pain, their shame, and they have learned to love the entire package.

You are who you are. You have done what you have done. You had the parents you had. Some things you can change, some you can't. So you have a choice: You can either fight and loathe and remain a victim of your past and the parts of yourself you don't like, or you can lovingly accept them. You can ride the horse in the direction it is going. That's self-love.

In an earlier book, *If I'm So Wonderful, Why Am I Still Single?*, I related this incident:

> I took a friend of mine out to lunch for her fortieth birthday. "So how does it feel to turn forty?" I asked her.
>
> "I really like it," she told me. "I finally feel that I'll take what I've got and be happy with it. If I haven't accomplished all my self-improvement goals by now, I figure I probably never will, and that's just fine. I'm going to quit pestering myself to get better organized and write more letters, and bake for the kids more, and all that stuff. I'm not perfect. I'm not even where I thought I'd be at forty. But I'm very content. Somehow turning forty seems to give me permission to let go of the struggles and enjoy myself."

That's self-love.

Self-love comes from learning to have compassion for yourself. "Poor thing, you've been through a lot. Let me help you and be kind to you. What you are undertaking here is a really difficult challenge; let me support you. I know you think you are awful in some ways, but there is nothing wrong with you. You are a wonderful person. We'll get through this. I love you."

When I was in junior high school, I kept a little sign over my desk, something I received from the Methodist Youth Fellowship. It had three words stacked on top of each other, like this:

God

Others

Self

I now believe this message was backward. It seems to convey that everyone and everything is more important than I am, that *I* should come last, the precise opposite of the spiritual values I now embrace. For I now know that unless I love myself and am taking good care of myself, I will have nothing to give to God or others.

Maybe, if we view this little sign more charitably, it was trying to convey that self-love is the foundation of everything else. That is more accurate.

LOVING OTHERS

If we put love on a continuum, on the left might be greedy, selfish, abusive behavior toward another, complete lack of love. And on the right might be Mother Teresa, who devoted her life completely to the alleviation of suffering in others, and the Dalai Lama, who is a model of compassion, even toward his oppressors. Over toward the right would be Johnny Appleseed, who put out his campfire because he saw that mosquitoes were flying into it (I think of him every time I vacuum up ants in my kitchen), my friend who gives a dollar to every street panhandler he passes, or a schoolteacher who encourages and supports children every day.

Spirituality calls upon us to move farther over to the right, little by little, as we are able; to cultivate our capacity to love.

It's a challenge, because our culture values money, not love, and the two value systems are incompatible. When a company exploits third-world child workers to increase its profits, it is using the money value system, not the love one. So is the person who works twelve hours a day, consistently neglecting his or her family. The money value system is staggeringly powerful in this society. Some would say that a society that trains its members to produce and achieve, to accumulate and consume, systematically and deliberately destroys their ability to love, that the unfettered drive toward growth and profit precludes love.

But love is the spiritual choice.

Everyone's expression of love is different. We won't all care for the sick or volunteer in homeless shelters. The point is to carry out whatever your life requires of you with as much love as possible.

What if, with regard to every decision we ever had to make, we would always ask the question, "What does love require?" In our complicated world, the answer might not always be clear. But certainly, many nonloving alternatives could quickly be eliminated.

It's not a question we ask very often, but it is what the spiritual life requires of us. What a different world this would be if corporations operated in accord with that question! But for them it's "What does profit require?"

Love is not just kindness, but is actually a manifestation of authenticity. In our pure essence, all of us are loving. Only when we abandon our true selves in favor of selves that fit in better with our money-oriented society will we behave in ways that are not loving.

Consciousness

If most of us remain ignorant of ourselves, it is because self-knowledge is painful and we prefer the pleasure of illusion.

—ALDOUS HUXLEY

Consciousness, or awareness, is the spiritual tool that we use to achieve the first three aspects of spirituality: connection, authenticity, and love. It is not enough just to live your life. As a spiritual person, you make a commitment to yourself to experience your life, to reflect upon it, and to become an active agent in your own being.

Becoming conscious is like climbing a mountain with an ever elusive peak. At each level of the mountain, you assume that you are seeing everything there is to see. Then something nudges you into climbing higher, and when you do, you see how limited your previous view was. You can never know what lies above you on the mountain, but you will know everything that is below you. As long as you are only partway up the mountain, you may still be living with illusions or misconceptions. Your view of the world will be limited.

The challenge in becoming more conscious, or expanding your awareness, is that you may not know just where you are limiting your own thinking or your capacity to experience something new. Or, even if you do, you may like your station on the mountain and want to stay there. It is risky to keep climbing. Who knows what comfortable viewpoint may be threatened, what old truth may be shattered?

The higher you climb, the more you will learn, not only about the real world, but also about yourself. The summit, the ultimate spiritual goal, is an accurate view of yourself and of everything and everyone else. Most of us normal folks never reach the summit, but we learn from spiritual teachers who have.

The experience of becoming increasingly conscious is different for each of us. Roughly, however, it consists of two parts: (1) receiving new information, and (2) paying attention to the new information. New information alone isn't enough.

1. There are endless ways to acquire new information
   about yourself. Journaling; talking with friends;

recording your dreams; meditating; joining spiritual or personal growth classes or groups; working with a spiritual teacher or therapist, are just a few examples. Sometimes you receive new information or insights through deliberate effort, but often they come through serendipity or chance.

In this book we will single out your relationships as a source of new information. It certainly isn't the only source, but it is a good one because it is already an integral part of your life.

2. On Aldous Huxley's utopian *Island,* mynah birds flew around all the time calling out, "Attention. Attention. Attention." We should all carry those mynahs around inside our own heads, for paying attention is the second necessary stage of raising your consciousness about yourself. You can't just acquire new information; you need to reflect upon it and integrate it. Pay attention: Do you have emotions inside you right now that you are not acknowledging? After you just now made that remark to your partner, how are you feeling inside yourself? What might you have said instead? Are you exercising choice about your relationship, or simply repeating routines? Are you doing what you most want to be doing right now? Have you had a new insight about yourself lately?

Paying attention to yourself may give you new information that can be life-changing for you. A woman in one of my groups, Bobbi, was often told that she talked too much and that she interrupted. She was always stunned to receive this feedback and did not agree that she was offensive. Bobbi's response was to curtail her behavior deliberately, but angrily. She would arrive at the next group determined to keep her mouth shut. Her resolve usually lasted about a half hour, because she would become resentful, and besides, she had valuable contributions to make to the conversation.

I suggested to Bobbi that she make no effort at all to change her behavior, but that instead she start paying attention to herself. At first nothing changed. But then Bobbi reported to us, "I actually caught myself interrupting this week! I was amazed. And you know what? *It didn't feel very good to me.*" Over a period of time, as Bobbi took more notice *of how she felt* in conversations, she saw what others had been trying to tell her.

Even more important, Bobbi began to experience what it felt like to be more quiet, to listen without adding her own comment every time. To her surprise, she would sometimes feel very sad and even become tearful. As we explored what the tears were about, she discovered she was afraid she would be left out, that she had a deep fear of being invisible. This fear evoked a great deal of pain for Bobbi. She sobbed relentlessly. It turns out that she did feel invisible in her family as a child. Revisiting that old pain was very hard for her. But can you see that her willingness to experience that pain enabled her to "update" her fears, to see that her pain was old pain, and that she no longer needed to live in fear of it?

Psychologist Carl Jung says that neurosis is a substitute for real pain. Bobbi's interrupting, her neurosis, was a substitute for her real pain of feeling invisible. Only by experiencing your real pain will you stop running from it.

Over time, Bobbi kept paying attention to herself in conversations. Eventually she found that she could be appropriate, letting others speak, adding a comment only occasionally, and that now she felt far more "seen," accepted, and loved than before.

It is easy for us to see that Bobbi's compulsive interrupting was her protective personality trait that she invented so she wouldn't have to feel the pain of being ignored. Interrupting had become so habitual for her that she quite literally didn't notice it. Ironically, as is often the case, her habitual behavior exacerbated the problem she was hoping it would solve. But it enabled her to hide the terrible pain of feeling invisible to those around her. She hid that pain from herself and others for many years. The deep pleasure she felt when she chose to shed her annoying habit while still being accepted, was the pleasure of discovering her authentic self. Bobbi had "raised her consciousness." This is an important aspect of spiritual growth.

Note that Bobbi's spiritual journey toward authenticity also enabled her to move toward connection. This will be true of you in your own relationship also. It is why Spiritual Partnership heals the wounds of love so much more effectively than the "Old Model" of communication and problem solving.

The important point here is that this entire chain of discovery, this climb up the mountain of consciousness, started because Bobbi began paying close attention to herself, in particular to the "information" that others felt she interrupted too much. She (1) received information, and she (2) paid attention to it.

Perhaps it is not too radical to say that all of "spirituality" boils down to paying attention. By paying attention, you become aware of your isolation; you discover what is real for you and what is protective, habitual behavior. By paying attention you discover deeply buried, old pain. And by paying attention, you learn that you can, after all, love the real you, not just the dressed-up, public you.

As an experiment, identify one characteristic about your personality, or one habit you have. Do you exaggerate? Are you an advice giver? Do you correct or contradict people? Are you quiet, giving, controlling, passive, shy, loquacious, critical, funny? Do you tease?

Now, don't do anything to change this quality, but start paying close attention to it. Just catch yourself doing it. Notice it. See what happens as you tune in to this one quality over a period of time.

Paying attention will help you decide what is moral for you. For example, when you truly pay attention to how you feel when you hear yourself spreading malicious gossip, that habit will stop all by itself because it will feel toxic to you. And, if you keep paying attention, you will discover *why* you were engaging in that behavior, which will help you move closer to your authentic self. Your life, just as it is now, is the only teacher you need, if you can pay close enough attention. The role of spiritual teachers is simply to help you learn to pay attention, to do it more often, and to help you work with what you discover when you pay attention.

In contrast to Bobbi, I know a woman, Betsy, who has a delightful personality but who has a habit of correcting other people all the time. She virtually always takes the opposite point of view and has no awareness that she consistently does this. Others, including her husband, have tried to point it out to her, but she becomes defensive, not open to looking at this aspect of herself. She doesn't want to take the risk of climbing up the mountain one more step. She likes the view from where she is.

With this protective habit or "neurosis," Betsy has learned to cope in the world, to protect herself from having to feel inadequate or exposed. But unless she becomes willing for some reason at some time to pay attention to this habit, she will be stopped in her spiritual growth. She is unwittingly creating separation between herself and other people, when what she truly longs for is connection.

What behavior or habit might you pay closer attention to in your own life?

Observer Self

We might call your ability to pay attention your "observer self." It is as if there is a part of you that is always able to pull back from your life drama and watch the drama happening. So now there will be two parts of you: One part is all caught up in, let's say, an argument, fighting for your point of view, passionate about the importance of your cause, utterly absorbed in the moment. The other part is able to pull back from the little scene and watch yourself arguing. "My, I certainly am passionate about this!" your observer self might think. Or, "That last thing I said wasn't quite accurate."

When you activate your observer self—that is, when you become conscious—you can make choices about what you are doing. On the other hand, if you are completely immersed in yourself, you will operate on automatic pilot, with no bigger picture, no sense of the consequences of your action or its impact on other people, no understanding of why you do what you do, no awareness of how your behavior fits into the larger drama of your life.

As you begin to develop your observing self, one of the first obstacles you will encounter is that you can't see what you aren't aware of. This is frustrating, but it doesn't matter. What matters is that you *become aware* that you can't see what you aren't aware of, that you open yourself to possibilities. As spiritual writer John Welwood says, "My awareness of being lost, confused, or

stuck *is never itself lost, confused, or stuck.*" In seeing that you
are lost, you are already less lost. You are on the path; just stay
on it. Keep paying attention.

BELIEFS

It is important to pay attention to what you believe, because your
beliefs affect everything in your life, and beliefs can change in
the wink of an eye.

Annie told me a remarkable story. Her sister, Vicky, was a
state senator, very active and visible in the community and
extremely bright and successful. Annie herself was a gardener
who felt lucky to have a job she loved. Annie loved Vicky and
they got along well, but Annie always felt inferior to her shining,
exuberant, successful sister. That was just the way it was.

One day in a casual conversation, a friend said to Annie, "Did
it ever occur to you that you may be as smart as your sister?"

The remark stunned Annie. The truth was, this *had never*
occurred to her. The whole family had always taken for granted
that Vicky was the smart one. But in an instant Annie realized
she could change this belief and adopt a new one: I am as smart
as my sister. It was like an earthquake in her life. She began
finding a great deal of evidence to support her new belief. Her
self-image gained a huge boost.

Nothing had changed but her belief!

Beliefs can be limiting. A belief is a point in life at which you
have decided to stop growing, at least for the time being. It is
natural and important to have beliefs. But being open to expanding your consciousness means being open to reexamining your
beliefs when you hear something that lures you beyond what you
believe now.

Beliefs may have momentous impact. In my work with single

men and women who are looking for love, I often ask them to identify their self-limiting beliefs. They say things like:

> I believe I can't be the person I want to be and be in a relationship.
> I believe that what I would gain by being in a relationship is not worth what I would have to give up.
> I believe there is a true shortage of suitable men and that my chances of finding one that suits me are very small.

These singles will have a very different experience from the woman who told me this:

> I believe there is no way in the world that I will end up single.
> I know absolutely that I will end up with a wonderful man.

We always behave in a manner that is consistent with what we believe, so the woman who believes she will find love is actually much more likely to find it than the people who believe that love is beyond their reach. Those people will see all of the world as evidence that what they believe is true. If they could change their belief, they would find plenty of evidence to the contrary. Your beliefs greatly color the way you see the world.

So what are the beliefs that govern your life? Do your beliefs enhance or diminish your life? Are they part of your conditioned personality, or do they come from deep within you, from your authentic self?

As you pay attention, beliefs you take for granted may begin to surface and beg for reexamination.

RESISTANCE

Most of us resist expanding our consciousness. Just as no one wanted to hear from Galileo that the sun did not circle around the earth, we don't want to hear that our perch on the mountain isn't just fine the way it is.

Resistance is a normal and common part of the spiritual journey. The secret is to view your resistance as one more opportunity to pay attention. Now, you pay attention to your feelings of resistance. That's all you need to do. Alan Lew in *One God Clapping* puts this beautifully:

> Real mindfulness comes about not by an act of violence against our consciousness, not by force, not by trying to control our consciousness, but rather, by a kind of directed compassion, a softening of our awareness, a loving embrace of our lives, a soft letting be.

We will talk more about resistance when we look more specifically at Spiritual Partnership.

EVIL

If we understand spirituality to be a climb up the mountain of consciousness, every step affording us a more accurate view of our world and allowing us to become more authentic and more connected, then the problem of evil is easy to understand. Evil is not some independent force, like Satan, who lives a separate life and does battle with the forces of good. Evil is simply ignorance, a lack of consciousness. "Evil people" live at the very bottom of the mountain, with limited awareness and a tiny vision. They have not exercised their capacity to pay attention to themselves even a tiny bit. They are completely identified with their protective habits, maintaining a frantic effort to stay far from their inner pain. Their evil behavior is their public self, their neurosis, the behavior they have adopted to fend off pain and cope with their environment.

The spiritual response to evil, therefore, is not hate, but compassion. Hate and anger are moves toward separation, not connection. When you feel hate or anger, you are diminishing yourself, allowing habitual feelings to overwhelm your spiritual values of understanding and compassion. And, you will have no impact on the person you hate. You cannot help to heal someone else's limited vision if you are trapped in your own feelings of anger or hate. If you have no compassion in your heart, you become like the ones you hate, the "evil" ones who have no consciousness, who behave out of habit. You enter their realm, way down at the foot of the mountain.

When you think about the areas of dissatisfaction in your marriage, you may not think of your partner as "evil," but you probably feel anger and maybe even hate. If you can instead view your partner with compassion, as a fellow human being who is doing the best he or she can under the circumstances, you will be raising your own consciousness and moving toward connection.

Hate, anger, envy, and hurt are one perch on the mountain. If you pay attention to them, to how they feel and what results they bring, you will gradually begin to rise above them, to find a higher consciousness that replaces them with compassion.

That higher consciousness is exactly what we will be trying to achieve when we look in detail at the Five Sacred Acts of Love.

Surrender

> *And which of you by being anxious can add one cubit to your*
> *span of life?*
>
> —MATTHEW 6:27

The invitation to trust, to relinquish control, to "let go and let God," as they say in the recovery movement, is pervasive in spiritual teachings. Do not try to superimpose your own will on the universe; instead be receptive, for life may not turn out as you plan or expect.

Interestingly, many differing "beliefs" or theologies lead to this same conclusion. Some religions say your fate is already predestined and nothing you can do will change that. Others say that you come to self-love and authenticity only through grace; "salvation" is a gift, and nothing you do will affect it. Some say that events in the universe are completely random, that they aren't "fair," or just. Bad things happen to good people, as Rabbi Harold Kushner explains. Don't look for a reason, but look for what these random events can teach you. Others believe in the great cosmic energy of karma, that viewed over eons of time, what you do now will come back to you, or what you did some time ago is coming back to you now. Some see the world as a great spiritual school where everything that happens should be viewed as the particular lesson you needed to learn.

But all of these worldviews end up at exactly the same place: relax. Let go. Be open to what is really happening, not what you think should happen or wish would happen. Don't try to control the river; flow with it.

Letting go does not mean that you no longer want the things

you want or that you no longer have any goals or desires. It means that you are no longer *anxious about* achieving these goals or fulfilling these desires. If they don't happen, your inner peace will not be destroyed. It means that you do everything you can to bring about what you want, while still trusting that whatever the universe provides is okay.

I was once a finalist for a big, highly visible job at the University of California. When they chose someone else, I was shattered. But now I see that if I had taken that job, I might still be a frazzled bureaucrat and might never have written any of my books. I could have avoided a great deal of suffering at that time if I had been more trusting, more able to surrender, less attached to my fervent desire. One of the earliest Sunday school lessons I remember is, "When God closes a door, another door always opens up."

Definitely, some of life's happenings are harder to accept than others. Some things are terribly hard to accept. But spirituality is not just for the easy times.

Letting go is a deep trust that, even without your intervention, things will work out. It is recognizing that trying to force other people or events into your own mold will cause you stress, that clinging feverishly to a particular outcome will cause you suffering, and that the universe will go ahead anyway. It is seeing that you are helpless by yourself; that only when you surrender to the great cosmic flow, the rhythms of nature, God's purpose for your life, will you be strong. You can work *with* the forces in the universe that make things happen, but you don't have to make everything happen yourself.

Surrender is something you can practice. But it also arises naturally when you are connected with your authentic self. When your self-love is as strong as a giant redwood tree, terrible storms, fires, even earthquakes cannot destroy you. Anxiety and controlling behavior are substitutes for inner strength.

Think of a disappointment, an unachieved goal, or a loss in your own life. It is natural for you to experience emotion: grief, sadness, and anger. But to develop spiritually is to develop the ability to move on so your loss does not destroy you, but makes you stronger. Christopher Reeve stands as an extraordinary model of someone who was able to accept the unacceptable and move forward with his life.

Julia Butterfly Hill, the remarkable woman who lived in the top of an ancient redwood tree for two years to save it from the ax, tells of the time she was in the grip of a violent storm with extremely high winds. "I was trying to hold on to life so hard that my teeth were clenched, my jaws were clenched, my muscles were clenched, my fists were clenched, everything in my body was clenched completely and totally tight."

Then the tree itself spoke to her: "Julia, think of the trees in the storm." She writes, in her book, *The Legacy of Luna:*

> And as I started to picture trees in the storm, the answer began to dawn on me. The trees in the storm don't try to stand up straight and tall and erect. They allow themselves to bend and be blown with the wind. They understand that power of letting go.

GRATITUDE

I once heard a spiritual teacher suggest that every prayer should be a prayer of gratitude. The idea appealed to me.

Later that day I found myself searching for the very first star I could find in the evening sky. Ever since childhood, I always use the first star as an opportunity for a little prayer of petition.

My brain automatically recites the verse I learned at my mother's knee, and I make a wish, but I do it in the form of a prayer.

That evening, I prayed for the health of a friend who was in treatment for cancer. But then I remembered, Make every prayer a prayer of gratitude, so I changed the prayer. I prayed something like, "Thank you for this wonderful friend and for all she has brought into my life. Thank you for letting her find her cancer so early and for all the treatments available to her. Thank you for all the doctors helping her. Thank you that she has such a positive spirit about all this that I know will help heal her."

Although this whole scene happened inside my head and took only seconds, it made quite an impact on me. After my first prayer, I felt sad and desperate. There was an urgency to the prayer, and a helpless feeling that went with it: Please, *please* help my friend to heal. You *have* to make her better.

After my prayer of gratitude, I felt strong and confident. I still had the feeling that I was in partnership with my "higher self" or my "higher power" and not alone in my struggle, but I felt more in touch with my own role in the drama. Besides, there was something that always bothered me about prayers of petition: They made me feel that I was trying to superimpose my will on God, as though I know better than God how the universe ought to go. Whenever I asked God for anything, like, "Please let my friend get well," or even, "Please let my book sell a lot of copies," I always felt compelled to add afterward—another rote sentence that survived from my youth—"nevertheless, not my will but Thine be done." After my prayers of gratitude, I didn't need that little tag line. I could express my desire and still imply that I was open to accepting whatever really happened.

I decided to experiment for a time using only prayers of gratitude. One thing I discovered is that I prayed more often. They were just little thoughts, really, about why I was grateful. Even when I didn't *feel* grateful, keeping gratitude in the front of my mind helped me focus on abundance rather than scarcity.

In his book, *Healing Words,* Larry Dossey tells about laboratory experiments called "The Spindrift Studies" that tested the difference in effectiveness between "directed" prayers, in which the petitioner had "a specific goal, image, or outcome in mind," and "nondirected" prayer, which "is an open-ended approach in which no specific outcome is held in the mind." The studies showed that while all prayer is effective, ". . . in these tests, the *non*directed technique appeared quantitatively more effective, frequently yielding results that were twice as great, or more, when compared to the directed approach."

I loved reading about that study, because now I feel confident that I am doing the right thing when I pray prayers of gratitude, which are open-ended. They keep me mindful of all that I have to be grateful for, and more important, they remind me not to tie my good feelings to specific outcomes. My little "ego" may want certain things, but may not know what is truly in the best interest of my soul. God has a bigger perspective than I do.

Happiness

The result of a spiritual life is happiness. The more you recognize your oneness with the essential nature of all things, the more you access your authentic self, the more you love, the more you expand your consciousness, and the more you bend with the wind, the more you will experience happiness. You will move through life from inner strength, with purpose and passion; you will know what you do best, and you will find a way to do it; you will feel enthusiasm and a zest for life, and you will love and be loved by beautiful people. Whatever the universe has in store for you, you will accept gratefully, even if it is not what you had in mind. Because you have compassion and love for yourself, you will feel it for others; you will be filled with a spirit of generosity and goodwill and will choose to help and support others.

Your relationships will bring you pleasure. Especially as you learn to practice Spiritual Partnership, you will bring a loving, upbeat energy to every relationship and group you are in. You will be accepting of a wide variety of people and their behavior. Since you will know how to manage conflict in a spiritual way, people will welcome your leadership and influence. You will be able to let go of any attempt to control the universe, and will operate from a deep trust. You will be filled with gratitude.

Of course, you won't feel that way all the time.

To be on a spiritual journey is to be like a well-tuned violin. The strings are taut and vibrant, but they can play a wide variety of songs: sad songs, exuberant songs, songs of passion, songs of grief, fiercely energetic music, or music that is quiet, almost still. You may find yourself in the grip of terrible disappointment, envy, indecision, or grief. You may feel depressed or lonely. But the more you develop your spiritual capacities, the more you will be able to bend and sway with these experiences. Don't resist them. Rather than thinking, "As a spiritual person, I shouldn't be feeling this," think, "As a spiritual person, I need to accept that this is how I feel now. This is real for me right now. It's painful, and I'm going to let it happen, let it run its course. I will see what I can learn from this experience. I will accept what is, and I will pay attention."

To be spiritual means to do the right thing as often as you can. It's a bit like parenting. You may learn good parenting skills, such as don't contradict your children; listen to them. But then you will catch yourself contradicting your children! Later you say, "Here's the way I might have handled that better."

Just so with spirituality. You know the right direction to go.
You practice the disciplines you need. You view every challenge
as an opportunity to learn. But you won't get it perfect every time.

Being perfect isn't what will make you happy; being on the
spiritual path is.

Spirituality, then, is the journey from:

- Isolation to connection
- Public, protective personality to authentic self
- Fear to love
- Sleep to consciousness
- Control to surrender
- Restlessness to inner peace

In the rest of this book we will see how Spiritual Partnership
promotes this journey. For example, imagine what your relationship would be like if you were always asking yourself this question:

If I were to act from my highest spiritual self, what would I
do now?

ᗠ EXPERIMENT #3:
   YOUR OWN SPIRITUALITY

Answer these questions in your journal or discuss them with your partner or a friend:

1. Do you agree with the six components of spirituality described in this chapter? What would you add, subtract, or change to create your own definition?

2. Which one or two of the six components represent the biggest challenge for you personally? Where do you feel a need to focus your own spiritual work for now?

THREE

The Essence of Spiritual Partnership: Five Principles

In this chapter we will examine five "axioms" from the Old Model of relationships and, in each case, the new Spiritual Principle that replaces it. From these discussions will emerge the Five Principles of Spiritual Partnership. These five guidelines offer you a completely new way to "do" your relationship.

After we examine the old and new principles in detail, at the end of the chapter we will summarize what we have learned in the form of five new principles.

Principle #1:
OLD MODEL: The Most Important Tool for a Good Relationship Is Good Communication
SPIRITUAL PARTNERSHIP: The Most Important Tool for a Good Relationship Is Sacred Actions

THE OLD MODEL: GOOD COMMUNICATION

In the Old Model, just about the only tool for improving relationships is communication. Most therapeutic approaches rely almost exclusively on helping partners to talk, listen, and learn more effective communication skills for use on an ongoing basis. Couples learn elaborate rules for negotiation, conflict resolution, and even fighting. When you have a conflict, what do you do? Find a way to sit down and talk it over, argue, negotiate. What else is there to do? When you want to feel closer, you sit down and have an honest conversation. Tell your partner what you need to feel loved. Listen to your mate's deepest feelings.

It turns out that communication is a weak tool for problem solving in a relationship—despite the fact that it's been virtually the only tool we've had until now. Communication fails, much of the time, for at least four reasons.

In the first place, one partner may be unavailable, unwilling, or even unable to talk. If the two are entirely dependent on communication and have no other tools available to them, they will be stuck, maybe even utterly frustrated, with nowhere else to turn.

In the second place, one partner is often better at communicating than the other. So when they use communication, they are relying on a skill that puts them on an unequal playing field from the start, and places one partner at a disadvantage.

A third problem with relying exclusively on communication to solve problems and create closeness is that effective communication does not come naturally to most people. It is a high-level skill that most people have not even begun to master. In fact, what we seem to be born with instead is a natural tendency to become defensive when attacked, to offer an immediate solution when someone cries or complains, to blame the other guy when there is a problem instead of looking at our own role, to gloss over feelings instead of acknowledging them, to ask for what we want indirectly, and to criticize others more often than we affirm them. All these extremely ineffective communication patterns are ubiquitous. Unlearning them and replacing them with effective skills is work most people never have the opportunity or interest to do.

When communication is done badly, it exacerbates the original problem, creating more confusion, frustration, and anger than ever. *Poor* communication doesn't solve problems—it creates them!

But the biggest drawback associated with communication is the hidden agenda it so often brings with it. When two people sit down to communicate about a problem, what they are really trying to do is get the other person to see things their way, to get the other person to change. Trying to solve a problem by getting your partner to change is by far the most common approach. Yet it is neither effective nor spiritual because (a) it never works and (b) it does not honor your partner.

It may be difficult for you to remove communication from your arsenal of relationship skills for the time being. Most couples depend heavily on talk and view it as the only way to solve problems or negotiate differences. But in fact, Sacred Actions are a powerful alternative to talk, as we shall see.

Of course, *good* communication between two people who love each other and who treat each other in a spiritually mature way is a valuable tool and a great pleasure. Excellent communication is the natural *result* of a highly evolved, thriving, intimate relationship. When two people love and respect each other and are motivated by spiritual values when they relate, they will naturally communicate well—even if it isn't perfect and doesn't follow all the rules—and this will be a great pleasure for them. *In Spiritual Partnership, good communication is a goal you strive for, not the means you use to get there.*

In Spiritual Partnership, for both problem solving and spiritual growth, actions speak louder than words.

Spiritual Partnership: Sacred Actions

A Sacred Act or Sacred Action (I will use the words inter-changeably) is an intentional behavior that is:

- Motivated by a desire for spiritual growth
- Unilateral
- An act of will, requiring discipline
- Experimental

In order to examine each of these characteristics of a Sacred Act, let me tell you about Lyle.

Lyle had gone to great lengths to plan a surprise for his wife, Wendy. An old friend of hers, Deb, was coming to town. Lyle arranged for Wendy to meet him at a restaurant at six o'clock, where Deb would also be waiting.

At a quarter to six Wendy called Lyle on his cell phone saying she wouldn't be able to make it.

Working late, usually unexpectedly, was a pattern of Wendy's that caused a lot of friction between the two of them. In the past, Lyle's pattern was to get a righteous tone in his voice and to lecture Wendy about how inconsiderate she was and how this just couldn't continue. He kept looking for ways to convince her that she was wrong, and his frustration would escalate, because he felt there was nothing he could do to make Wendy change her ways.

Wendy loathed the way Lyle became paternalistic with her, and she felt misunderstood and unsupported. She couldn't help these work crises. Her work was important, and she contributed a lot of income to the family. She needed some slack.

But this time Lyle had been attending one of my groups, so he decided to experiment with the Sacred Action "act as if," which we will examine in Chapter Six. Lyle was upset, but he deliberately acted loving and understanding, as an experiment. He asked Wendy, in an interested way, what was going on at work. While she was talking, he had a chance to pull his thoughts together and realized the surprise would be just as much fun if he and Deb waited until Wendy came home later. Then Lyle wished Wendy good luck with her project, said, "I love you," told her he'd see her later.

Lyle and Deb had a lovely time getting to know each other better, and later they all had a wonderful time with the surprise.

So, in what ways was Lyle's behavior a "Sacred Act"?

First, he was *motivated by his desire to grow as a spiritual person*. He knew from his own meditation practice and from spiritual tapes, books, and speakers that the spiritual path would be to return to a quiet mind, to let his inner calmness prevail rather then reacting out of habit to Wendy's work circumstance. "It's not what happens to you, but how you deal with what happens to you," said the voice in his head. He got a vision of his spiritual teacher and knew that *she* would not be so torn up inside, so helpless and out of control at Wendy's behavior. He wanted to do what he could to be a stronger spiritual person.

Second, Lyle's action was *unilateral*. He did not announce his decision to Wendy. He did not ask for her cooperation. He did not worry about whether his action was "fair." He moved beyond who was right and who was wrong to a different realm entirely by asking, "No matter who is right and who is wrong, what can I do to make a difference?"

The difficult part of taking a unilateral action is that you have to do all the hard work yourself. But the great part of it is that you *get* to do it all by yourself! You can skip altogether the monumentally hard step of having to secure cooperation from your partner! Suddenly, all the cards are in your hand. You don't have to wait until your partner "gets it," or until your partner cooperates or agrees, or until your partner changes. Being able to affect the situation all by yourself gives you enormous freedom. It empowers you! This is not power over other people, but inner power, inner strength. It lets you out of the prison of being at the mercy of someone else.

All Sacred Acts are unilateral. They may even have a kind of secret quality, as though you are a little elf or angel who did a good deed but will never tell. Sometimes you may never reveal your Sacred Action to anyone. You certainly can, of course, and may want to if you are in a spiritual support group, or if you and your partner are on a spiritual journey together. But the point is, a unilateral act is its own reward. Lyle did not ever need to tell Wendy what he did to salvage their evening in order to elicit her praise or to feel better about himself. He knows that he had the courage and discipline to take a Sacred Action, and that it brought him everything it promised: He became stronger in his spiritual life, and he single-handedly turned a potential fight into a pleasant evening.

Third, Lyle's action required *discipline and an act of will.* There is a reason spiritual "practice" is not spiritual "theory." Spiritual growth is about making difficult choices, and then practicing them over and over. Eventually, they will become less difficult and even more natural than doing things the old way. Spiritual growth is about turning back the strong tide of habit and conditioning. It is about overcoming laziness and apathy. When you are climbing a mountain, you won't reach the summit if you give in to the voices that say, "Hey, it isn't worth all this hard work. Just turn around and go back down. So what if you don't get to the top." Part of spiritual work is staying disciplined, keeping yourself motivated, because the work is hard and the rewards sometimes seem dim and remote (although that is less true when relationship is your spiritual path, for in your relationship, the rewards are sometimes more immediate, as they were for Lyle).

And finally, Lyle's action was an *experiment,* a fourth characteristic of all Sacred Actions. Lyle needed to try "acting as if." He had no idea what the outcome of his action would be. It was an experiment. The goal of his action was simply to see what would happen.

Lyle didn't say, "I'm going to 'act as if' I'm not angry so Wendy will feel guilty," or "I'm going to 'act as if' so we can have a good evening," or "I'm going to 'act as if' because then Wendy will appreciate me more and maybe even see the error of her ways." He undertook the experiment *without knowing what the outcome would be,* just like a scientist working in a lab. He may have had a hypothesis about what would happen, but until he conducted the experiment, he wouldn't know whether his hypothesis was correct. He "acted as if" because he knew this was one spiritual choice he could make. Now, he'd watch carefully to see what would happen.

No Sacred Act can ever fail, because every Sacred Act is an experiment, and the only goal of an experiment is to gain new information. When you try a Sacred Act in a relationship, maybe you will discover that you feel different inside; maybe your partner will respond more warmly toward you; maybe your partner will become angry and hostile; maybe you'll feel worse than you did. Whatever happens, you will have learned something. The more consciously you engage in your experiments, and the more carefully you observe the results, the more you will learn. This learning is the substance of spiritual growth.

So, to review, a Sacred Act is a specific, unilateral act of will that is motivated by a desire for spiritual growth and undertaken as an experiment, the results of which will be carefully watched and factored into future experiments.

Sacred Acts have two functions. First, they give you a taste of what it's like to be a fully evolved spiritual person. And second, they help you to become one. An evolved spiritual person in Lyle's situation would have such a highly developed inner calm and peace of mind that he would never have been thrown off balance by Wendy's behavior in the first place. Lyle isn't there, but by deliberately adopting spiritual *behavior,* as an experiment, he gets to experience something of what it would be like to be a spiritually evolved person. Also, he moves forward in his spiritual journey because his Sacred Act is one more effort at spiritual practice. After years of "acting as if," and whatever other spiritual practices he is doing, Lyle will have the quiet mind and inner strength that is the goal of spiritual practice.

In Section II you will learn five specific Sacred Acts that will go a long way toward transforming your relationship. If you are in a healthy, happy relationship, you may already be using some of them, and will find it helpful to recognize and apply them more deliberately. If you are in a relationship that is troubling you somewhat, or even a great deal, *these Sacred Actions have the power to transform your relationship.* I realize you may be skeptical about this. That doesn't matter, unless your skepticism keeps you from experimenting. All you need is the tiniest bit of willingness to experiment with these actions, even when they feel ridiculous, useless, strange, or even crazy. After all, the methods you have been using until now haven't worked. What is the harm in trying something entirely new? I promise you, if you put energy and effort into the Sacred Actions, age-old conflicts may actually disappear, and warm emotions will flow.

Bringing Spirituality into Your Relationship Requires Leadership

Whenever you use a Sacred Action, you are voluntarily offering leadership to your relationship.

A leader is someone who agrees to watch over not only his or her own needs, but also the needs of everyone in the group and of the group itself. A good leader promotes the goals of the whole group, not just his or her own personal goals, and wants the whole group to succeed. Above all, a leader takes initiative in order to accomplish these goals, both by setting a good example and by supporting each member of the group.

If you are a natural leader, applying that quality to your relationship will be easy for you. If not, this will be an excellent opportunity to push yourself, to reach outside your comfort zone and increase your skills and self-confidence. In Section II you will learn specific ways to lead. For now it is important just to see that using Sacred Actions is a form of leadership, which, by itself, is a substantial contribution to your relationship.

Leadership is not fair. Often, the leader has to do extra work. But the leader also receives the satisfaction of guiding the group to success. How often have you been part of a department or class or committee and had the feeling you could have done a much better job of leadership yourself? Here is your chance to do that: your very own relationship.

If both you and your partner have a Spiritual Partnership together, then you will both be providing leadership at different times. Often, however, one partner is more inclined to provide it than the other. If you are the one who seems to care more about the quality of your relationship or to experience problems more often, you have the opportunity to make an impact by voluntarily taking a leadership role. Or, if you are undertaking Spiritual

Partnership by yourself without involving your partner, you can enjoy the role of uncontested, voluntary leadership.

Another way to talk about spiritual leadership is that the spiritual leader is the "big" person in any interaction. This means that you voluntarily take the high ground. You make a sacrifice. You say to yourself, "The relationship is more important than whether I get my way this time." You put your ego in the backseat for the time being and don't worry about being acknowledged for what you do. Being the "big" person may mean that you give up being right, or making sure your partner knows you are right. You become more interested in good results for the relationship than in either "winning" or receiving praise.

My friend Erin, who is a real estate agent, was working with a family who found their ideal dream home but felt it was beyond their means. Erin knew that, in the current fast-paced market, within a year they would feel they had gotten a bargain, and she encouraged them to stretch their limit. She told me that she quietly gave up her own commission, though the family never realized this. "I didn't need the money," she told me. "And they really needed that home!"

Erin was the "big" person in that situation. She made a sacrifice, an unselfish gesture. She took pleasure in her good deed, and didn't need any recognition for it.

Every time you adopt that attitude in your relationship—and the Sacred Acts will help you do it—you will reap enormous rewards.

Being the "big" person means that you avoid getting caught up in the immediate action and take one step back so you can see the whole game you are a part of. Then you have the choice: simply not playing the game or maybe even inventing an entirely different game. Leadership is the simple switch from, "Why won't you *talk* to me about this? I really want to know how you

---

ℬ EXPERIMENT #4:
   KEEP YOUR MOUTH OUT OF IT

Even before you have learned any specific Sacred Actions, watch for an opportunity in your relationship to act instead of talk. Think of something you want to convey to your sweetheart. Maybe it is a compliment or an appreciation. Maybe it is a request or a complaint or criticism. Now, just for fun, see if you can figure out a way to convey this message with some kind of action instead of words.

In your notebook, make a note about exactly what you tried and how you felt it worked or didn't work.

---

feel!" to "Look, here we are, arguing about communication again. Let's go get some ice cream. I'm sure you'll let me know how you feel at some point."

Lyle was exercising leadership and being the "big" person when he deliberately decided to "act as if" he was not angry, even when, inside, he felt anger and frustration.

The great thing about deciding to provide leadership in your relationship is that you gain power—not power over your mate, but inner strength and confidence. You suddenly realize you have far more control over life-in-your-relationship than you realized.

Spiritual Partnership Principle #1: Use Actions instead of communication. Keep your mouth out of it.

Principle #2:
OLD MODEL: *You Will Be Happy When Your Partner Changes*
SPIRITUAL PARTNERSHIP: *You Will Be Happy When You Change*

OLD MODEL: PERSUADE YOUR PARTNER TO CHANGE

Most of us try to solve our relationship problems by using every means possible to persuade our partner to change.

- If only you would clean up your messes after you! This is a reasonable request, it's fair, and it's easy for you to do.
- Look, I'd like just one compliment a week. Is that too much to ask? Just one time, tell me I look nice or that you enjoyed the meal I prepared.
- It isn't fair for you to talk on the phone so much every evening. It leaves no time for us. You've got to find a way to cut down. It's only fair.
- You spend too much time on that computer! I'd like to make a rule that there's no computer time after eight in the evening.

Asking your partner to change is the most common relationship problem solving technique in the world—and the least effective.

Change *will* happen in your relationship when you use a spiritual approach, but probably not the changes you imagine, and not because you engineer them. When you try to change your partner, you are leaving Spirit out of your relationship.

Remember what Thomas Moore said: "Slight shifts in imagination have more impact on living than major efforts at change."

There are two major problems with the age-old technique of trying to change your partner: (1) It doesn't honor your partner, and (2) though it may create a temporary, Band-Aid solution, it will never truly work.

Your partner has a right to be sloppy or gregarious or absent-minded or workaholic or selfish or habitually late or rude to his or her parents. These may be personality characteristics that displease you, but your partner doesn't have to change them for you.

For one thing, your partner's "faults" were probably there when you fell in love. Either love blinded you to them, or the very same quality you once loved has transformed itself in your own eyes. What you originally saw as generosity, you now see as careless spending. What you originally saw as strength, you now see as arrogance. The iconoclasm you loved now seems weird to you. The ambition you so admired has turned into workaholism, or the free spirit you adored has now become a lack of ambition.

Your partner has personality tendencies, a family history, and difficult past experiences. He or she didn't just spring from whole cloth, ready to satisfy your images of love. Your partner has images too, and has a right to those.

Women often want more expressions of affection and affirmation from men. They want to feel more adored and to experience more intimate moments.

Men's ideal is often the opposite. They love to relax into a relationship and not feel they always have to be taking care of it. They like "parallel play," relaxing together while they both are reading, or puttering in the garage knowing their love is inside sewing.

You have a right to what you want, but so does your partner. So you may not end up with everything you want. This is not a problem, it is a fact of life. Badgering your partner to change will only create discord, upset, and distance between the two of you. It doesn't honor the precious person your partner has spent all these years becoming and is still trying to become.

When you constantly harp on your partner for being late or sloppy or inattentive, or even if you constructively negotiate for change, the message you are conveying to your partner is "You are not quite good enough the way you are. I would love you more if you would change." So your partner's experience is, "I'm being assaulted, criticized."

As we saw before, it is actually a *healthy response* for your partner to say back, "I'm not a bad person. I'm fine just the way I am. I love myself, even if you can't love me the way I am."

When you criticize a relatively healthy person, you actually trigger that person's self-protective instincts, and probably make the person even more likely to behave in the way you don't like, whether this reflex is conscious or unconscious. If you have a partner who acquiesces to your every desire and never stands up for himself or herself, then you have an even worse problem. You should be grateful for a partner who is trying to maintain personal integrity in the face of your criticisms.

"But," you may say, "I'm trying to persuade my partner to be more organized or more thoughtful or more competent *because I know it would be better for him or her,* as well as better for the relationship. I am trying to be helpful!"

Help is help only when it is perceived as help.

A person is not likely to change a deeply rooted personality trait for you. If the trait is something your partner doesn't like in herself or himself, then the more you convey your love and create an atmosphere of acceptance, the safer your partner will feel to risk experimenting with changes.

To reiterate then, trying to solve a problem by getting your partner to change doesn't honor who your partner is, and it will never work. Nevertheless, most people keep trying to change their partner for years and years, because it is the only thing they can think of to do.

Sacred Actions provide an alternative that does honor your partner and that does work: They give you a way to manage or even eliminate problems *without relying on your partner to change.* In Spiritual Partnership, you stop focusing on your partner and start focusing on yourself.

SPIRITUAL PARTNERSHIP: CHANGE YOURSELF

The mistake many couples have made in the Old Model is to focus all their attention on each other and the relationship.

In Spiritual Partnership, relationship work is inner work.

In Spiritual Partnership, it does not matter what is going on with your partner; it matters only how *you respond to* what is going on with your partner. Your work is to pay attention to yourself, to learn what you can, and then to provide leadership to move yourself and your relationship forward.

This Is About You

In one of my groups of eight people, Sharon became very annoyed with Tim, a man in the group who was not her partner. Tim was an advanced student of yoga. He talked about yoga all the time and even sat in our group in yoga positions. Sharon felt that he was "showing off," and that his self-centered behavior was disruptive to our group. She wanted to get him to look at his behavior. But every time she spoke to him, I would say to her, "Sharon, this is about you." I would invite her to look at exactly what her feelings of annoyance were and to pay attention to them. Sharon hated my interventions; she wanted me and the group to support her in conveying to Tim that he was insensitive and arrogant. But we all helped her to see that Tim had a right to be who he was, and that her feelings were offering her an opportunity to learn something *about herself.* Why did she find his behavior to be so upsetting?

It took Sharon several weeks even to understand what I meant when I said, "Sharon, this is about you." In her view, Tim was being glaringly disruptive.

Gradually, as Sharon *was* willing to look at herself, it developed that she had practiced yoga herself in the past, but that she had let her practice lapse and felt pangs of regret about it. Tim was evoking this regret. When Sharon discovered how strong her regrets were, she found a way to fit yoga back into her schedule.

Whenever you find yourself annoyed with your partner, remember the phrase, "(Your own name), this is about you." As a spiritual partner, you want to ask not, "Why is my partner doing this dumb thing?" but rather, "Why do I have such strong feelings about what my partner is doing? Where does this big 'charge' in me come from?"

The way to "fix" whatever you don't like in your relationship is to stop worrying about what your partner is or isn't doing and go within. The answers to your conflicts, to your longings and dissatisfactions, are not out there in someone else or some other situation. Everything you need for peace and happiness is within you, and that is where your relationship work has to start.

Spiritual attention to self is completely different from inappropriate selfishness, self-involvement, or narcissism, which lead away from connection. When you pay spiritual attention to yourself, this should not be apparent to other people. Paying attention to your own spiritual journey leads toward connection. It means that you stay aware of your highest spiritual aspirations and act out of them.

*. . . if you take good care of yourself, you help everyone. You stop
being a source of suffering to the world, and you become a reservoir of joy and freshness. Here and there are people who know
how to take good care of themselves, who live joyfully and happily. They are our strongest support. Everything they do, they do
for everyone.*

—THICH NHAT HANH

A deeply held belief in this society is that relationships are
hard work. Truly, many people experience this to be true. What's

---

ℬ EXPERIMENT #5:
ON CHANGING YOUR PARTNER

1. Look back at the list you made below the line in
   Experiment #1, the problem areas in your relationship.
   Choose one problem.

2. First, in your journal, write a sentence or two about how
   this problem could be eliminated if your partner would be
   willing to change.

3. On a scale of 1 to 10, with 1 being "Never Happen" and
   10 being "Extremely Likely," give the scenario you wrote
   for the above point a number. How likely is it that your
   partner will change in this way?

4. Now, with regard to this same problem, write, "The reason
   I react so strongly to (your partner)'s behavior is _____
   _____."

5. Assume that your partner will never change with regard to
   this behavior. Do you think you could ever change your
   reaction to this behavior? Explain your answer.

sad is that most people spend their whole lives doing the *wrong hard work*, trying either to change or to put up with their partner. This is futile and frustrating hard work. Becoming spiritual, waking up to who you truly are, learning how to operate from love and empathy—*that* is hard work, but it leads somewhere! It takes you beyond the hard work! It is the kind of hard work that is enormously satisfying and makes your relationship into the one you wanted in the first place. Spiritual Partnership is learning how to do the *right kind* of hard work!

Spiritual Partnership Principle #2: Never try to solve a problem by asking your partner to change.

Principle #3:
OLD MODEL: *Usually, One Partner Is Wrong. The Partner Who Is Behaving Inappropriately Needs to Change*
SPIRITUAL PARTNERSHIP: *Far More Important than Being Right Is Having a Spirit of Goodwill*

OLD MODEL: WHEN YOU'RE RIGHT, YOU'RE RIGHT

Name an ongoing problem in your relationship.

I'll pick the biggest problem Alice and Jack have, as an example, but throughout this discussion, I suggest you substitute your own problem.

> *Jack:* Alice is involved in way too many activities. She goes out almost every evening. I love our cozy evenings at home, and

I don't think it's fair for her to leave me alone so often. All I ask is a little moderation.

Alice: I feel as if Jack wants me to stop the rest of my life. He should see how much these activities mean to me. When am I supposed to see my women friends? He never appreciates how much I do give up so I can be home more. No matter how much I do, it's never enough.

Jack is right. So is Alice. And the way they have been dealing with this problem for years now is to discuss it, argue about it, and negotiate it. They even see each other's point of view. Alice sort of likes that Jack wants her home more. Jack admits that he likes Alice's gregarious nature and admires her community involvement. Jack gives a little. Then Alice gives a little. But the problem remains, because deep inside, Jack still believes he is right. And deep inside, Alice still believes that she is right. And neither can convince the other.

In your own relationship, what are you absolutely right about? Your partner should be more affectionate, should help more with household tasks, should stop nagging and criticizing you? Pause now and pick one thing that you know you are right about. Do you have something in mind?

First understand: I am not suggesting that you are not right. Let's stipulate that you *are* right about your analysis of this problem. Probably any reasonable person would agree with you.

But as a Spiritual Partner what you need to understand is that being right will never get you anywhere. Being right is the booby prize of life, because you do get to be right, but that is all you get.

You don't get to feel closer to your partner.

You don't get to allow your partner to feel closer to you.

You don't get to solve the problem.

You don't get to reduce the conflict and upset in your relationship.

All you get is, you get to be right. It's a dead end.

When you insist on being right, you are signing up for years of an endless tape loop. How likely do you think it is that your partner will suddenly one day just roll over and say, "Yeah, honey, I see your point. I guess you have been right all these years. And I've been wrong."

Being right is useless.

There are three problems associated with being right:

1. Insisting that you're right prevents you from expanding your vision.

What if there is an off chance that you have the whole thing figured out wrong, or that there is a dimension that you are not seeing. What happened to Don and Sarah was a good example of this.

Sarah was upset with Don because he rarely made conversation with her. When they first got together, they talked intensely all the time, and Sarah loved this. But now Don was always either reading or watching TV. He didn't want to talk about movies they saw, friends and family, or even his work. He just gave her one sentence answers.

Sarah approached this problem by trying to convince Don that she was right, that what marriage is about is staying in touch on a day-to-day basis, sharing ideas, and enjoying casual conversation. Don didn't disagree, but he felt annoyed by what felt to him like nagging and criticism. He would make small efforts to make conversation occasionally, but only to try to appease Sarah.

After several years with little change in this situation, Sarah and Don had occasion to visit Don's sister, who lived two thousand miles away. Sarah and Don had married later in life, and Sarah had never met this sister.

The household was chaotic. Radios and TVs were going on everywhere. Two teenagers and their friends took over various common rooms. Dogs barked and required attention. Neither Don nor Sarah could take it for very long. "This is exactly what my house was like growing up," Don told Sarah.

The incident opened Sarah's eyes. She also knew that Don's mother, who was now dead, had been an extremely invasive woman. When she put these facts together, she began to see Don's quiet as a way of protecting himself from chaos, of carving out some privacy for himself. She saw how precious privacy would be to him. She even saw herself as a shadow of Don's overly intrusive mother. Something inside her shifted. She saw how inappropriate it was for her to take Don's reserve personally; she felt herself wanting to help protect his quiet.

Sarah didn't exactly let go of her position, but she softened. Her vision expanded.

Shortly after the visit, Sarah mentioned to Don that she could now see why quiet was so important to him. And she stopped talking about it as though hers was the only correct position. When there was quiet in the household, she decided to relax and enjoy it herself. She began to see an evening at home as a little retreat for herself, a welcome respite from her hectic days.

What Sarah found over a period of time was that, as she herself became more quiet, Don started to talk more!

So one problem with insisting that you are right is that, often, there are several "right" ways to look at a situation, and your right way is only one of them. Being right may be keeping you from expanding your vision.

But there is an even worse problem associated with being right.

2. Being right makes you helpless.

Usually your "right" view of the situation is that the problem is your spouse's fault. When you think about your own relationship problem, it probably starts out, "My partner won't . . . " or "My partner is too . . . " or "My partner isn't . . . "

If the only solution to the problem is that your spouse needs to make a change, this puts you in a terribly weak position, because you have no control over what your spouse does or doesn't do! You can rant and rave and flail about, but it will gain you nothing. Or, you can sulk in silence, feeling betrayed, cheated, and angry. Those are about your only alternatives, and neither achieves anything that you want.

But you still have that precious booby prize: You are right. And when you talk it over with your friends, they will agree with you. Poor you, your partner is so ⎯⎯⎯⎯⎯⎯⎯. And you are helpless to do anything about it, try as you might.

The third problem associated with being right, we have already mentioned:

3. As you're trying to get your partner to change, the indirect message you are consistently giving him or her is: "You are not good enough the way you are. I would love you more if you were different. You are not okay."

You are actually, indirectly, diminishing your partner all the time, instead of offering support and love. Remember that inner flame we talked about that is always striving to burn brightly within each of us? When you cling to your righteous position, you are tossing little handfuls of sand on your partner's flame. Wouldn't you both feel better if you could find a way to fan the flame?

By being right, you give your partner a reason to withdraw from you, when what you would truly like is more closeness. You may view the problem as your partner's fault, but by harping on it all the time, *you are the one who is creating the distance!*

Being right is the booby prize of life. But it is actually worse than a booby prize. It is more like the monkey's paw, because it brings you nothing but pain.

What to Do When You Know You Are Right

But you *are* right. So how can you just give that up?

Here's the secret: No one is suggesting for a second that you are not right. You probably are. All we are saying is, being right makes absolutely no difference to anyone. It is completely irrelevant. And one of the least effective and least spiritual things you can do in your relationship is to keep insisting that you are right, and to keep making your partner wrong.

In Spiritual Partnership, instead of asking who is right and who is wrong, you exhibit a spirit of goodwill by asking, "No matter who is right or wrong, what can I do to make a difference?"

What can you do?

There is always a Sacred Action that will be appropriate. After you learn the Five Sacred Actions, you will be able to find one that will work in every situation. Choosing a Sacred Action in a spirit of goodwill brings you far better results every time than insisting that you are right ever will.

Being Right as a "Defense"

For some people, being right is their defense, the personality trait that they have assumed to protect themselves from feeling foolish or unseen or left out. Being right all the time is a superficial way of saying, to yourself and to everyone else, "See, I'm a great person. I'm very knowledgeable, and I always have the right answer. Aren't I clever? Aren't you impressed?"

When you use being right as a defense, you don't stop with

being right about conflicts with your partner; you are right about religion, politics, current events, family history—everything. You will often contradict others, add the correct information in every conversation, and even go out of your way to point out to people when they have been wrong.

If you (or others) notice this tendency in yourself, as with every other personality characteristic, just start paying attention to it. Begin to catch yourself doing it. See how you feel after you have corrected someone or added additional correct information. See if you can catch yourself before you are about to correct someone, and try being quiet this time. See how that feels. That's all spirituality requires of you. Pay close attention, and see what happens. This is the route to your authentic self, and to connection instead of separation.

SPIRITUAL PARTNERSHIP: GOODWILL IS MORE IMPORTANT THAN BEING RIGHT

As I mentioned in Chapter One, in extensive interviews with thriving couples I found one outstanding quality that separated couples who thrive from couples who don't. It wasn't that happy couples all came from stable, loving homes. It wasn't that happy couples all had excellent communication skills. What set happy couples apart was a spirit of goodwill.

Goodwill is an overall feeling of generosity toward your partner. It is the attitude, "I am on your side, no matter what. I am your ally, not your adversary." When you approach a situation with a spirit of goodwill, it means you value your relationship far more than whatever this one little incident is. You are willing to acknowledge that your partner's point of view, while you don't agree with it, might have some validity *for him or her.* You realize that positive, spontaneous acts of thoughtfulness are important expressions of love. You understand that love has nothing to do with fairness. Love is love. The more you give it away, the more you receive.

When your relationship operates on a foundation of goodwill, it means that even when you are angry, you can be reasonable, you can be "nice."

Gail and Jeff were both exhausted one evening, and they got into an argument. Jeff was late for a meeting, and so at the height of Gail's tirade, he slammed the door and left. Gail was furious and felt dismissed and abandoned. She was sobbing.

About five minutes after Jeff left, he pulled over to a convenience store that had a pay phone and called Gail. "I'm still angry," he told her, "but I love you. I'm sorry I left so abruptly. We'll talk when I get home. I know we will work this out. Don't worry."

Jeff wasn't worried about who was right or wrong. His goodwill prevailed, even when he was angry. If this had been a couple in which there was little goodwill, this fight might have escalated, with much name-calling and blaming and bad feelings being carried around for days.

Alice, a participant in one of my groups, told me that just the idea of goodwill turned her marriage around.

As soon as I heard the idea, I saw right away that I didn't have any goodwill. If I wanted the window open at night and Peter wanted it closed, all I could think about was that I needed to protect my interests. I spent a lot of years learning how to be assertive and how to "get my needs met." I blamed Peter for everything, but the truth is, I was never generous or thoughtful—or even kind, really. No wonder he wasn't nicer to me!

Now, in a situation like that, I actively think about goodwill. It's not that I always give in. It's that incidents that used to create a fight are just nothing now. I let things roll off my back. I'm much kinder to Peter now, and it pays off incredibly every single day. We don't go around anxious that we are not going to get our fair share. The idea of goodwill has transformed our relationship.

Goodwill sounds as though it is designed to help the other person. But in fact, extending goodwill toward another person is one of the kindest things you can do for *yourself*. A kind or generous gesture toward another person puts you in control of a situation, eliminates conflict, and lets you experience the pleasure of giving to someone you love.

And goodwill can actually solve problems.

Although she knew it was minor in the grand scheme of things, Julia tried in vain to get Mike to put away his newspapers and magazines after reading them. The dining room table and the couch always seemed to be cluttered, no matter what she did. Mike said he never felt like he was really finished reading, and besides, he didn't view reading material as clutter. He would make a halfhearted effort after they talked, but then revert to his old habits. Julia felt thwarted.

Then, one day, she had a long conversation with a woman who was upset because her husband was gambling more and more. Julia became aware of how lucky she felt to be with Mike and how many things she adored about him. She made up her mind to view the messy newspapers as a little reminder of how much she loved Mike, and to view cleaning them up as a little love ritual, a secret gift to herself.

This story reminds me of a favorite passage from Lao-tsu:

> As the soft yield of water cleaves obstinate stone,
> So to yield with life solves the insoluble.

In a spirit of goodwill, Julia yielded, and the problem disappeared.

The term "goodwill" actually covers a range of specific behaviors like being grateful for what you have, emphasizing the positive traits in your partner, accepting your partner just as he or she really is, tolerating the aspects of your partner that you wish you could change, and practicing thoughtfulness and generosity. We will become far more specific about exactly how you can exhibit these qualities in Section II.

It is important to note that acts of goodwill must always be balanced with a willingness to take care of your own needs. This is the subject of Principle #5, which we will discuss in a few pages.

Goodwill goes against the grain of much of what we have been taught. This country was founded on an ethic of rugged individualism and watching out for number one. Also, in the last several decades both the women's movement and the recovery movement have encouraged us to identify and take care of our own needs. Above all, we must avoid the dreaded "codependency."

The pendulum needs to swing back now. We must balance our hard-won self-care and independence with a willingness to be thoughtful, gracious, and generous.

Let's be clear that goodwill has nothing to do with being codependent. Codependence means attempting to do for other people work that they must do for themselves, as when you try to "help" someone to stop drinking. Or it can be behavior that actually encourages someone else to continue dysfunctional behavior, as when you call in sick for your friend who is too drunk to go to work. There is a huge range of generous, loving, kind, thoughtful, giving behavior that is in no way related to codependence.

Goodwill must also be distinguished from what psychologist Beverly Engel, in her book *Loving Him without Losing You,* calls "the disappearing woman." Goodwill is not about "giving in" or losing your feeling of control. It is not about becoming a doormat and letting your partner determine everything. Quite the opposite, an act of generosity comes from a self that is so strong and well-developed that it can easily tolerate not getting its way. A deliberate decision to make a kind gesture is *empowering.*

Even when you are not feeling strong, engaging in deliberate acts of generosity will help you build your inner strength and help you develop your growing spiritual self. When you "think goodwill," you will begin to experience more compassion for your partner. You will become more forgiving, and more able to see a different point of view. You will start to recognize that your partner is doing the very best he or she can, and that your love and support—far more than your nagging or your watching out mainly for yourself—will expand your partner's ability to do well and to love you back.

Goodwill is definitely part of a spiritual approach to love. And it is also high on the list of effective strategies for good relationships. John Gottman, who studied couples in a laboratory setting, also encourages couples to develop a spirit of goodwill. "Turn toward your partner, instead of away," he says. Also, "Let your partner influence you." What a concept! Let your partner's needs and desires have an impact on you. It is profound advice! Especially coming out of the decades where all the emphasis seemed to be on getting your own needs met.

You may be thinking now, This is never going to work in my relationship. I've been giving in all along, and it does nothing. Besides, it doesn't sound fair. If I show "goodwill," my partner will just take advantage of me. I don't think I can do it anyway; I'm not a saint.

These anxieties are natural, and we will address them all in Section II. Don't expect yourself to start behaving differently on the basis of this short discussion of goodwill. In Section II you will learn specific Sacred Actions, which might also be called "acts of goodwill." Here, we are just laying the foundation for Sacred Actions, clarifying the philosophy that underlies Spiritual Partnership.

In his *Treatise of Human Nature,* the eighteenth-century philosopher David Hume wrote this about love:

> 'Tis plain, that this affection, in its most natural state, is deriv'd from the conjunction of three different impressions or passions, viz., the pleasing sensation arising from beauty; the bodily appetite for generation; and a generous kindness or good-will.

How has it taken us so long to learn this wisdom? Let's not miss it this time around.

ℬ⃝ EXPERIMENT #6:
THINK "GOODWILL"

1. Again select a problem from your list in Experiment #1.
2. With regard to this problem, who is right and who is wrong? In your journal, write, "_____ is wrong about _____."
3. Now write, "No matter who is right, the way I could make a positive difference, in a spirit of goodwill, is _____ _____."
4. If what you wrote above is something you are willing to do, do it. Make a note in your journal about what you tried and how it turned out.

Spiritual Partnership Principle #3: Don't worry about who is right.
Instead ask yourself, "What can I do to make a difference here?"
Think "goodwill."

Principle #4:
OLD MODEL: *Great Relationships Are Always Fair;* *Both Partners Participate Equally*
SPIRITUAL PARTNERSHIP: *As a Spiritual Partner, You* *Balance Your Own Level of Giving and Taking*

OLD MODEL: GREAT RELATIONSHIPS ARE FAIR

Fairness and equality have been the bedrock of relationships for at least fifty years. Marriage is a fifty-fifty proposition. Both partners have to give equally for the marriage to feel good. No one partner should be burdened with most of the giving or most of the work.

Sounds good. But if you are approaching your relationship by watching over your own spiritual growth, it is not a useful model.

Relationships may not be fair. The question isn't, Are we giving and taking in exactly equal proportions? The question is: Do we feel good? Is this marriage nurturing each of us as individuals?

People's capabilities and propensities are different. Both of you may be giving 100 percent of your ability to express emotions. But your 100 percent may look like a gallon, and your partner's 100 percent may look like a teaspoon. Is that equal? Barbara does eighty percent of the actual housework measured in time or number of tasks, but her partner's willingness to do all the grocery shopping and to wake up with the children on weekend mornings feels like way more than twenty percent to her.

The rest of the housework feels easy to her, even enjoyable, and she knows it would be a burden to her partner.

What works is not equality and fairness, but a spirit of goodwill.

The problem with envisioning a giant balance scale with your partner's contributions on one side and yours on the other is that when you feel the scales are out of balance, your only alternative is to negotiate with your partner to change. Oops! We just saw that persuading your partner to change lies outside the spiritual approach to relationship. And you can't keep that scale balanced by yourself, because you have no control over what your partner does or does not do.

Socially and politically speaking, equality remains an important struggle. Some of the inequities between men and women are still appalling. And the equality that has been achieved between men and women has made a difference within individual marriages. But when you use fairness and equality as a measure within your own marriage, you don't have a marriage, you have a contest.

Spiritual Partnership: You Balance Your Own Giving and Taking

As a Spiritual Partner, the balance you need to strive for in your relationship is not, "Am I giving 100 percent and is my partner giving 100 percent?" but instead, *"Am I giving 100 percent and am I taking 100 percent?"*

This way, you have complete control over the balance that makes you feel good. And when you feel good, both you and your partner will enjoy you more.

In Spiritual Partnership you have two big jobs: You need to stand up for and take care of your partner, and you need to stand up for and take care of yourself. Whatever *your partner* is giving and taking, your spiritual task is to accept that. Your partner is a given in this. What lies within your control is (1) how much and how often you take care of your partner, even if it is at your own expense, and (2) how much and how often you take care of yourself, even if it is at your partner's expense.

Watching over this balance is challenging work.

Each of us is better at one-half of the task than the other. Are you someone who is very good at taking care of yourself, at meeting your own needs? Are you quite self-sufficient and decisive about what you want? Then your work will be to stand up for your partner more, to practice generosity and thoughtfulness, even if it may be at your own expense sometimes.

Or are you someone who is very good at taking care of others, at keeping peace, and at thoughtfulness and generosity, even though it may be at your own expense? Then your task will be to stand up for yourself more, to be assertive, to take initiative, and to insist on what you need, even though it may be at your partner's expense sometimes. You will no longer be dependent upon your partner to have a well-balanced relationship that meets both of your needs.

Your task may differ depending on your relationship too. If your partner is self-oriented, controlling, or insensitive, you will need to make a huge effort all the time to stand up for yourself and you may need to do very little to take care of your partner. If your partner has a weak sense of self, is indecisive and often ambivalent, you may have to do more giving and supporting and be careful that you don't take advantage of this situation.

Recently, a friend of mine, Tammy, was agonizing because she and her husband had decided they could not afford for her to fly back East for her best friend's wedding. When I saw her in tears, I questioned her about the "joint" decision and suggested this might be a time when she needed to act on her own, to be loving but decisive. We thought through what it would be like for her simply to announce to her husband, Tom, that she had decided to go. *This idea had never occurred to her,* and she determined to try it, as an experiment. When she did, Tom was more surprised than anything. He was angry at first, but the next day they both realized it was a better decision. Tammy felt wonderful. She saw that this was spiritual progress for her too, because it brightened her

---

ℬ EXPERIMENT #7:
BALANCE GIVING AND TAKING

1. In your journal, complete these sentences with the appropriate words:
   - In our relationship, I am better at taking care of (myself) (my partner).
   - I need to pay better attention to taking care of (myself) (my partner).
2. Make two columns. In one, list ways you have taken care of yourself in the past month or so. In the other, list ways you have taken care of your partner.
3. Make a list of ideas for specific ways you can take better care of yourself in your relationship.
4. Make a list of ideas for specific ways you can take better care of your partner in your relationship.
5. From whichever list represents your "weaker suit," choose two items and make a specific plan to do them within the next couple of days.
6. Make a note in your journal about what you tried and how it worked out.

inner flame. It raised her consciousness about what was possible for her. And because Tom ended up respecting her for her assertiveness and could see that she was more her real self after this decision—more relaxed, happier, and stronger—the decision ended up bringing the two of them into closer connection.

On the other side of this coin, I recall a couple I worked with several years ago, Richard and Diane. Richard wanted desperately to go to graduate school in philosophy, and Diane was dead set against it. They had two small children and needed both incomes. Besides, Diane worried that his degree would be useless in terms of increased income for them. I invited the two of them to look carefully at the proposed plan, to lay it out in detail. As they talked, I could see a shift in Diane. She saw how clear Richard was about his desire, how animated he became when he talked about it. She began to come up with suggestions for making the plan work. She also talked about how hard it was going to be for her. She was quite afraid. But she had opened the door a crack, and little by little she was willing to walk through it. Richard was quite demonstrative with his appreciation.

Sometimes it's "spiritual" to stand up for yourself, sometimes to give up what you wanted and support your mate. A great relationship brightens the inner flame of both partners.

Balancing goodwill with self-care is the very heart of Spiritual Partnership. It's an ongoing, never-ending task within every relationship. The more you strengthen your weaker muscle, the more you will appreciate the importance of it, and the easier the balancing act will become.

Spiritual Partnership Principle #4: At any time, you can choose to take care of yourself or your partner. Strive to keep these in balance.

Principle #5:
OLD MODEL: *First You Need to Solve Your Problems;*
Then You Can Be Happy
SPIRITUAL PARTNERSHIP: *First You Need to Be Happy;*
Then Your Problems Will Diminish

OLD MODEL: YOU NEED TO SOLVE YOUR PROBLEMS TO BE HAPPY

Most couples believe: If only we could solve our problems, then we could be happy together.

The far more productive (and spiritual) way to think is: If only we could be happy together, our problems would diminish.

Put another way, you may think, "We have problems; therefore we don't feel good together." But what is far more likely is, "We don't feel good together; therefore we have problems." Problems are not the *cause* of unhappiness in marriage, they are the *symptoms* of unhappy marriage.

The traditional approach to improving marriage is to work on resolving conflicts and differences, to *focus on problems* as though the road to happiness is *through* the brier patch of problems. Sadly, this strategy has left many couples hopelessly stuck in the brier patch.

In Spiritual Partnership you use the opposite approach: Always focus *first* on creating a harmonious atmosphere and a spirit of goodwill between the two of you. Only then, within this harmonious atmosphere, should you begin to resolve conflicts or solve problems.

In his book *Divorce Is Not the Answer,* psychologist George Pransky used this metaphor: If you have a sore on your arm, the last thing you should do is poke at it, dig around in there, examine it more thoroughly. You'll make it worse! Instead you should create a gentle, healing environment for the wound, and allow it to heal itself.

Relationship problems should be treated the same way.

Most Problems Can't Be Solved

Usually, "working" on problems *won't solve them.* Why? Because most marital problems can't be "solved." When your problems are based on fundamental differences in personality or values, there is no "solution," and the search for one will increase your frustration and drive you further apart.

> *All the greatest and most important problems of this life are fundamentally insoluble. They can never be solved, but only out-grown. This "outgrowing" [requires] a new level of conscious-ness. Some higher or wider interest appears on the horizon ... and the insoluble problem loses its urgency. It is not solved logi-cally in its own terms but fades when confronted with a new and stronger image.*
>
> —CARL JUNG

Jung had an elegant way of describing the very core of Spiritual Partnership: Focus primarily on your own spiritual growth, and the "new level of consciousness" you will achieve will transform everything, including what you thought were problems in your relationship.

Many relationship problems aren't truly "problems" at all, they are facts of life. If you label something as a problem, you imply that it has a solution. If you label it a fact of life, you understand that you simply need to learn to live with it, to "accept the things you cannot change," as the Serenity Prayer says. Learning to accept what you can't change is an important aspect of spiritual growth. Not only will it create an atmosphere of harmony in your relationship, it will expand your awareness and open you up to new possibilities. As the Dalai Lama says, "If you intend that your relationship with your husband or your wife become harmonious and loving, that intention will open you to new perceptions." That is a deeply profound statement. And remember, "new perceptions," expanded awareness, higher consciousness, is a key part of spiritual development.

A conflict or problem in your relationship always represents an opportunity for spiritual growth, not an opportunity to solve the problem. Train yourself to think: What can I learn about myself and about us from this conflict?

I do not mean to be glib about conflict in relationships. My point is that the Spiritual Partnership approach to problems is fundamentally different from the old "conflict resolution" model, and that the spiritual approach is not only more enlightened, it is also more effective. It is what Thomas Moore means when he says that change is more likely to happen as a result of "slight shifts in imagination" than because of "major efforts at change."

To reiterate, all couples have problems. But when you focus most of your attention on the problems—because you have the illusion that if you focus on them, you will solve them—then pretty soon all you have is problems. The weakest, most dissatisfying parts of your relationship will be receiving all your attention, leaving little time for fun, affection, and mutual support. "Problems are like goldfish," says Pransky. "The more you feed them, the bigger they get."

Spiritual Partnership: If You're Happy, Your Problems Will Diminish

Think of the ongoing problem that plagues your relationship. Or the problem you happen to be dealing with right now. Are you having a "power struggle" over something? Is your partner too controlling? Do you disagree about something? Does your partner have certain traits that feel annoying or even intolerable to you?

Does it surprise you to hear that the best way to "solve" the problem is to ignore it?

Probably, because most of what you have heard before is about how to talk so that you will be heard, how to negotiate with your partner, how to "fight fair," how to work at understanding your partner, how to find time to sit down and talk.

Spiritual Partnership suggests that you prepare a special meal for your sweetheart this evening, or take him or her out to a cozy restaurant—*even if you don't feel like it*—just as an experiment. Find an unusual way to say "I love you," like writing it in shaving cream on the mirror or making a heart-shaped pancake. Write your loved one an unexpected little love note. Bring home a CD or book that you know will delight your honey. Give your partner a sincere compliment. Plan a surprise erotic evening. Make reservations for a B&B in the country for this weekend. Have your partner's favorite friends over for Sunday brunch. Surprise your partner by "giving in" on some difference you are having now, not with anger or as a victim, but as a gift you freely decide to give.

If you are short on ideas, buy a copy of Greg Godek's book, *1001 Ways to Be Romantic,* and find something thoughtful to do for your sweetheart every day. Even ten minutes with that book will inspire you. Also, any of the Five Sacred Acts of Love in Section II will work.

If you have been feeling deprived in your relationship, maybe the best way to feel better is to do something wonderful for yourself. Take a vacation day from work and treat yourself to a day fishing, hiking, or shopping. Plan a special lunch with a good friend. Hire someone to take care of lingering household projects. Find a way to "act on your own" (Sacred Act #3) to resolve something that has been troubling you.

That's the spiritual approach to solving the problems in your relationship. Deliberately create a harmonious atmosphere between the two of you, *even if all of your problems have not been solved.* Just think, you don't have to solve your problems in order to be happy!

Suppose right now you feel terribly distant or upset or betrayed or furious. This is painful; I've been there too, and so has every other intimate partner at one time or another. I'm not suggesting it will be easy, but now is exactly the time for you to muster up your willingness to try an experiment, *even if you don't feel like it.*

The spiritual journey is difficult, remember? You are climbing a steep mountain in bad weather, not sauntering along a level path in the summertime. You have to care about your spiritual growth. You have to be willing to try something you've never tried before, even if it seems impossible, even if it sounds absurd.

What are your excuses?

"I can't bring myself to do anything nice right now. I'm too hurt."

"My partner won't even notice anything I do."

"It's just too corny."

"Anything I do will backfire on me."

"This is so unfair. I already do all the giving."

"I already do all those nice things. We are beyond that."

Well, even Jesus on his way to the cross prayed, "My Father, if it be possible, let this cup pass from me." He didn't want to do what he knew he was called upon to do, but he went ahead with it. Your task isn't as hard as his.

The harder this challenge to "create an atmosphere of harmony" seems to you, the more important it is for you to try it.

Remember that this is an experiment. It can't "fail," because no matter what happens, you will have learned from it. There is no wrong outcome. Just try what you now know is the spiritual alternative, and carefully observe the results. Pay attention.

Again, in Section II you will learn specific ways to "create

 ♉ EXPERIMENT #8:
 CREATE HARMONY

 1. Make a new list of everything you consider to be a
    problem or negative aspect of your relationship.
 2. Next to each item write either a T for "Tolerable" or DB
    for "Deal breaker."
 3. Now consider not discussing or working on any of these
    problems at all for the next eight weeks.
 4. For now, make an agreement with yourself that you will
    not discuss any of these problems for one day.
 5. Think up one action you can take to create harmony in
    your relationship, a favor for your mate, a surprise, a
    special treat. Do this *even if you don't feel like it*, just as
    an experiment.
 6. Make a note in your journal about what you did and how it
    worked out. Remember, avoid anticipating any particular
    outcome. Just note what actually does happen.

harmony first." Here, we are just talking about the principle: Focusing on your problems won't solve them and won't make the two of you happy. Focusing on your friendship and on enjoying each other will.

Spiritual Partnership Principle #5: Don't discuss problems. Instead, create a positive, harmonious atmosphere—right now.

Let's review.
Spiritual Partnership is *not:*

- Improving your communication skills
- Persuading your partner to change
- Determining who is right and who is wrong
- Insisting on fairness and equality
- Solving your problems

From now on, whenever you catch yourself in any of these habits from the Old Model, *stop.* The spiritual alternatives, and the Five Principles of Spiritual Partnership, are:

1. Use loving actions instead of communication. Keep your mouth out of it.
2. Never try to solve a problem by asking your partner to change.
3. Don't think about who is right. Instead, ask yourself, "What can I do to make a difference here?" Think "goodwill."
4. Strive to keep in balance the times you stand up for

your partner's needs and the times you stand up for
your own.

5. Don't discuss problems; don't try to solve problems.
Instead, create a positive, harmonious atmosphere,
right now.

The Five Sacred Acts we will discuss in Section II offer specific, concrete ways to practice these principles.

Keep in mind as you practice Spiritual Partnership that you
are voluntarily providing your relationship with spiritual leadership. As the "big" person, you are quietly following spiritual values to the best of your ability and letting your relationship reap
the benefits.

How to Use the Five Sacred Acts: An Introduction

The following suggested program may be the easiest couples-work you have ever attempted. There's no preparation (except for the chapters you just read). There are no long questionnaires to fill out. You don't have to set aside big blocks of time or persuade your partner to sit down and do a structured exercise with you. The Five Acts are just a new way to be, a new way to think, a new way of doing what you already do in your relationship.

All you need is a little willingness. Even an ounce will do. It doesn't matter if you are skeptical or pessimistic. It doesn't matter if you don't feel like doing an act. Just do it, for a set amount of time. That's all.

Each of the Five Sacred Acts of Spiritual Partnership stands on its own and can be used at any time or place, separately or combined with other acts.

What follows is a suggestion for using the acts as a deliberate program for improving your relationship. The program consists of six steps:

GET READY

1. Assess your relationship
2. Make a commitment to your relationship
3. Make a commitment to the program

GET SET

4. Set up support appointments
5. Read through all of the Five Sacred Acts of Love

GO

6. Begin experimenting with the Five Sacred Acts

1. Assess Your Relationship

On a scale of 1 to 10, one being just this side of calling a divorce lawyer and ten being completely fabulous, where would you put your level of satisfaction and happiness in your relationship right now. Go ahead, choose a number.

Be assured, the Five Sacred Acts will improve your relationship *no matter where you are on the scale.* I have literally seen twos and threes move to ten, and I have seen tens make discoveries that moved them into even closer intimacy.

Now, if you haven't done so earlier in this book, take a moment to list what you see as the biggest problems in your relationship, the main obstacles to happiness. Then list what you see as the greatest strengths in your relationship. What do you adore about your partner? What do the two of you do well together?

I suggest you write these lists in your journal. Take time with them, and be completely honest with yourself.

2. Make a Commitment to Your Relationship

This program using the Five Sacred Acts assumes that you want to improve your relationship, that you love your partner and are committed to making the relationship work really well for both of you. If you feel that commitment, skip to step three.

If you are not certain that you feel that commitment, this program will be extremely useful for you. Here is how it will help:

If your relationship is so bad that you are thinking about leaving your partner, either you are genuinely ambivalent or you haven't mustered up the courage to do what you know you need to do: walk away. In either case, this program will give you great help.

If you are ambivalent, then what you need is more information. That's exactly what doing the Five Sacred Acts will give you: more information. Do a Sacred Act, and take careful notes about what happens. Notice how it makes you feel. Even angrier? Softer and more understanding? Every subtle feeling counts. How does your partner respond? Notice and write down everything.

It's a known axiom that if you keep doing the same things, you will keep getting the same results. That's what has been happening in your relationship for years. The Five Sacred Acts give you *something new to try*, and you are absolutely certain to get different results. You have no idea what those new results are until you try the experiments. By the end of this "program," either you will know for certain that you want to leave or you will be clear that your own new attitude has created positive changes that you like.

For the purposes of this program, then, if you can't make a

genuine commitment to your relationship, make a commitment to finding out exactly what your level of commitment is.

Exception: If your partner is abusing you, either physically or emotionally, do not use this program. If your partner is addicted to drugs or alcohol, do not use this program. Instead, call someone and ask for help. Find a minister, priest, or rabbi in your area, even if you don't know the person. Look in your phone book for psychotherapists or for domestic abuse programs or substance abuse programs. If you can't find anyone else, call your local police department and ask for a referral to a domestic abuse program or a counselor. You must take care of yourself. If you don't, no one else will. Don't let fear stop you from asking for the help you need. *You cannot manage this problem by yourself.* No one else ever has. You must call someone and be totally honest about what is happening.

Special Warning to Singles: Do not use this program to stay in a relationship when you know you are settling for less than what you truly want or deserve. While you still have the opportunity to choose the person who will be your lifelong partner, *choose carefully!* Don't make the mistake of staying in a relationship you are less than enthusiastic about, or that has significant problems, just because you aren't paying attention!

One of the most common mistakes singles make is to spend months or years in what I call "BTN" relationships: better than nothing. BTNs keep you out of circulation for finding the true love of your life, and they lower your self-esteem. I have written extensively about BTNs in my book, *If I'm So Wonderful, Why Am I Still Single?* and about exactly how to keep your standards—and your spirits—high as you search for your soul mate. Here, suffice it to say that if you truly desire a committed relationship and are not yet in one, that in itself might be a reason for you to end your relationship. Move on, and hold out for what you truly want; only then do you have even a chance of getting it. Save your skills as a spiritual leader for a relationship you are certain you very much want to be a part of.

As Benjamin Franklin so wisely said, "Keep your eyes wide open before marriage and half shut afterwards." (By "half shut afterwards," I'm sure he meant "be accepting," not "be unconscious." There is a world of difference.)

3. Make a Commitment to the Program

I suggest you give this program at least eight weeks. Make a commitment to yourself right now that you will, to the best of your ability, follow the principles and try the Five Sacred Acts for eight weeks.

If your relationship is seven to ten on the scale in step one above, maybe just reading this book is all you need to do. A shift in attitude and a few Sacred Actions when they are appropriate here and there will enhance your already thriving relationship. You may not need this program.

If you are from one to six on the scale, I encourage you to be extremely deliberate, set up an exact program, and follow it precisely. Make this program a major priority for yourself for the next eight weeks. *It is impossible to do this program seriously and not see changes!*

If you are going to set up a precise and deliberate program for the next eight weeks, you will need three allies: a journal, a calendar, and a support person.

If you haven't already done so, find a notebook or an attractive blank bound book that you can use as a journal. And find a calendar to keep with your journal.

Also, you will need a support person. Even if you and your partner are doing the program together, find someone else. A second person is necessary to help you pay attention and keep you focused. When you talk through an experiment you did, you will learn more from it. And, since you will be accountable to this person, you are more likely to stay on track.

The ideal support person is a friend who is using this program at the same time you are. Do it together.

When you find your support person, make an appointment to talk with him or her *every week at the same time.* You will report exactly what experiment or experiments you did that week, the results, and exactly what experiment or experiments you will do for the following weeks.

Reminder: Set Aside Your Problems

For the eight weeks of this program, do not discuss your problems. The point of this program, remember, is not to solve your problems, but to create a "new level of consciousness," a "higher or wider interest," so that through this broadening of outlook, "the insoluble problem loses its urgency." (Carl Jung)

If you catch yourself discussing your problem; having an old, familiar argument; or even *experiencing* your problem (your partner is criticizing you, you are doing all the housework, your partner falls asleep in the middle of your conversation, your partner doesn't listen to you, etc.); *immediately do something positive yourself.* Either take care of yourself in some way, give yourself a nice gift, or do something thoughtful and generous for your partner. Deliberately create a positive atmosphere. Remember that your relationship is far more important than this annoying incident.

REMINDER: KEEP YOUR
EXPECTATIONS OPEN

Avoid fantasizing or hoping for any particular results from your experiments. This is not easy; it is a spiritual value that we work on for our whole lives: Do not become attached to any particular outcome. (Reread "Surrender," in Chapter Two, page 74.) The Five Sacred Acts will give you a very fine opportunity to practice this value.

There are two reasons it's important to keep your expectations open: First, it will help you avoid pain and disappointment if what you hope for doesn't occur. Second, if you are riveted to one outcome, you may miss wonderful serendipitous results that you never even imagined might occur.

Winifred was an avid Balkan folk dancer. More than anything, she wanted her husband Jonathan to take up the hobby too. He sort of liked it, but in order to enjoy it fully, he would have had to dance every week so he could learn a number of dances well. This he was never willing to do.

Winifred tried Sacred Act #3. Acting on her own, she hired a folk dance teacher to come to their home every Thursday evening for a lesson. She told Jonathan she was doing it for herself, but invited him to join her. Jonathan did the lessons, but he still would not go out dancing with her, except occasionally.

They both enjoyed the teacher and found themselves involved in long conversations with her after the lessons. Jonathan suggested that she bring her husband with her the next time and that they all go out for dinner after the lesson. Over dinner, the other couple talked about how much they missed playing bridge because none of their friends played. Since Jonathan and Winifred both played, they set up a bridge evening and had a wonderful time. Now they all play bridge regularly. Winifred still goes dancing without Jonathan, but she doesn't care because they have found a different hobby they enjoy together.

That's serendipity. "Acting on her own" worked for Winifred, but not at all in the way she had anticipated or hoped for.

REMINDER:
KEEP IN MIND THE FIVE PRINCIPLES
OF SPIRITUAL PARTNERSHIP

The Five Principles of Spiritual Partnership weave themselves throughout the Five Sacred Acts, as I will point out over and over. Actually, each of the five acts *is a way of putting all of the principles to work.* In other words, whenever you are performing a Sacred Act, you will automatically be in alignment with the principles. I will demonstrate this when I discuss each act. For example, when you "act as if" you feel loving, even when you don't you will be (a) acting instead of talking, (b) changing yourself instead of your partner, (c) exhibiting a spirit of goodwill, and so on. The five acts are a concrete way to put the principles to work for yourself.

So let's review the Five Principles of Spiritual Partnership once more:

1. Use loving actions instead of communication. Keep your mouth out of it.
2. Never try to solve a problem by asking your partner to change.
3. Don't think about who is right or wrong. Instead, ask yourself, "What can I do to make a difference here?" Think "goodwill."

4. Strive to keep in balance the times you stand up for your partner's needs and the times you stand up for your own.

5. Don't discuss problems; don't try to solve problems. Instead, create a positive, harmonious atmosphere, right now.

There definitely are exceptions to each of the five principles. There are times when it is appropriate to ask your partner for a change. Sometimes it is necessary and useful to discuss problems. We will look at these exceptions in detail in Chapter Ten.

However, *you will not know when to make appropriate exceptions to the principles until you have the principles themselves firmly under your belt.*

My strong suggestion is, for the first eight weeks that you deliberately try Spiritual Partnership, adhere unswervingly to the Five Principles to the best of your ability. Do not knowingly or deliberately make any exceptions at all. This whole project is an experiment from which you can expect to learn a great deal about yourself and your partner. The more strictly you abide by the principles, the more you will learn. Be rigid with yourself. It's only eight weeks. Follow these principles with no exceptions, and see what happens.

4. Set Up Your Support Appointments

Call your support person and set up an exact appointment each week for the next eight weeks (see page 129).

5. Read Through All of the Five Sacred Acts of Spiritual Partnership

6. Begin

A. First, set up the first week of your program. Choose one or maybe two of the five acts. Look at your calendar and write down in your journal exactly when you plan to try one of the five acts. For example, "Next Monday evening from seven to nine P.M., I will act as if I feel loving and supportive toward my mate, even if I don't." Or, "One time this week, when I find I am angry, I will act as if I feel loving, even if I don't. I will do this for a full half hour."

Always try one of the five acts *as an experiment,* and always for an exact set time with a beginning time and an end time. The amount of time can be anything from five minutes to the entire week.

B. Now, when the appointed time arrives, do the Sacred Action you have selected. Remember, it's an experiment.

C. As soon as possible after each experiment, find some time to write in your journal about it. Think of yourself as a scientist, trying for a purely objective report of the experiment. Always include:

- Exactly what happened
- How you felt during the experiment
- How you feel now
- Exactly how your partner responded

One of the things that may happen is that you will find a
way not to do the experiment. This is very common. You may
have a reason, like someone came over, or your partner went
out for the evening. Or you may just have been unable or
unwilling to do it. Period.

This is a result! Remember, with an experiment, there is no
such thing as "failure." No matter what happens or doesn't happen, you learned something, and that is all we ever ask of an
experiment.

I worked with a woman who stayed in a support group for
eight weeks but did not actually carry out a single experiment
until the last day of the last week, and even that was halfhearted: She attended a business dinner with her husband but
left early. After eight weeks, by paying attention to her unwill-
ingness to experiment at all, this woman began to see how
debilitating her own anger was, and that she was the only one
who could change it. That was a big lesson for her.

Or, you may do an experiment and see no response whatsoever from your partner. This is also very common. No notice-
able response is a response. Write it down. Or all you may
notice is a tiny glance or gesture, or a single remark. Everything counts. Pay attention. Notice everything, and write it all
down.

D. If you like, sometime during the week find time to do the
boxed "experiments" that are associated with the Sacred Act
you chose.

E. At the end of the first week, set up the Sacred Act or Acts
you will experiment with for your second week. It's fine to
repeat your first week exactly. Or you may want to try something different. If you aren't sure what to do, discuss it with
your support person. The truth is, it doesn't matter too much

what you try. Just keep experimenting, paying attention, and recording your experiences. Use each of the Five Sacred Acts at least once during your eight weeks.

That's it. That's all you have to do. The rest will happen by itself.

Don't make the mistake of saying to yourself, "I'll do all this sometime, after _____." Don't put this program off another minute. Start right now.

Now we are ready to learn the Five Sacred Acts of Love.

Part II

The Five
Sacred
Acts of
Spiritual
Partnership

FIVE

Sacred Act #1:
Practice Restraint

According to my thesaurus, some synonyms for "restraint" are: moderation, prudence, judiciousness, equanimity, self-control, poise, presence of mind, level-headedness, good taste, discrimination, and subtlety.

These are exactly the qualities we strive for on the spiritual path. Composure. Coolness under pressure. Serenity. Inner peace.

The quest for these qualities requires discipline. But sometimes it isn't clear exactly how spiritual discipline translates into daily life. Sacred Act #1 offers you highly specific opportunities to practice restraint, and all those wonderful synonyms that go along with it. We will learn three specific Sacred Acts of Restraint:

- Avoiding negative comments
- Avoiding defensive responses
- Avoiding fights

Avoid Negative, Critical, and Demanding Comments

Make a pact with yourself that for two full weeks you will refrain from making any negative, critical, or demanding comments to your partner.

This assignment is easy to understand, simple, and direct.

And extremely educational.

Virtually always, when people who have agreed to this experiment report back to me, the first thing they mention is how surprised they were to discover *how often they make* negative, critical, or demanding comments to their partners.

I strongly encourage you to do this experiment. Starting right now, and for two full weeks—mark it on your calendar—just agree with yourself that you will not make any negative, critical, or demanding comments to your mate.

I warn you, there is a learning curve.

If you are like most people I've worked with, first, you will realize that you have said something negative, critical, or demanding *after* you have said it. That is major progress. You are waking up! You are paying attention! You are expanding your consciousness about yourself.

Next, you may realize that you are saying something negative, critical, or demanding *as* you are saying it. Congratulations! You have moved to phase two. More progress.

Then, I hope, there will come a magical moment when you are on the verge of saying something negative, critical, or demanding, and you actually decide not to say it. You practice restraint.

This is spiritual growth. This means you have exercised your will and your discipline instead of living unconsciously on automatic pilot; you have been "spiritual"! You have just practiced moderation, prudence, judiciousness, equanimity, poise, level-headedness, good taste, discrimination, subtlety, *self-control,* and *presence of mind.*

After you are successful in practicing restraint several times, you may begin to feel a sense of accomplishment and a strengthening of your inner power. You will be more in control of your own behavior.

Also, as you keep paying attention when you are tempted to make a negative, critical, or demanding comment, you will learn what types of comments you tend to make. This can make an immeasurable contribution to your self-awareness and to your spiritual growth. What was motivating you to say what you were about to say? What was your remark going to accomplish? Are your negative remarks typically critical, controlling, whiny, sarcastic, invasive? Do you sound like your mother or father when you make these remarks? What can you learn by closely observing your own behavior and then choosing to modify it? I can't overemphasize the importance of the learning that can take place if you take this experiment seriously.

Of course, by the end of two weeks you will almost certainly begin to notice a difference in your household, and in your relationship.

Many negative, critical, or demanding comments by themselves may sound fairly harmless. You may even think you are being helpful when you say them:

"Honey, be careful. You're being too rough with Johnny."
(Critical)

"I didn't think your remark was very funny! It was rude!"
(Negative, critical)

"Would you please stop talking about that!"
(Demanding)

"Don't interrupt me!"
(Critical, demanding)

"If you hold the bagel this way, it would be a lot easier to slice."
(Controlling, invasive)

"Don't follow that car so closely!"
(Demanding)

It doesn't take many such apparently helpful comments before your mate feels invaded, criticized, or belittled. And for the most part, the remarks are useless. Your partner isn't really going to harm Johnny. She isn't going to stop making corny or crude jokes. The bagels will get sliced. He has been arriving successfully at his destinations when you're not in the car.

But even when they are harmless and not numerous, such comments still bring down the energy between the two of you, however slightly. Pay attention. You'll see.

And of course, for some couples, negative, critical, and demanding remarks are not so harmless. They make up the majority of all conversation.

Dennis came to me on the verge of leaving his wife, Mary.

She's not affectionate, she's not warm and cuddly. She's too involved with her work, and she's always tired at night. I mean, why did she get married? She's supposed to kiss me when we both get home, cozy up in front of the fireplace. She's always off doing more work.

Dennis belonged to a spiritual study group and viewed him-self as a spiritual person. I asked him to try the above experi-ment and pay attention to his negative, critical, or demanding statements. After two weeks he came back astonished.

I was spending a lot of time criticizing her. I had no idea of this. But I was always trying to prove to her how unaffectionate she was, and of course, this came out as criticism. And demands. And negative! I was being so negative. It took me a long time to truly stop, but by the end of this week, our household was much more peaceful, and I feel I have made a spiritual discovery. I've seen something about myself I never saw before.

This is the discovery Dennis made: In his mind, the problems were all the fault of his wife, who just wouldn't get affectionate and lovey dovey. But he found out that *he was actually the cause of all the upset in the relationship.* By criticizing her so much, he was making the relationship a very unpleasant place to live. He was pushing Mary away, when his desire was to bring her closer. It was he who needed to make a change, not Mary.

Using the one simple Sacred Act of practicing restraint, Den-nis actually invoked all five of the principles:

1. He stopped trying to communicate, and used a Sacred Act instead.
2. He stopped trying to change his wife, and instead he made a change.
3. He let go of being right and instead asked himself, "No matter who is right and who is wrong, what can I do to make a difference?"
4. He stood up for himself, by trying a new spiritual prac-

tice, and he stood up for his wife by letting go of his incessant nagging, and instead accepted her for who she truly is.

5. He stopped trying to solve the problem, and instead deliberately created a harmonious atmosphere.

After Dennis discovered how liberating it was for him to stop his criticism, I encouraged him to begin "acting as if" he felt loving and adoring, behaving the way he wanted his wife to behave toward him, even when he didn't feel like it.

Guess what?

Mary became more affectionate, and more receptive to Dennis's affection.

That's not why Dennis made the change; he stopped all criticism because that was the spiritual thing to do. He experimented.

But he was amazed at the outcome of the experiment. Mary didn't magically transform into a totally different person; she had been raised in a repressive household and would never be completely free with her body. But she opened up to Dennis. And Mary's strength was her high energy, happy, upbeat personality, and childlike playfulness. All those wonderful qualities had almost disappeared under Dennis's assaults. Now they reappeared, and the two of them began enjoying each other's company much more.

Dennis still wishes Mary were more cuddly and sexy. But he adores her cheerfulness, and he single-handedly turned their relationship around, just by practicing restraint.

It is important to note that before this experiment, Dennis did not see himself as negative, critical, or demanding. He could not see beyond the obvious fact that he was "right." "Wives should be affectionate." He would tell me: "Mary should be more loving." If he had continued trying to convince her of this, they would surely have ended up in the divorce courts. He would have lost his marriage, but he would have kept his precious booby prize: He would have proven he was right.

Alex is another person who learned about himself by using the First Sacred Act. When he first heard about practicing restraint, he realized that he was demanding a great deal of his wife. On his own, he decided to reduce his requests. Rather than pestering her to find a time to cut his hair, he went out to get it cut. And even though he felt he wasn't good at buying his own clothes, he decided to begin managing that on his own. He found stores where the salespeople were helpful. His initiative eliminated two areas of negative energy in their relationship.

Alex never mentioned this to his wife, and it was a couple of months before she even noticed the changes. But after she saw a haircut she didn't do and noticed a few new shirts, she expressed her surprise—and then her gratitude. Alex was happy, not only because two areas of tension in his relationship were gone, but also because his increased self-sufficiency felt great to him.

Helpful Hints

As you begin the experiment of deliberately stopping all negative, critical, or demanding comments within your relationship, you may find it useful to ask yourself this question: "What is it like to be loved by me?"

Actually talk with a friend about this, or take a half hour and write your answers in your journal.

Put yourself in your partner's shoes. Think about your interactions in the last several days or weeks. What have you been like in the relationship? How do you suppose your partner felt about you? What contributions do you make in general? Are there ways you could brighten the life of your loved one? Are

there behaviors you might let go of that would make you an easier person to be around? What is it like for your partner to be
loved by you?

If you think your partner would be receptive to it, you might
even want to ask him or her this question, sometime when you
are both relaxed and in a talkative mood. You may become aware
of something new that your partner does or doesn't like, something about which you had no awareness before you asked. If this
conversation "raises your consciousness" or expands your
awareness, it is spiritual growth.

Here's a little "mantra" that is useful to some people as they
practice restraint: "The relationship is more important than this
one incident." Or: "The relationship is more important
than ＿＿＿＿＿＿ (socks on the floor, my doing the dishes,
that thoughtless remark, etc.)." One woman told me:

> That phrase comes up so often for me, and it is always on tar-
> get. Most of the events I start to comment on are so trivial, and
> my comment won't change the situation anyway! I'm sure I say,
> "The relationship is more important than ＿＿＿＿＿＿" to
> myself ten times a day now. It works with my kids too. What's
> most important is for everybody to feel good and be happy. Nag-
> ging or corrective "help" from me is going to spoil the good
> feelings. That sentence has a big impact on my family!

If you, dear reader, do not act on any other specific experiment in this book, I encourage you to try practicing restraint. I
know of no one who has seriously done this experiment and not
learned from it.

> ∂つ EXPERIMENT #9:
>   BAN NEGATIVE COMMENTS
>
> 1. Mark your calendar for two weeks, and promise yourself
>   that for those two weeks you will not make any negative,
>   critical, or demanding comments to your mate.
> 2. For these two weeks, keep paying attention. Listen to
>   yourself.
> 3. Find a good half hour to spend with your journal, and
>   write about this question: "What is it like to be loved
>   by me?"
> 4. Memorize the phrase, "Our relationship is more important
>   than _____." When you are about to say
>   something negative, say this to yourself instead.

Be Open Instead of Defensive

Now we move on to a more advanced level of practicing restraint:
learning to refrain from making a defensive, knee-jerk response
when someone is attacking you. Refraining from making negative, critical, or demanding comments is a bit easier, because
you are initiating the remarks. Avoiding defensive responses is
harder, because you are usually caught off guard. But as you
read here about alternatives to being defensive, and you begin to
pay attention, sometime soon you will catch yourself being
defensive. That is an extremely important first step. Right then
and there, maybe you will be able to shift gears, as I suggest
below.

Being defensive is a natural and normal response. Here are some examples:

"I thought that was a rude remark you made to Mrs. Thomas."
      "It wasn't rude, she wanted to know the truth. I was just being honest!"

"You never do anything around this house!"
      "I do too! I swept the porch last night. I'm too tired when I come home. I do stuff on weekends."

"Can I tell you something I would like you to do when we make love?"
      "You mean you don't like what I'm doing now?"

Defensiveness is as old as humankind. Someone throws a stone at you; you put your hands in front of your face to protect yourself. Maybe you throw a stone back. We do the same thing with words: verbal assault, verbal self-protection. It is a survival instinct.

But, as we know, part of being spiritual is becoming "conscious" of habitual behaviors and making a decision to change them if they are counterproductive. Defensiveness is usually part of your conditioned personality, not your authentic self. It is not loving, and it definitely creates distance, not connection. When you become defensive, even if the other guy started it, even if you're being unjustly accused, even if you're "right," you are escalating the hostilities. Spiritual practice requires you to be the leader, the "big" person. It requires you to exercise your will and discipline, to make a move toward connection, and to overcome bad habits.

Whenever you have any interaction with your loved one,

whether you are being attacked or just having any kind of discussion or interaction, you have only two modes available to you: Is your heart open or is it closed? The point of spiritual practice is to be able to keep your heart open to your partner as much as possible. Can you yield to your partner, moving with his or her mood, comment, opinion? Or are you resisting your partner, arguing back, becoming defensive and self-protective?

One way to start overcoming the bad habit of becoming defensive and closing your heart, especially when your partner is assaulting you in some way, is to memorize the phrase, "I feel defensive." The urge to make a defensive remark comes up fast. It's hard to catch yourself before you do it. But if the phrase "I feel defensive" is on the tip of your tongue, maybe it will fall out of your mouth instead of the knee-jerk "Yes I do!" or "I did not!" or "You're not so great yourself!"

"I feel defensive" is a noncombative comment. It buys you time to calm down and decide what to do next. It names what's going on without placing blame anywhere. You are simply telling the truth.

The next level of nondefensive, peacemaking response to a verbal assault is to use the martial arts model. As you know, in martial arts, when someone throws a fist at you, instead of throwing up your own arm and trying to stop it, which will probably hurt both of you (the defensive move), you simply grab the fist and pull it, continuing in the direction of your opponent's momentum and pulling him or her off balance.

In conversation, a martial arts response—or continuing in the direction of your opponent's remark—would be to repeat the remark, or ask about it, like this:

"I thought that was a rude remark you made to Mrs. Thomas."
"You thought it was rude?"

Or like this:

"We never go out anymore!"
"You feel like we never go out anymore?"

Another option is to make a response that seems as if you're agreeing with the remark, even if you actually aren't. At some later occasion you may be able to bring the topic up and express your own, different opinion. But at the moment someone is angry with you and invested in being right, if you try to bring up another view, you will only be contributing to negativity and bad feelings, and you'll be passing up an opportunity to provide spiritual leadership, to de-escalate the hostilities. You can avoid disagreeing without actually agreeing either. For example:

"You never do anything around this house!"
"I know it seems that way. You do a lot of the work, it's true."

As another example, if your partner says, "We never go out anymore!" a typical, knee-jerk defensive response might be:
"Yes we do! We went to the movies last night! We went out for dinner last week!"
In this case, consider these nondefensive, peace-promoting responses:

"You feel like we never go out anymore?"
"It does seem like we never go out anymore."
"We do enjoy it when we go out. I love to go out too."

Recently, Tina and Ron had a serious misunderstanding while spending a few days with us. Ron thought Tina was going to get up early and go for a run. Tina thought Ron was going to get up early with her. When Ron sauntered downstairs about nine-thirty, Tina was fit to be tied. The conversation went something like this:

> *Ron:* Gee, it felt good to sleep in. Did you go for your run?
>
> *Tina:* Now I know what it's like to live with someone who doesn't keep his agreements!
>
> *Ron:* Agreements?
>
> *Tina:* I thought we were going to get up early! I just wasted this whole morning.
>
> *Ron:* Was I supposed to get up early too?
>
> *Tina:* You know you blew it. Don't sound so innocent. You are just so selfish. You only think of yourself! You're just being defensive because you know you're wrong.

Listening off in the corner, I knew this was the critical moment. I thought Ron would say something like, "I did not blow it! We never had an agreement that I would get up early. The last thing you said last night was . . . " And the fight would be on.

But Ron was brilliant. Here's what he said:

> *Ron:* I'm being defensive because I'm feeling attacked (pause). I am so sorry I misunderstood this. You must feel awful waiting around for me. I don't blame you for being angry. Honey, I'm so sorry you missed your run. That really makes me sad.

Ron didn't take Tina's bait. He didn't feel he needed to defend himself. He felt genuine empathy for Tina, in spite of her lashing out, and he decided to express that. Tina's anger toned right down.

Sometimes it takes several days to reverse your initial defensive response. I recall when a friend became angry with me because I broke a date with her. At first I was hurt and blamed her for not being more flexible. I felt she was deliberately trying to make me feel guilty. But after a few days, as I calmed down, I saw the validity of her position. I said to myself, "It doesn't matter who is right and who is wrong here. The relationship is far more important to me than this incident." I faxed her an apologetic note, which she appreciated. By letting go of being defensive, I mended my valuable friendship.

THIS HAS NOTHING TO DO WITH ME

One of the most challenging of all spiritual tasks is learning how to practice restraint when you have a nagging, critical, or controlling mate. If this is the case, consider that the universe is offering you an extra special opportunity to learn the Sacred Act of Restraint.

When your partner criticizes you, or continually nags or harps away at you, it is of course tempting to fight back, to defend yourself, and in fact to work very hard at getting your partner to discontinue this behavior. Your partner is the "wrong" one, you will feel, for picking away at you all the time.

If trying to get your partner to stop this behavior has not worked for you, here is a new strategy that does not involve making your partner wrong or trying to get him or her to change.

Learn the phrase, "This has nothing to do with me." Now, whenever your partner starts in on you, say it over and over *to yourself.*

The truth is, your partner's behavior probably does have very little to do with you. He or she has a natural tendency to be nagging, critical, or controlling, and almost certainly behaves this way with other people besides you. The behavior is coming from your partner's own fears or perfectionism or insecurity, and is not greatly affected by anything you do or do not do. If she is nagging you to lose weight and you do lose weight, she will probably start in on you about something else. Or if he is constantly telling you how to drive, he'll keep doing it, no matter what you do behind the wheel.

If the nagging, criticism, or controlling comments are habitual with your partner, they are not about you. You may be annoyed by them, but do not feel you have to defend yourself or change in any way. As much as you can, let the remarks slip off you, like water off a duck's back.

Sherry and Arthur were a couple for whom "This has nothing to do with me" worked well. Sherry was a backseat driver, but she didn't save her behavior for the car; she gave Arthur unsolicited advice about virtually everything he did. Arthur felt utterly frustrated when he came to one of my groups. Every attempt he made to persuade Sherry to stop not only was futile, but usually ended in a big fight. His comment to me was, "If she thinks I'm so helpless, why did she marry me?"

I asked Arthur to observe Sherry's behavior with other people, and sure enough, he began to realize that Sherry backseat-drove with everyone. Often, her advice was actually quite good, and friends didn't mind it so much because they received it in limited doses. But it began to dawn on Arthur that Sherry was not singling him out for special treatment. She didn't give him advice because she thought he was inadequate or "helpless," but so she could feel more in control. Her advice made her feel good about herself. It gave her the satisfaction (or the illusion) of helping other people. It had nothing to do with him! When he was able to stop taking her comments personally, he was much better able to let them roll off his back, change the subject, and move on. Sherry's controlling comments didn't change, but the atmosphere in the relationship was transformed because Arthur stopped making a crisis out of every remark.

The "martial arts" strategy we discussed above, of sounding like you agree even if you don't, can also be helpful with chronic criticizers or advice givers. You can respond by saying something like, "You're right, I wish I could be better," or "That's a good idea. Thanks," and then just go on your merry way. On your own, think through your partner's advice to see whether it has merit. If you can follow it or change what he or she is critical about with no compromise of your own desires, then do it. But it is perfectly okay for you to go right ahead with your way of doing things if that feels better to you, as long as you're being reasonable. But then, don't defend yourself. Simply don't engage with your partner. Just keep telling yourself, "This has nothing to do with me." It's one more way of practicing restraint, of taking leadership, of being the "big" person, thereby opening up more possibilities for closeness, connection, and mutual enjoyment, which after all is the real purpose of your relationship.

Becoming defensive is unenlightened, habitual, thoughtless behavior. Learning not to respond defensively is spiritual practice.

If you think seriously about the true meaning of spiritual practice, it has to do with the development and training of your mental state, attitudes, and psychological and emotional state and well-being. . . . For example, if you find yourself in a situation in which you might be tempted to insult someone, then you immediately take precautions and restrain yourself from doing that. Similarly, if you encounter a situation in which you may lose your temper, immediately you are mindful and say, "No,

ℬ EXPERIMENT #10:
ON DEFENSIVENESS

1. In your journal, list incidents or times that you can recall when you reacted defensively. It might be a big, classic fight from some time ago, or small incidents from the last couple of weeks. If you can't think of any, start paying attention until you catch yourself being defensive. Then return to this exercise.

2. Next to each defensive incident you recall, write a nondefensive response you might have given.

3. Memorize the phrase, "I feel defensive." For these eight weeks, associate the phrase with something you do every day, like brushing your teeth, getting into your car, or turning on the dishwasher. Now, every time you do that activity, pause, close your eyes for just three seconds, and say the phrase to yourself three or four times. The idea is to keep the phrase in the front of your mind so that when an incident arises where it might be useful, you will remember it.

4. When you hear someone else being defensive, either with you or with some third party, to yourself say a sentence that would have been a nondefensive response. It might be, "I feel defensive," or "Yeah, you could be right," or "That's an idea."

5. The first time you catch yourself *before* you make a defensive response and you actually make a nondefensive response, congratulate yourself. Record the incident in your journal.

this is not the appropriate way." That actually is a spiritual practice.

THE DALAI LAMA

Avoid Fights

The third aspect of the Sacred Act "Practice Restraint" is to stop destructive fighting.

Virtually all couples have arguments, lose their tempers, and become upset with each other from time to time. Fights are normal, and certainly not a sign of a "bad" relationship.

Some fights are even useful and actually assist spiritual growth and move a relationship forward. And some fights may not be useful, but they are harmless.

A fight is useful when it helps to clarify and to convey true feelings. Maybe you are feeling uneasy but you aren't sure why. Or you know your true feelings but have been reluctant to express them to your partner. By letting the emotions fly, you may learn what is truly upsetting you, and it is important for your partner to see how deeply you feel.

For example, Michael, a lawyer, had a difficult case and needed to work evenings until it was over. Jill tried to be understanding but found herself complaining about it now and then. Finally, one night, to her surprise, she erupted. As she went on for a while in great anger and with tears flowing, she discovered why she was feeling upset: She was afraid that working nights would become a pattern for Michael that would continue forever. Plus, she was feeling a great deal more strain over her lonely evenings than she realized. It was important for both of them to see all the emotion that was there and know exactly what they were dealing with. Jill's deep emotion was her authentic self speaking.

In this case, Michael helped to make the fight useful for both of them, because *he did not become defensive.* He listened to Jill. He could understand that she was not blaming him; she was expressing her own feelings. Michael knew he did not need to "fix" the problem then and there. He told Jill that he had no idea she was having such a hard time and that he was really sorry. And he reassured her that he too did not want to make a habit of working evenings. This fight was definitely a move toward connection for both of them.

A good fight, with expressions of rage and anger, is a way for the body to discharge built-up energy, and sometimes it just feels good. Even though one or both partners may be very angry, at some level they both know that this is simply a good blowup and that it will pass.

Harmless fights are the ones that happen when both partners are exhausted, under stress, or even depressed. They bicker or complain. They are irritable or edgy. The next day, when they feel better, it all goes away.

But the vast majority of fights between couples are destructive. They have no useful function. They create negative energy and leave the household in a doom and gloom atmosphere. Partners may say things that are truly hurtful or malicious. The people involved are *not* being authentic, but are acting out of habit, exercising no control over their feelings. Most often the subject of the fight has little or nothing to do with the true source of conflict. No progress is made in resolving any problems. Since the partners are not paying attention, they are making no progress in their spiritual growth.

One easy way to tell whether a fight is useful or destructive is that useful fights happen only once, or once in a great while. Or, a useful fight may happen in several stages over a period of weeks. It's the same fight, but each episode builds on the last, and progress is made each time. Also, in useful fights, you will be talking about your own feelings, not about your partner's behavior. Your partner's behavior may be contributing to your feelings, but what you are really talking about is your own feelings.

Destructive fights are the same fight over and over and over with no progress ever being made. The participants are not observing themselves or making any attempt to be conscious or to exercise choice. Destructive fights are characterized by habitual, thoughtless behaviors like blame, defensiveness, accusations, criticism, sarcasm, name calling, insisting that you're right and your partner is wrong, and making yourself into a powerless victim.

The spiritual remedy for destructive fights is to avoid them altogether.

This is not easy, because fighting can be addictive. When you are in a rage and your adrenaline level is up, it is hard to resist showing your partner how right you are, or how he or she blew it again.

But the spiritual approach is to walk away.

You have a choice. You do not have to behave the way you feel. Pay attention. Bring consciousness to the situation. Discipline yourself to do something difficult. Be willing to experiment.

The way in which you walk away is critically important. If you throw in the last word and then rush out in a fit of pique, slamming the door, this is not spiritual. The ideal is to say, in as calm a voice as possible, "I'm very angry right now. I want to talk about this, but not when we are both so emotional. I'm going to leave so we can talk about this later when we're both calmer."

Then leave the scene altogether. Very decisively, walk away.

If you are full of emotion, find a way to discharge that emotion *not* in the presence of your partner. Go for a run or a vigorous walk. Hit your bed: Stretch your arms way over your head and, as you exhale, come down hard on that bed with your fists, over and over. Or call a friend and express your anger to a third person. This can work even if you get an answering machine—if this is a very understanding friend. You will feel better if you let your body discharge its buildup of energy.

One of the very best ways to calm yourself down is to let time pass. If you are boiled over about something in the morning, chances are you will already feel less "charge" about it by afternoon. So, after you discharge your angry energy, find a way to distract yourself.

In the end, you may or may not choose to talk about the problem again later. If you were fighting about something that needs to be decided, like where you will go on vacation, or who's going to stay home with the children on Thursday evening, or even whether or not you are going to have a baby, then you will have to resolve it later. But if your real fight is about who has more power in the relationship, for example, that issue will respond far better to unilateral Sacred Actions than it ever will to long discussions. You'll never be able to resolve your power issues by discussing them; you probably won't even be able to agree on the problem, since you each see it from a different point of view. So instead of discussing it, choose a Sacred Act and do that. Figure out what you need and figure out how you can manage that need on your own. And let your partner go ahead and be who he or she is.

I once attended a lecture on a particular type of psychotherapy. An audience member asked the speaker, "Will this method help us to stop fighting?" The speaker replied, "The way to stop fighting is to stop fighting."

I agree. And avoiding fights is the spiritual path too. Don't indulge your immature urges to punish your partner or get your way. Take your anger out on a pillow or a friend with a sympathetic ear, not on your partner. Your job is to nurture your own and your partner's sacred inner flame. Fighting will only dump sand on both of them.

Practicing restraint can be an educational and life-changing Sacred Act. Put your attention on refraining from:

- Making negative, critical, or demanding comments
- Responding defensively when attacked
- Fighting

Practicing restraint helps you learn how to pay attention. It helps you distinguish between your personality and your authentic self. And it moves you toward love and connection.

Truly, all you have to do is start paying attention. You will be able to hear yourself being negative, critical, demanding, defensive, or bellicose. When you do, that is a major first step. Just notice what you said. Notice how your remark made you feel. Notice the impact of your remark on those around you. If you

---

℘ EXPERIMENT #11:
STOP DESTRUCTIVE FIGHTS

1. In your journal, list the last several fights you had with your partner. Using the criteria above, label each fight "useful" or "destructive."
2. Next time you find yourself starting to become involved in a destructive fight, experiment with a spiritual leave-taking.

can't stop yourself right away, don't worry. Just pay attention as you do it. Gradually, as you actually hear yourself, you may find that you naturally become less negative and defensive, because you yourself will find your negativity to be unpleasant.

Most of us will never achieve perfection with any of these Sacred Acts. Perfection is not the goal. Learning is the goal, spiritual growth, always moving in the direction of greater connection, authenticity, love, consciousness, receptivity, and happiness. Practicing restraint is one good way to achieve self-awareness, self-control, and spiritual growth.

Meanwhile, you will create a much more harmonious and joyful household.

SIX

Sacred Act #2:
"Act As If"

One of the great keys to success in life remains a closely guarded and little known secret: You don't have to behave the way you feel.

Let's say your friend, Janice, shows up late for an appointment, for the fourth time in a row. You are angry and frustrated, and of course you will behave that way. "How can you do this to me again? This is going to mess up my whole day. I even called to remind you. I just don't understand why you can't get it together. Damn, this makes me angry!"

Here's the big secret: You have a choice. You can *feel* angry and frustrated inside, but *behave* in a loving way. Not as a thinly veiled disguise. Not as a "passive-aggressive" strategy (being nice with a big fist right behind your smile). Not as a manipulation. But as a deliberate, spiritual exercise.

What would Buddha do in this situation? Or Jesus? They would already have a well-developed inner calm, and a larger perspective or "consciousness" that would help them realize how minor this incident is in the grand scheme of the world. Instead of wanting to be right ("I was on time! You are the bad person here, you are the one who blew it!"), they might feel compassion for Janice. Maybe they would be thinking, I've done things like this myself. I know how bad it feels. She must be upset with herself too. Maybe she is irritated with me and doesn't know how to express it. Maybe she just doesn't have very high self-esteem.

They would be motivated by wanting to make connection, and would automatically know that the relationship is more important than this incident.

EXPERIMENT WITH "ACT AS IF"

Of course, most of us are not there. We have not spent the last thirty years fasting and meditating so that nothing upsets us. But we can learn by deliberately "faking" what we think the spiritual response would be, *even if we don't feel like it.* If you superimpose spiritual behavior onto a situation as a conscious experiment, it will give you a taste of what it is like to be more spiritual, and gradually, over time, it will help you get there.

Let's say you would like to feel nonjudgmental, but you don't; you are filled with judgments. Do you have to wait until nonjudgmental feelings arise spontaneously? No. *Behave* in a nonjudgmental way and see if the new feelings you hope for follow.

Now, of course, like all spiritual disciplines, "acting as if" is not easy to do. It requires enormous effort, especially at first, and especially if your feelings are very strong. But the more you do it, the easier it becomes. You will like the feeling of being in control instead of at the mercy of everything going on around you. And you will like the results.

"Acting as if" is a Sacred Act, because it is a way for you to emulate spiritual behavior. Also, it is an exercise that will help you grow spiritually: As you pay attention to how you feel when you do it, it will expand your consciousness, help you separate your personality from your authentic self, help you become more loving, and increase your self-love. "Acting as if" is a move toward connection and away from separation. As you become more experienced, you will definitely feel happier more of the time, because you will not be at the mercy of other people's behavior.

Always behaving exactly the way you feel is the Old Model. Your behavior is a "knee-jerk" reaction, like a tape being flipped on. Now, you are not part of an "experience"; you are part of a familiar old tape, just running itself again.

Probably, you always become angry when Janice is late, or when _____ (substitute your own ongoing relationship problem). We already know what that produces. You get to be right and to make Janice wrong. You get to feel distant from Janice and angry at her. You make it hard for Janice to feel warm and close toward you. Maybe your frustration (because you can't get Janice to change) will hang around for a few days. Then you'll feel better; then she'll be late again; and the whole cycle will repeat itself. Probably for years.

Think about a problem in your own relationship. You have no doubt tried the same approach over and over (probably trying in some way to get your partner to be different), and every time you repeat the same behavior, you actually still hope that something might change! It never will, because it is a law of the universe that when you keep doing the same thing, you'll keep getting the same results.

"Acting as if" gives you something brand-new to try. Something that has probably never occurred to you before.

And when you try something new, you might get new results! No guarantees here. Remember, every time you "act as if," you are conducting an experiment. Don't be attached to any particular outcome. You have no idea what will happen. Just pay close attention to the results.

One possibility is that your partner's response to you might change. Never "act as if" as a manipulation, but just watch the results. Janice's chronic lateness is far likelier to change if you keep the atmosphere between you warm and stop blaming her, than if you go off on your anger every time she's late, just as you always have. We've seen that people are more likely to change in response to love and support than to criticism and anger. By "acting as if," you provide leadership and engage in a creative act of love.

A second possibility is that your own feelings might actually change. That's what happened for Karen.

Karen and Al didn't fight often, but when they did, it always took Karen days to feel good again. The arguments left her feeling belittled, frustrated, and helpless.

After learning about "acting as if," Karen determined to try it after her next argument with Al. They argued one Sunday morning about whether to buy a new rug. Once more, Karen felt as though Al insisted he was right and had no regard for her opinions or feelings. The familiar anger and frustration set in. Unfortunately, the two of them had planned a whole day together, taking their niece to the zoo.

Karen decided to "act as if" she felt just fine. Even though she was actually on the verge of tears, after a little time and with great effort, she made a cheerful, normal-sounding comment to Al: "I think I'll take this blanket in case we want to sit by the lake after the zoo."

"Yeah, that's a good idea," Al replied.

After fighting off tears but continuing normal-sounding conversation for another five minutes or so, Karen found that she actually began to feel better inside. The longer she continued her experiment, the better she felt. Her mood shifted. The anger actually abated, and they went on to have a very pleasant afternoon.

"Acting as if" actually incorporates all five of the building blocks, or principles of Spiritual Partnership. To see how, let's look at Karen's Sacred Act again:

1. Instead of communicating ("I'm angry. We have to talk about this"), she experimented with a unilateral Sacred Act.
2. She didn't insist that Al change; she changed.
3. In a spirit of goodwill, she created a harmonious atmosphere in which Al could feel warm toward her.
4. When she looked at whether she wanted to meet her own needs or Al's right then, she decided to take care of herself: She stopped the fight without resolving the issue, and set about making herself feel better. In this case, Al benefited also.
5. She let go of the illusion that if she and Al talked about their problem, they could solve it.

"Acting as if" is not new, it's been around for a long time. But we have underused it, and have failed to recognize it as a spiritual practice. Remember Anna in *The King and I*? She whistled when she felt afraid as a way to fool those around her. But she goes on to sing, "When I fool the people I fear, I fool myself as well." She "acted as if" she was brave and had no fear at all, and her own feelings were transformed.

The strategy of changing your feelings by acting the way you want to feel is a fundamental principle of the new science called Neurolinguistic Programming. To change your feelings or your "state," change your physiology. The same principle is involved when you are feeling blue and you go for a run or take a bike ride, and afterward your mood has changed.

SOME EXAMPLES

Let's see how "acting as if" worked in several real-life situations.

When Ed and Nancy left for a two-week vacation in Italy, Ed had just been laid off and was considering taking a job Nancy thought was a big mistake. They felt a great deal of tension over this and had several fights. On the plane on the way over, they read and just kept their distance. Nancy told me:

> At first I felt like we should talk about the job and the fact we'd been fighting so much lately and see if we could get to a better place. I didn't want to spend the whole two weeks feeling rotten about him. But it never seemed like the right moment, and I kept putting it off. Then I remembered "act as if." Right away, it was a huge relief. I started to relax and focus on having a good time. When we arrived at our gorgeous Tuscan villa, we were both so impressed, we got sort of playful and giddy as we began to unpack. The tension we had been feeling seemed gone. I let go of the whole problem and focused on having a good time and on all the things I adore about Ed. I was amazed at how quickly and easily it worked. Over dinner, I began feeling very loving toward him. By the next day we were feeling as close as ever and having a wonderful time.
>
> I never brought up the job issue again. He took the job, and while I thought he'd be out of there in six months, he's now been there two years.

A woman I interviewed, Charlene, told me this story, which I have related before:

> "Acting as if" works well for me with sex. Often when Michael wants to make love, I don't feel in the mood. I used to say no a lot, and he'd be upset and it would become a big deal. Now, I "act as if" I'm in the mood, and it doesn't take long for me to be in the mood. I "act as if" in a spirit of goodwill toward Michael, because I really do want to give him what he wants. Now that I know it works, it's not hard to do. I virtually never say no to him anymore. Michael is so happy about the change—and so am I!

A two-career, two-child couple I interviewed for my second book have a similar attitude. They call their policy "mood schmood," meaning that if they waited until they felt in the mood, they might not ever make love. They act as if they are in the mood, and soon they are.

Peter also had a revelation about his sex life when he began to "act as if":

> I've always had a clear fantasy about what I wanted in sex, and when I married Kelly, I thought she was everything I wanted. But we had a baby right away, and things really changed. I was pretty sad about it, and I would talk with her, but it just made her feel bad. She would just say, "I can't be what I'm not." I lost interest too. I was very skeptical about "acting as if." [Peter resisted our suggestions in the workshop for almost the full eight weeks.] But finally, I decided to "act as if" she were the sexy lover I imagined. She loved the change in me. The big difference was, I was not judging her, I was just being me to the

fullest. She was actually very responsive. I saw that I needed to let go of my ideas of what she ought to be and just be who I wanted *me* to be. I am so grateful that we have our sex life back now. It is right for who we really are, not some fantasy I had in my head. I feel now that sex is truly an expression of our love for each other.

I was very surprised that this experiment changed anything. I found out that *thinking about* doing something is very different from *doing* it. I was certain that nothing would change after the experiment. I was so wrong.

"Acting as if" can work very well when you apply it to your own moods, even if you are by yourself. Anne told me this:

When I get up in a blue mood, or I come home from work tired and cranky, I have learned not to talk about it and "milk" it. When I hear myself make a bitchy remark, I'll just turn around and make a cheerful one. I "act as if" I feel good. Then either my blue mood continues but I'm not forcing those around me to suffer through it, or the mood fades away and I start to feel better.

I didn't believe in "acting as if" at first because it seemed to contradict the philosophy I was raised on, that it's healthier to express emotions, to examine them thoroughly and not to sweep them under the rug. I can still do that when I think it's appropriate, but now I have a choice, and I have been able to brighten up a lot of my own days.

Of course, it is appropriate to examine your feelings sometimes, and to allow a blue mood to come over you. Our dark sides have much to teach us. But when "acting as if" is one of your tools, you have a choice about when you want to go deeper for yourself, and when you want to at least behave in a brighter way to see what happens.

Guidelines for "Acting As If"

"Acting as if" simply means choosing "nice" behavior, *even when you don't feel like it*. It means not allowing your feelings to dictate how you will behave, but instead, by an act of discipline and will, motivated by your desire to become a more spiritual person, *choosing* how you will behave. When you "act as if," you are no longer at the mercy of your feelings or your mood.

Start small. You can "act as if" you are a loving, adoring spouse even if you don't feel that way, for just five minutes, or for a half hour, or for one evening a week.

The next time something upsets or angers you, think about "acting as if." Try it for just one minute.

Recently, as I returned to my car because I knew my parking meter would be running out, I saw a meter maid writing out a ticket. "Wait! I'm here. The meter just ran out!" I cried out. But she wouldn't tear up the ticket. I don't do well when I have no control over what I consider to be a dumb situation. I felt my face get flush, my heart start to race. But since I was writing about spiritual behavior every day, the thought "act spiritually" went through my head. I took a deep breath. And then I smiled. Not a sarcastic smile. It was an "act as if" smile. I couldn't bring myself to say anything nice to the meter maid, but at least I didn't say anything nasty to her. I kept smiling. By the time I was driving away, I was thinking, So a parking ticket, so big deal.

You can also "act as if" as a proactive way of taking initiative or providing leadership, rather than in response to a situation.

Try directly creating the feeling you wish you had in your

relationship. What do you want from your partner? Do you wish he or she were more demonstrative? Do you wish you had fun more often? Would you like more thoughtfulness, more romance?

Create these activities yourself. Ask yourself, "How would I behave if I were a totally loving spouse?" You might do favors for your partner. You might greet him or her enthusiastically when you come together at the end of the workday. Maybe you'd fix your partner a drink and suggest a little cocktail hour.

What do you wish you could do with your partner? Don't wait.

As one workshop participant told us after two weeks of experimenting with "acting as if," "It's so easy to get affection; just give it."

Don't be discouraged if your feelings or your mate's responses don't change quickly and dramatically. Patiently proceed with acting like a loving spouse on a regular basis, even if it is just for a few minutes at a time, even if you see no direct results or changes. Pay attention to what is happening inside you.

Remember, in the midst of a difficult incident or when you feel very bad, you cannot change your *feelings*. They are simply there. You feel angry. You feel afraid. You can't make your feelings go away by an act of will. Also, you can't change the other person who is part of this situation, as we have already discussed.

But you do have control over your own behavior. You can make a deliberate choice to "act as if" you feel good. And when you do, you open up a whole range of new possibilities.

Be prepared for voices of resistance within you:

"My partner doesn't deserve this loving behavior."
"This is too one-sided. I shouldn't have to be nice."
"This is too fake. I *can't* pretend I feel loving. I don't!"

It is okay for these voices to be there. Just don't let them win. Talk back to yourself. Be your own cheering section:

"You can do it."

"Remember, this is for your own spiritual growth."

"If you never experiment, you'll never move forward."

As Dan Millman observes in *The Way of the Peaceful Warrior*, "Old urges will continue to arise, perhaps for years. Urges do not matter, actions do."

Actions matter. When you are trying to create a happy, safe atmosphere in your marriage, actions are what will make this happen. Apathy won't help you. Talking won't make any difference. Blaming will keep you stuck for years. Only new behavior, even when you don't feel like doing it, will make changes start to happen. You will never think your way to a new way of acting, but you can act your way to a new way of thinking.

One woman told me:

The difficulty I have with "acting as if" is that it sometimes literally makes me anxious to behave in ways that run directly counter to how I feel. "Acting as if" makes me feel like I'm abandoning myself.

If you feel anxious, realize that your anxiety—or any other form of resistance to "acting as if"—is a gift to you, because it is a window into your authentic self. Rather than running from the anxiety, gently allow it to be there. See how much you can tolerate. What is your anxiety telling you about yourself? This is all an integral part of your experiment. It's precisely the reason you are doing the experiment: to learn more about yourself. Just keep paying attention, and let the results unfold.

Experiment. Try going back to behaving in accord with your real feelings. Does that feel better to you? Does it produce less anxiety? What results? You don't always have to "act as if." Maybe sometimes it is not right for you.

But definitely try "acting as if" again in a few days, even if it is just for a short while. And keep paying attention to how you feel.

You might also take the time to write in your journal about your anxious feelings. Describe them. What other situations evoke anxiety for you? Are there any similarities? Dialogue with your anxiety. Ask it what purpose it serves for you, and see what it says back.

More Examples

I have seen this one spiritual tool, "acting as if," transform even the bleakest of relationships. The following is just one of many such stories.

Becky and John had been married ten years, and there was little left of their marriage. Becky came to one of my groups, thinking she would get support for leaving John. She had a list as long as her arm of the qualities she didn't like in him. He was controlling. He never discussed anything with her. He was rough with the children. She actually didn't like him very much at all. What puzzled us in the group was that other people seemed to like John a lot, and he didn't sound like a bad fellow as she described him.

I suggested to Becky that she "act as if" she felt loving toward John for just five minutes during one evening. For several weeks she reported that she couldn't bring herself to do it and was filled with excuses. Trying to make it easier for her, I suggested that she try just giving him one genuine compliment. The next week, she reported:

On Saturday morning when he returned from soccer with our son, I said to him, "Thank you for taking Sam to the soccer game. I really appreciate what a good father you are, and all the interest you take around all this soccer stuff." Of course, it surprised him to hear this. He did give me a little look, not quizzical, but more like a smile. And that night while we were watching TV, he reached over and gave me a little kiss on the cheek. That really got my attention.

Over the next weeks, Becky began to see that she was actually as big a part of the problems as John was. It was a stunning revelation to her.

He was controlling and too hard on the kids and self-centered, but *I wasn't being a loving wife at all.* Why would he want to be nice to me?

Becky began "acting as if" on a regular basis. She stopped making John wrong about everything and began exhibiting a spirit of goodwill more often. She was surprised at the differences she began to see in John, and even more amazed at the feelings that began to stir in her. Admitting these changes was a very difficult and courageous act for her, and we gave her a tremendous amount of support.

When Becky started behaving as a loving wife and focusing on John's strong points instead of his weak points, he was pleased and began to respond in kind. Becky also started to take better care of herself in the relationship, and stopped depending on John for things he would never provide. When I spoke with them a year later, they were doing very well together. Becky said:

I didn't believe that I would ever feel so different about John. He hasn't changed a lot. He's still controlling. I don't like that, but now I stand up to him a lot more. I see that I have to take care of myself. And that has made a big difference. I *like* John, and I feel grateful for our relationship. Most of the time, we're enjoying our life. And the children are so much happier!

Here is another marriage that was greatly affected when one of the partners acted as if she felt loving even when she didn't feel like it.

Allison came to me quite distressed. Her husband, Ken, was part of a group of four guys who had been backpacking together for years. Two times each year they took ten days to go off to the wilderness. Allison had been stricken with polio when she was three and was left with one very weak leg. She could walk, but with a severe limp and only for short periods of time. She had been putting up with these trips for years, but now that they had three small children, she reached her limit.

"It's so unfair!" she said to me. "You can't believe how hard it is for me to manage for ten days without him. He just doesn't care. All he ever says is, 'You knew about this when we got married.' The other three guys are all single! His situation is different. I feel like he just has to give this up for a few years. Eventually, he can take the kids with him or something. But every time he goes off like this, I get so angry, I feel like I want to leave him. He won't even talk to me about it. Where is *his* spirit of goodwill? It doesn't work for only one of us to have it!"

Allison was putting out her best effort under the Old Model of relationships. She insisted that she was right. Probably most of us would agree with her that Ken was being thoughtless and unfair, but being right did nothing for Allison except make her more frustrated. She had tried in vain to communicate with Ken and had focused endlessly on "the problem," believing that if Ken would help her, they could come up with a solution. One solution they had tried was to hire help for her while he was away, but they both felt bad about spending the money, and they couldn't find reliable people. Allison was riveted on the only solution she could think of: Ken needed to change. He had to give up or modify the trips!

After working for a time with Allison, I suggested that she try an experiment: to "act as if" she felt loving, even if she didn't. We talked in some detail about how she would do that and exactly what she might try.

Several weeks before the next backpack trip, Allison started asking Ken about it. Where were they planning to go? How much climbing would they do? What kind of food did they pack?

Ken was delighted. He took out maps and marked their route for her. He cooked up one of their favorite camp meals one evening. Allison was so interested in what she was learning, and so surprised at how little she knew about what they did, that she found she had more and more questions. Suddenly, they were talking more than they usually did, and enjoying it. Ken never said anything about the changes in Allison, but he obviously liked them. He even became somewhat affectionate with her, a habit they had lost in recent years.

The morning Ken left, Allison got up at four A.M. and cooked up a special breakfast. She gave Ken a big hug and told him to have a great trip. This was a huge contrast from previous trips, when they would have a fight the night before, and then Ken would steal off in the morning—alone.

I had been talking with Allison about taking more initiative concerning her own needs. She had a good friend who was a single mom with a big house, and they decided to have a great big "house party" for a few days. Her friend took some vacation days, they hired a high school girl to provide some entertainment for the children in the afternoons, and they interrupted all their usual routines and just hung out together. They took the children to the zoo one day and to a lake another day.

Then, an amazing thing happened: Ken phoned to say he was coming home early, that he wanted to take the whole family car camping, if Allison were open to it. Her story about herself was that she hated camping, but she hadn't done it for many years, and decided to go along with the idea. She ended up having a wonderful time, and was thrilled because it was the first activity they had done as a family for a very long time.

Of course, not all experiments work out so tidily. Yet this story is not unusual. Whenever a couple, or one member of a couple, is willing to try something new, even when it feels bizarre and is really difficult, new things happen.

Several years ago I spent a day helping some friends move into their new home. Meredith and I were organizing the kitchen. Her husband, Cliff, was keeping his usual critical and controlling litany going, all directed at Meredith:

"Don't spend so much time sorting through that stuff. We'll never get finished. You're being way too fussy. It doesn't matter where stuff goes. Just put things away. You are so messy and unorganized, whatever you set up today won't last anyway."

Cliff is a nice guy, and very bright. I waited until Meredith ran out to get us some lunch and then asked him if he minded my giving him a suggestion or two. He was receptive. For about fifteen minutes I explained to him about having a spirit of goodwill. I suggested that Meredith would probably be much more open to him if he made supportive rather than critical remarks, and I tried to show him how much negativity he was creating. I explained how much she needed his support, with all the stress she was under. And I also tried to show him that he was probably never going to change her but might instead see her for who she really is and accept her. He seemed to take in what I was saying, and thanked me. (By the way, I had spent a lot of time giving Meredith suggestions too, about letting his comments roll off her back and taking more positive initiatives toward him.)

A week later Meredith phoned. "Things are really different around here," she told me. "Cliff made up a little mnemonic about what you said: 'Slago: Supportive, Loving, Accepting, Giving, Open.' We go around saying 'Slago' to each other all the time now. It's sort of a joke, but he's really doing it. And so am I. I can't thank you enough for having that little talk with him. It has truly made a change."

Cliff probably still feels critical of certain aspects of Meredith's personality. But he saw right away the value of *behaving* more positively toward her, of "acting as if" he fully supports her. Now, she *feels* supported, so she is much warmer toward him. They will never "solve their problem" of her lack of organization or his desire to control everything, but they are happier together.

One man whose sense of discovery was similar to Cliff's wrote this to me in a letter:

> . . . what attracted me most of all was the idea that the solution to improving my relationship with my wife did not involve "sitting down and communicating." I can't tell you what a relief that was. I had a newfound hope and confidence, and experienced the most peaceful sleep I've had in years.
>
> If I had the unenviable task of picking just one of the many valuable tools and ways of thinking that [Spiritual Partnership] offers, it would be the idea that "You can be happy together even if you don't solve all your problems." Again, what a relief! [These ideas] helped me to keep trying new things but to retain a spirit of experimentation and be open about the results . . . Now, when some irritating problem resurfaces, I remind myself

what my real goals in this relationship are: intimacy, support, and pleasure.

What are the real goals in your own relationship? To solve some problem or other? To make over your partner? Or to increase your intimacy, mutual support, and pleasure? If they are the latter, start experimenting by "acting as if" sometimes. Remember, don't preprogram what you think the results will be. Just watch carefully. With an experiment, you can never fail, only learn. Think "Slago"! Have fun with this. And good luck.

ॐ EXPERIMENT #12:
"ACT AS IF"

1. In your journal, write your answer to these questions:
   - If you were completely in love with your spouse, totally adoring and in love, how would you behave? You may want to write a paragraph or make a list. Let your imagination take over.
   - What are your goals for your relationship? Again, write a paragraph or make a list, whichever fits for you.
   - What needs to happen in order for you to achieve these goals? Do you believe you have to solve certain problems first? Can you imagine having what you want in your relationship right now by "acting as if" you have it?

2. Set a specific time—from five minutes to an evening or a full day—to "act as if" you are a loving, adoring partner.

3. Record what you did in your journal and how it turned out.

4. If you find the reminder "Slago" useful (Supportive, Loving, Accepting, Giving, Open), try thinking about it every morning as you get ready for your day. Incorporate it into your prayers or meditation. Even if you don't feel "Slago," try acting as if you feel "Slago" for a specific period of time with your mate.

5. In your journal, record exactly what you did and how it turned out.

SEVEN

Sacred Act #3:
Act on Your Own

It may come as a surprise to you that you do not need to obtain your partner's agreement for everything you do. Sometimes acting on your own is the greatest gift you can give to both of you.

Rhonda wanted very much to get season tickets to the ballet, but she could never get her husband Bill to agree to it. "I don't like ballet well enough," he'd say. "Let's just get tickets to one performance." For several years that's what they did. Rhonda saw it as a reasonable compromise, but she also felt anguish every time she read the reviews of the performances she was missing.

One year, when she was agonizing over which performance to choose, like a bolt of lightning the idea came to her that she could buy a season ticket for herself. "The amount of time between the instant I got this idea and the time I picked up the phone to order myself a season ticket was a nanosecond," she told me. "I couldn't believe the idea had never occurred to me before." She enjoyed every performance immensely, and the next year persuaded a good friend to buy tickets with her.

Tina and Max bought a much needed new car. Their second car was old and clunky, possessing no new conveniences like power locks or even power steering. Somehow, from the beginning, there was an unwritten assumption that the new car would be Max's. Occasionally, if Tina had a good reason, like attending a luncheon, she would ask Max if she could have the new car that day.

One day Tina found herself asking Max for the nice car, and she felt like an idiot. "It's our car," she said to herself. "Why does Max get to call the shots here?"

After thinking it over all day, that evening Tina said to Max, "Y'know, honey, I got to thinking, we both like driving the new car. I would enjoy taking it to work more often. From now on, let's alternate. You take it one day, I'll take it the next."

At first Max came up with a few objections. Remembering Principle #1, "Keep your mouth out of it," Tina wisely made the comment, "Just think about it," and then dropped the subject.

The next day Tina said, "So I'll take the new car today, okay?"

"I've been thinking about it," Max said. "What would feel better to me is if we alternate weeks. Then for a whole week we can feel like, 'This is my car.'"

"That's an even better idea! I like it," said Tina. "I'll start with today, if that's okay." Then she gave him a big kiss, climbed into the new car, and drove off.

Notice: Tina did not start out by making Max wrong, by pointing out that he wasn't being fair, or that he wasn't being thoughtful or considerate. She didn't even bring up the "power struggle," that it had somehow quietly evolved that Max got to have the final word on the new car. She just quietly and firmly changed the power dynamics. She didn't ask for the "power" she needed in this situation, she took it. By instituting a workable solution, Tina followed all of the principles:

1. She didn't discuss or communicate with Max; she acted decisively.
2. She didn't try to change Max, she asserted herself.
3. She didn't ask who was right or wrong; instead, she asked herself what she could do to make a change.
4. She saw that, in this matter, her inner scale felt out of balance; she was giving, but not taking care of her own needs. So she found a way to take better care of herself.
5. She didn't bring up a problem and discuss it. When Max wanted to argue, Tina instantly knew that keeping the atmosphere harmonious was more important than the car thing, and she changed the subject. And she still felt in control.

If you have a need you feel is not getting met in your relationship, chances are very good that you can find a way to meet that need by acting on your own. Many common problems respond to this Sacred Act:

- If your husband hasn't gotten around to trimming the hedges, hire someone to do it.
- If your wife doesn't like to talk about movies after seeing them, invite a couple to join you when you see a movie.
- If your husband is withdrawn and preoccupied when he comes home at the end of the day, use that time to call a friend and share your day with her.
- If your wife spends too much time talking on the phone in the evenings, take her out to dinner occasionally, or plan other times when you can have her attention.
- If your partner spends too much time on the Internet, either take an interest in it yourself so you can do some of it together, or spend the time on a hobby of your own.

When you can find a humorous way to address the problem, so much the better. One woman told me that her husband kept putting off fixing the leaky bathtub faucet in the spare bathroom, so she put the plug in the bathtub! When he saw the tub filling up, he got the point.

A man told me that he couldn't get his wife to stop picking lint off his suits. So he put a little thread on his lapel—which was attached to a spool of thread in his pocket. Their children got a huge laugh when she tried to take that piece of lint off!

It is impossible to describe "acting on your own" completely, because it requires something different in every situation. Sometimes the most significant part of it is just realizing that you have the *option* of acting on your own, and then the needed action will be obvious. But sometimes the solution isn't obvious and you have to free up your creative energy, be brazen, and do the outrageous.

Dallas radio personality Susie Humphreys threw her own surprise party. After fifteen years of hinting, she figured her husband was never going to get the idea. So one night at a gathering of friends, she announced that she was going to surprise herself with a party and told everyone to save the date. They all laughed—until they received their invitations in the mail. Susie included a little map and told people to park around the corner so she wouldn't be suspicious. She filled her house with helium balloons and a big sign that said, "We love you Susie!" Then she assigned two of her best friends to take her out for a drink so people would have time to gather. When she arrived, the house was dark. Then the lights came on and everyone yelled, "Surprise!" And Susie cried!

If You Don't Take Care of Yourself, Who Will?

You are the only person who knows what you want, where you feel deprived, and what changes will make you happier. No one else can climb inside you and find out what you truly want, what your fondest hopes and dreams for yourself are. And no one else can make those dreams come true.

When you need to take a nap, no one else is ever going to do that for you. No one else can! And what's more, no one else may even notice that this need didn't get met.

If you forget an appointment, or you forget to make dinner for your children, other people will care. But if you want to take dance lessons and you put this off for months and then for years, only you will miss out. If it is going to happen, you need to make it happen for yourself.

No one else cares about the quality of your life as much as you do.

Where are you neglecting yourself? Is this neglect a trade-off you are willing to make for the sake of some other goal you value even more? Or would you feel better if you act on your own to fill this void in your life, or to correct this imbalance?

Julia's Spiritual Solution

Listen to how Julia "outgrew her problem" by acting on her own rather than trying to "solve the problem" by persuading her partner to change.

Julia was a salesperson for business-related software and made a good income. She was married to Rick, who was having a hard time with his career. He had a low tolerance for bureaucratic regulations and wasn't much of a company man. And the business he started on his own had run into problems. Rick was proud of his determination to do something meaningful and useful, and had confidence in his abilities. He kept telling Julia he just needed time to figure it all out.

Julia agreed with Rick's values and loved his independent spirit, but they had four children, and they needed two incomes. She understood that she couldn't "help" Rick figure out what to do. She made a few suggestions, but she knew that this was Rick's problem and that he had to work it out on his own. She was patient and supportive. They did have some savings and would be okay for a while.

After one year was stretching into two, Julia became more and more anxious. She and Rick had several fights, which was unusual for them. Julia found that as she lay awake on sleepless nights, what went through her head were ideas for making more money on her own. One of these ideas began to excite her: She had been a craftsperson years ago, and she thought she could design a bracelet that might appeal to high-end fashion stores. One weekend she gathered all the materials she would need and went to work. One of her daughters became interested in working with her. In six weeks they felt they had sufficient samples to begin showing the work, and the first two stores they tried gave them an order.

After several more months of work, Julia and her daughter took the bracelets to a gift show, where they wrote enough orders to keep them busy for a year, supplementing the family income.

If this family were operating according to the Old Model, it is easy to imagine Julia becoming angrier with Rick, blaming him for the problem, pointing out how unfair he was, trying to convince him that he should just take a job, and focusing more and more attention on "the problem." Julia would have been "right," but that approach would have led to a most unhappy and upset family.

By *acting on her own* in a spirit of goodwill, Julia instead created a very happy family. She and her daughter became closer. Rick was given the gift of the time he needed to find his passion. And the income problem got handled.

But notice: This solution was not fair or reasonable. Julia was not asking, "Who is right and who is wrong?" but rather, "What can I do to help out here?" She did not solve the problem by talking it over with Rick, and she was not badgering him to change. She believed that he was doing the best he could, and that her support would be far more helpful to him than putting pressure on him. Julia put herself in charge of getting her own needs met, and her spirit of generosity was a gift to both of them.

Shifting from hoping your partner will take care of your needs to being willing to take care of yourself is at the heart of Spiritual Partnership. When you are getting what you want, even if you had to make it happen yourself, you will feel increased inner power and self-love. As you gain respect for yourself and an increased sense of well-being, giving generously to your partner will become a pleasure too. You will be able to give without feeling resentful.

Acting on your own fills all of the qualifications of being "spiritual," as we defined it in Chapter Two:

1. You will be moving toward *connection*, not separation.
2. Since you need to be very clear about what you want, when you act on your own, you will be helping your *authentic self* emerge.
3. When you solve a problem by your own actions alone,

you will feel personal freedom leading to increased self-esteem and self-*love*.

4. You will be expanding your *consciousness* about your own capabilities.

5. You will be *receptive* to events turning out in a way you never imagined, open to what the universe has in store for you.

6. You will definitely be moving toward *happiness* and well-being.

Two Important Guidelines for Acting on Your Own

1. If acting on your own is going to have an impact on someone else, and especially if you are acting on your own over the objection of someone else, do not act on your own when you are ambivalent. Save this Sacred Act for situations that feel truly "non-negotiable" to you. When you aren't sure exactly what you want, that may be the time to go along with your partner's clearer desires. If you act assertively and later realize you may have made a mistake, it's far too easy for your partner to come back and say, "I told you so." Also, acting on your own has a greater impact for good if you reserve it for things that are truly important to you.

2. When you act on your own to do something that you know may make your partner unhappy, the way that you tell your partner what you plan to do is critically important. *You must always use two steps:* First, express understanding of your mate's position.

Second, be clear that you will not be dissuaded from your own. In other words, be both empathic and decisive. When you are empathic, you take care of your spouse to the best of your ability. When you are decisive, you take care of yourself.

For example, when I once took a trip to New York over the objections of my husband, I hope I said something like this: "I agree this is a strain on our finances. I realize it makes you uncomfortable for me to spend this money. And I'm sorry about that." (Empathy.) "But I'm very clear that I would be just crushed to miss this trip. It feels to me like one of the most important opportunities I have ever had. I've decided I'm going." (Decisiveness.)

Because expressing empathy does not come naturally to most of us, you may find it useful to memorize a few sentences, or keep a bookmark at this page so that whenever you are going to act on your own and you need to be empathic and decisive, you will have the words ready. Here are some useful empathic-and-decisive statements.

"I don't blame you for feeling _____. I'd feel that way too if I were you. But I'm very clear I need to do this for myself."

"I know you don't feel good about this, and I am really sorry about that. That is not why I am doing this. I'm very clear I need to do this for myself."

"I agree with you that _____. And I feel bad that it is making you unhappy. But deep inside, I know I could not live with myself if I didn't do this. It is very important to me for my own spiritual growth."

Remember, *you do not need to persuade your partner that you are right*. If your partner becomes angry or tries to change your mind, do not argue back. Just continue to be empathic and decisive. "I don't blame you for being upset. I can understand why you feel the way you do. But this is very, very important to me, and I am going to do it. I'm genuinely sorry you don't like this, but I have to honor my own strong inner needs."

Your Partner's Response

When you act on your own, your partner will have a response.

Surprisingly often, the response will be positive. Most people want to be married to a capable, independent, fully functioning adult, and they will like the person they see taking charge. Your decisive clarity emanating from your increasingly spiritual essence is likely to be appealing to your partner. Even if what you are doing makes your partner angry for the moment, in the long run he or she is likely to be attracted to the inner calm and happiness you exhibit by being clear about what you want and willing to take care of yourself.

In some cases your partner may be upset by your emerging independence. It is a seemingly abrupt change that he or she wasn't expecting and doesn't know how to explain or respond to. Especially if your partner is used to having all the power in your relationship or you have a longstanding habit of acquiescing most of the time, your solo actions may seem threatening. Since you are upsetting a well-established pattern in your relationship, you may both feel confused and uneasy for a while. Don't let this stop you. Avoid arguing with your partner. Remember what Tina said when Max started arguing about her taking the new car: "Just think about it." Drop the subject rather than "discussing" it. Continue to be both empathic and decisive. Remain firm in your conviction. Your partner will most likely respect you for this as time goes on and you both become used to the new relationship pattern you are creating.

In the vast majority of situations in which you act on your own, you will be eliminating a problem that has been difficult for both of you, and your partner will love you for it. Most of the time, you can meet your own needs without disturbing your partner at all. In fact, you will be supporting your partner as well as yourself.

A man who attended an all-day workshop of mine without his wife spoke with me several months later. I was impressed with how much of the general message of Spiritual Partnership he had absorbed. He told me this story:

My wife and I were experiencing a lot of tension about church. She wanted me to go with her every Sunday, and I had made a clear decision within me that I did not want to attend church at all. We were deeply enmeshed in the belief that if we could just talk this through enough, we could somehow arrive at a solution. And we were exhausted trying.

When I heard you say that you can't solve problems by talking them through, and that you don't have to solve all your problems to be happy, I can still remember the relief that swept over me. There was a rightness about this idea that made me feel incredibly relaxed.

I decided to act on my own and to be decisive about my choice. So instead of just hanging around on Sunday morning, so there was always this implication that this time maybe I'd go with her, I planned every Sunday morning for myself. I'd go hiking, go to an art museum, or plan some other definite activity.

I knew I would feel better. But what amazed me is the impact my actions had on her. We stopped arguing. She never brought it up again. The issue disappeared. Suddenly, it was not a problem anymore, it was a fact of life, and we both adapted to it.

I never told my wife I had a "strategy." I never told her anything about what I learned in the workshop. It makes it a lot of fun for me to experiment. Of course, it is obvious that we are much happier together now, but we don't talk much about why.

Affection and Affirmation: Solved!

Two of the most common problems for couples concern affection and affirmation.

- "My partner is not affectionate and loving enough. We don't have enough gentle touching."
- "My partner takes me for granted. I just don't get complimented or praised or thanked nearly enough. Sometimes I feel as though my partner doesn't even notice the things I do."

Both of these problems will disappear when you act on your own.

Affection

If you don't get enough affection from your partner, you can solve this problem by initiating affection on your own. One workshop participant told me this, more than a year after our work together:

For years I felt sad that we weren't a more physically close couple. Our sex life was okay, but I was married before, and I loved the way my former husband was always grabbing me to hug me or plant a big kiss on my lips. We'd hold hands when we walked, or cuddle up while we watched TV.

At your suggestion, I started initiating affectionate touching on my own. Bob responded just fine. Now, I would call us a pretty lovey-dovey couple, but I initiate virtually all of it. That's totally fine with me! Once I gave up the useless idea that it didn't mean anything unless he initiated it, I started getting everything I wanted. Now, we are so used to kissing before we leave in the morning and just before we go to sleep at night that he'll seek me out for a kiss if I forget!

A key idea here was that this woman "gave up the idea that it didn't mean anything unless he initiated it." When she touched her husband or gave him a hug or kiss, there was no judgment in her action whatsoever, no resentment, no irony. And that is always important when you offer affection. You need to do it graciously, generously, as a free gift with no strings attached, no blame, and no expectations that your partner will change.

An extremely effective and much underused form of affection is the freely offered, nondemanding smile. Anytime you are together, just glance over at your mate and smile, then look away. You are not asking for anything; you don't have to wait for a reason to smile. Just catch your partner's eye and smile. It can be a little knowing smile, an "I feel happy" smile, a big smile, raised eyebrows, or just the tiniest little bit of a smile. It might include a little wink, or not. Right now, as you are reading this, practice a few different types of smiles.

You can toss your partner a little gift smile anytime. Maybe you are in the middle of a conversation, putzing around the kitchen, about to get into the car, playing with the children, standing on the subway train together. You can smile when you are feeling good just to convey that. Or you can smile when you are feeling blue or stressed out, as a mini-"act-as-if" smile. It is a gift to your partner, and it will make you feel good. It's free, legal, nonfattening, nonpolluting, and doesn't take extra time.

A spontaneous, no-special-reason, warm smile is a little spiritual move toward connection. It is one of the easiest and most powerful ways to create harmony by acting on your own, no matter what else is going on around you.

Don't take my word for it, try it. Experiment.

It may be that when you initiate affection toward your partner, he or she will not respond warmly in return. Try to refrain from any judgments about this. Though it may be a challenge for you, don't take your mate's lack of response personally. Your partner is just being himself or herself. Keep gently offering affection, but keep it at a level that seems comfortable for your partner. As a spiritual leader, your job is to take care of your own needs *and* your mate's needs at the same time, as much as possible. As you experiment over time, you will be able to achieve a level that works for both of you. It could be that you are with someone who is never going to be the warm, cuddly teddy bear you fantasize. But this person has other wonderful qualities that you love. Think about those, and let the level of affection you have when you take as much initiative as you can be just fine. You can't change it, so go with it. But keep initiating affection, if that is what you like.

Affirmation

Acting on your own works for eliciting the verbal affirmations you crave too. Workshop participants are always skeptical about this one and spend a lot of time role-playing it as if it were absurd. But all you need to do is take the idea seriously and try it once, and you'll be hooked. I use this particular strategy in my own relationship all the time.

Suppose your partner never comments on your appearance, your cooking, your parenting, your generosity, or whatever else you know you are good at. Your partner takes all your good qualities for granted and just never thinks to mention them.

The solution to this problem is amazingly simple: Wait until the two of you are alone, and then say something like this:

> "I changed the oil in both of the cars this weekend. It always feels good to me to keep up with that."

Or,

> "I feel so good about the way this party went. I loved the candles, and I thought the table looked so beautiful."

Or,

> "I just love this dress on me. The color is so good, and it's slenderizing. Don't you think?"

You don't even need to end your comment with a question. Your partner is likely to say something like, "Yeah, you are right. The table did look nice," or "That is a lovely dress. You are gorgeous in it," or even the standard, "Honey, you always look beautiful." But even if he or she doesn't respond at all, you have accomplished your purpose: you've brought about your partner's participation in acknowledging something you feel good about.

Another strategy is to tell your mate about compliments you

received from others: "You know, several people actually mentioned how pretty they thought the table looked tonight. It made
me feel good because I spent so much time on it. I'm really good
at this sort of thing." Your mate may reply, "It's true, honey, you
really are."

We sometimes think of scant or nonexistent verbal affirmations as a male propensity. Gender difference specialists tell us
that the part of a man's brain that feels emotions doesn't talk. I
have found that when I ask my husband Mayer whether he
appreciates something I did, he says he does, and he will be
amazed that I didn't know this. He was actually thinking it, but
his thought didn't make it over to the verbal part of his brain.

But in my experience, women fall short of verbal apprecia-
tions too. When our sweetheart does something that was his job
anyway, we don't think to say anything. After all, that's what he
was supposed to do.

Men often rely on their competence, dependability, and
thoughtfulness as a way to express their love, and they want
these qualities to be recognized. They enjoy being appreciated
for just going about their daily routine, especially when their
daily routine contributes to the family.

So it is important for you, both men and women, to learn to
*acknowledge your own accomplishments in the presence of your
loved one.* You can receive all the verbal affirmation you crave
by acting on your own in this important way.

One man told me:

> Donna's mother was coming for a visit, and I went to some trou-
> ble to rearrange my work schedule so the visit would go well.
> Donna never said anything about this. Before, I would have felt
> resentful and unappreciated. But I tried "acting on my own." I

just casually told her what I had done, and she was in fact very appreciative. But I don't think she ever would have mentioned it on her own. She was too preoccupied with other details of the visit.

It feels wonderful when someone compliments you spontaneously. But when that doesn't happen, would you rather sulk and be sad, complain to a friend, and continue to feel deprived? Or would you rather act on your own and find a way to meet the need yourself, thus brightening your life and everyone else's too?

Feeling deprived of affection or verbal affirmations will melt away when you act on your own to meet these needs. Try it, you'll see.

Fulfill Your Passionate Desires

I have a friend whose business is creating large displays for store windows and trade shows. She's extremely creative, and loves working on a large scale. A monumental hero figure in her life is the artist Christo, who creates works of art the size of buildings, or even entire countrysides or islands.

One day she heard that Christo was looking for volunteers to help him wrap the Reichstag building in Berlin. She became riveted on this opportunity. It was a fantasy almost beyond her imagining, something she thought was too outrageous even to contemplate, and she passionately, with all her heart, wanted to volunteer.

Her husband was against it.

She sold some family jewelry to pay for the trip, arranged for her aunt to watch her children, and made it happen for herself.

She came home elated, a changed person. She had fulfilled a dream.

In the end, her husband saw that this was the right thing for her to do, and rejoiced with her.

On the other hand, I know a woman, now ninety-one, who started a jewelry business in her home when she was twenty years old. She learned about gems and went to New York on buying trips. When she married at age twenty-seven, her husband took over the business and decided to sell cheaper, costume jewelry. My friend never worked in the business; her job was to stay home and raise the children. She went through her whole life angry that she was never allowed to pursue her own dream. Why didn't she go off and start her own jewelry business? we all wonder now. Why didn't she insist on taking over a part of the "family" business, starting a branch with fine jewelry? Of course, in the years all this was happening, there was no support for women who wanted to "act on their own," and probably, at some level, she never truly realized that any of these choices was an option for her. She poisoned her marriage all those years with her resentment, and never figured out a way to act on her own, to make her own dreams come true.

As my friend Roseanne Packard says, "There is no cancer like regret." She calls deep, passionate desires, "life agenda items." She says, "Marriage should never stop you from fulfilling a life dream. Just because you marry, you do not relinquish your most primitive longings."

If you have a "life agenda item" that truly matters to you, act on your own. Don't wait for support; create your own. It is truly a blessing to know what you want to do in your heart of hearts. Then never to do it is a tragedy.

Both your smaller, everyday desires and your "life agenda items" are equally important. Practice acting on your own with

🐦 EXPERIMENT #13:
ACT ON YOUR OWN

1. Review the list of problems you made in Experiment #1.
   With regard to each one, think, Is there a way I could
   make an impact on this problem by acting on my own? If
   there is, try it.
2. If you don't already do this, experiment with initiating
   affection with your partner. Later, make notes in your
   journal about how this is going.
3. Think of something you would like your partner to notice
   and appreciate. The next time you see him or her,
   acknowledge yourself for this thing as suggested in this
   chapter. Later, make notes in your journal about what
   happened and how it made you feel.
4. Sometime today or tomorrow, smile at your partner and
   then look away, a nondemand, no-special-reason smile. If
   you like this, don't forget about it. Do it again every now
   and then.
5. In your journal, make a wish list for yourself of desires
   and goals. They can be tiny little goals or great big "life
   agenda items." Star the "life agenda items," or put them in
   a separate list. For each item on the list, what would be
   required to make this happen? If you discover something
   you are not willing to wait for, is there an action you can
   take to start the ball in motion?

   Remember, if you don't take care of yourself, who will?

smaller desires, and be willing to act on your own for the dreams in your life that truly matter.

Acting on your own is a powerful Sacred Act.

Acting on Your Own Creates Balance in Your Relationship

I hope you can see how empowering acting on your own can be. The minute you take charge of a situation and are no longer dependent on your partner to obtain the results you seek—whether smaller desires or "life agenda items"—you have more control over your own life.

And you will be giving a gift to your partner also, by freeing up an area of your lives together that has been clogged. Usually, your partner will be heartened to see you happier, more independent, maybe even fulfilling a life dream.

Think of a way you can act decisively about something you deeply want, some way in which you can take initiative, be proactive, and meet your own needs without depending on your partner.

Taking a Stand When Your Limits Have Been Violated

As we've seen, you can't solve a problem by trying to persuade your partner to change. This strategy never works, and it doesn't honor your partner.

However, there are times when you need to let your mate know that you have reached your limit with his or her behavior.

When your partner does something that violates your own boundary, you need to take a stand. Your partner cannot yell at you, manipulate you, ignore you, be rude to you, be too hard on your children, or, certainly, abuse you, *without your compliance.* You may not be able to change your partner, but you can take care of yourself. Indeed, if you want to grow spiritually, you *must* take care of yourself.

Krysta's husband, Frank, was an intelligent man who ran his own nautical equipment shop. He read voraciously and once single-handedly defeated a team of five other people at Trivial Pursuit. Krysta loved all these qualities about him. But Frank had a violent temper and sometimes became critical and self-righteous toward both Krysta and their two daughters, who were nine and twelve when I met them. Sometimes he even grabbed the children and shook and frightened them. Frank's outbursts upset Krysta terribly. She would fight back, but never felt on an equal footing with him. Frank always "won." Sometimes after an outburst, the two of them wouldn't speak for three or four days. Then, eventually, Krysta would make a peace gesture, and life would be okay for a while, until the next episode.

Krysta was desperate when she came to one of my groups. "I want to do something about this, but I have no idea what to do."

At some level, she was allowing these outbursts to continue, because she couldn't find a way to communicate to Frank that she would not tolerate them. As a result, not only did tension in the family continue, but Krysta's self-esteem suffered too. She began to believe that she was powerless. It is hard to feel good about yourself when day after day you feel like the victim of an intolerable situation.

So how might Krysta take a stand in this situation?

Here is a set of guidelines for taking a stand, for communicating to your partner that your limits of tolerance have been reached and that you will not allow yourself to be treated badly any longer:

1. If you feel afraid or reluctant to act, enlist the help of a friend or support person. Do not try to do this alone. Stay in close touch with your friend throughout all these steps.

2. Admit that what you are about to do is difficult. You may feel afraid: afraid of how your mate will react, afraid that you won't be able to pull it off, afraid of what the consequences might be. That's natural. Just be clear that you don't have to wait until your fears go away before you take these steps. Feel your fear, and take a stand anyway. Courage is not the absence of fear; courage is the ability to act in the presence of fear.

3. Decide exactly what you want to declare to your mate. When you take a stand, you are not asking your partner to change. You are also not willing to negotiate. So you need to have your plan crystal clear in your own mind.

   If what you are declaring is a change in your own behavior, your task is easier. For example, one man in our group simply told his wife that he would no longer attend choir practice with her on Thursday evenings. He realized he had felt manipulated into going, and that he did not want to continue. Acting on his own, he was both empathic and decisive.

   What's more difficult is taking a stand about

something your partner is doing. In this case, your "stand" will consist of two parts: (1) exactly what you are no longer willing to tolerate, and (2) exactly what you will do if the behavior occurs again.

The hardest part of taking a stand is always figuring out the second part: What consequences will you carry out if the behavior occurs again? Here's where you have to be creative. Brainstorm with your support person or some of your friends for ideas. If you are not ready to separate from this person, thinking up your consequence can be a challenge.

Krysta's limit was Frank's anger and violence toward their girls. For a consequence, she told him that if he ever became violent with them again, she would ask a protective services worker to come and talk with them both. (I'll tell you how this strategy turned out in a moment.)

Another couple I spoke with, Sue and Rick, were feuding because she refused to get a job. They both agreed they needed her income. But she had been working for two years to start a mail order business, and even though it was actually draining their resources, she didn't want to give up and go back to a real job. Rick told Sue that if she didn't get a job within three months, he would take a second job that would keep him away from home every evening. Sue enjoyed their evenings at home and desperately needed his help with the children. She knew her guilt would be unbearable if Rick were working two jobs. His consequence worked with her.

Here are some other consequences couples have established:

- For leaving newspapers strewn all over the house, I will stop our subscription to the daily paper.
- For not throwing dirty laundry in the hamper, I will stop doing your laundry.
- For talking on the phone for more than forty-five minutes after dinner (this had been mutually agreed upon), I will disconnect our phone.
- For making critical remarks, I will go out with friends every evening for ten weekdays in a row.
- For failing to get the screens put up for six weeks after warm weather began, I will hire someone to put them up.
- For yelling at me, I will start seeing a therapist (even though they both felt they could not afford this).

4. Decide whether you want to write a letter to your partner, with the understanding that he or she will read it in your presence and you will then discuss it, or whether you want to speak directly to your mate. The advantage of writing your limits in a letter is that you will be giving a clear signal that this concern is different and special and you really mean business. Also you avoid the possibility of losing your nerve or becoming fuzzy-headed in the middle of your conversation. But either way can be effective.

5. Whether you write a letter or pick a time to make a verbal announcement, *begin with something positive.* Even if it is just, "Honey, you know I love you. And there is something I need to tell you," this makes a difference. It's even better to be specific: "Honey, the

garden looks gorgeous. I get so much pleasure from it. You are really good," or "Thank you so much for taking the kids to a movie yesterday. That was thoughtful, and I appreciate it."

People always complain to me that a positive opening sounds contrived or fake. So what? It's excellent practice for you, and I promise you, it will make a difference. Even if your partner can hear the *but* coming, it's a law of the universe that people can always accept bad news more easily if they hear good news first. Don't skip this step.

6. Speak or write only with *I* statements; avoid *you* statements altogether. Never say, "You are too hard on the children. You lose your temper too often." Instead say, "I am not willing to stand by when you hit the children anymore. I feel horrible when it happens. I have reached my limit."

7. State your position very simply. Do not give elaborate explanations or illustrations. Do not drag up past incidents. Do not give reasons for your position. Your partner might start arguing with the reasons or explanations and get the whole thing off track. For example, if Krysta said, "Your outbursts are hard on the children," Frank could say, "No they aren't. Discipline is good for them." This is beside the point. What Frank needs to get is that Krysta is not willing to tolerate the outbursts anymore—for whatever reasons. You don't owe your spouse any reasons; you have a right to your position. *The more simply you*

state it, the stronger it will be. Usually, your letter or statement will be very short, just a few sentences, or even one.

8. When you take a stand, your mate will react in some way—possibly with anger, defensiveness, pleading, or silence.

    Remember, you are not responsible for your partner's response, and you do not need to make your mate feel better. You are not causing your mate to feel bad; you are doing what is right for you. Focus on that. Again, as we discussed above, be both empathic and decisive. You can express genuine concern and understanding: "I'm really sorry if this makes you angry," or "I don't blame you for feeling bad about this. I know this is a very hard problem for you." But you should never try to either "fix" your partner's pain or blame yourself for it. You cannot be both the disease and the doctor. The most loving thing you can do for your partner is to be decisive and firm about your position, and understanding about your partner's feelings.

9. If you need to take a stand with your partner about something that is seriously dangerous or threatening, consider asking for professional support. If there has been physical abuse or destruction of property, you can ask a police officer to "stand by" as you let your mate know that you will no longer tolerate abusive, destructive behavior. If you are a woman and are afraid your husband might become violent when

you take a stand, call a shelter for battered women.
An experienced person will be able to guide and
assist you.

Let's return to Krysta and Frank to see what happened when
she announced that she would call a protective services worker
if Frank became abusive with the children ever again. Since
Krysta had never before taken a stand with Frank on this matter—she only cried and distanced herself and made it obvious
she was unhappy—her consequence startled Frank and made
him realize she was serious. For a time her declaration seemed
to have the desired effect. But inevitably Frank lost his temper
again, and Krysta, without hesitating, actually called a protective services worker. It helped that she was in a weekly support
group and was being coached and reminded every week about
what she needed to do.

Frank didn't show up for the appointment, but Krysta learned
a great deal from the social worker about alternatives for protecting her children from Frank's outbursts. Then the worker
sought out Frank at his place of employment. After some time,
he agreed to attend an anger abatement workshop run by the
county.

Once you decide on a plan, the very next time the behavior
occurs your consequences must be immediate and inevitable. If
you hesitate for a moment, or your partner agrees to try harder
and you give in, you have not taken your stand. It's okay. Since
taking a stand is something new for you, it may take you a while
to get the hang of it. Remember, in spiritual work we are always
more interested in the journey than the destination. If you
"chicken out" on your consequences, for any reason, remember
that this whole exercise is an experiment. Look back at your

behavior. Don't judge yourself. You did the best you could! But do see what you can learn about yourself from this incident. You will learn not just by having an experience, but by having an experience *and then reflecting upon it.* Write in your journal, talk with your support person. And then start over and take your stand again.

Let's recall Spiritual Partnership Principle #4:

> Strive to keep in balance the times you stand up for your partner's needs and the times you stand up for your own.

Sacred Act #3, "Act on Your Own," is an important tool in following this rule. Acting on your own and taking a stand are primary tools for taking care of yourself in your relationship. If you aren't willing to take care of your own needs, the whole system of Spiritual Partnership will collapse, because you can't give endlessly without filling up your own cup as well. Acting on your own is the most direct way to identify what you are missing in your relationship and to find a way to fill in that hole by yourself. The stronger and more self-sufficient a partner you become, the more you will contribute to the health of your relationship.

If you have never been a strong, assertive person, or you come from a family in which one of your parents was timid and unassertive, acting on your own will have a steep learning curve for you.

It may not come naturally or easily for you. That's okay. What is important in spirituality is moving in the right direction, not being there already. Standing up for yourself is what you need to work on. Take baby steps. Figure out one small way in which you are not standing up for yourself, and one small action you can take to act on your own. This is the cutting edge of your own spiritual growth. You won't believe how wonderful you will feel when you stop blaming your partner and take positive action for yourself. You will want more of that feeling of inner strength, and you will be on your way.

🐍 EXPERIMENT #14:
     TAKE A STAND

Is your partner doing something that you can no longer tolerate?

Carefully follow the steps in this chapter, and take a stand.

Remember, your partner cannot "get away with" any behavior without your compliance. Figure out a way to interrupt the destructive cycle, and take action.

EIGHT

Sacred Act #4: Practice Acceptance

Marcia feels that Todd is overly negative and pessimistic. (But you substitute your own real issue.)

Marcia has two basic options for making this problem disappear: (1) She can work on Todd to help him to become a less negative person, or (2) she can accept Todd the way he is and find a way to work with his negativity.

We have already discussed the first option at some length. If Marcia tries, however gently, to negotiate with Todd to become less negative:

- She will be setting herself up as right and Todd as wrong.
- She will be creating conflict and upset, not harmony.
- She will be giving Todd the underlying message that he is not okay, that she would love him more if he changed.
- She will be making it hard for Todd to feel close to her.
- She will unwittingly evoke defensiveness from Todd rather than cooperation. In other words, Tom's negativity is more likely to persist *precisely because* she is criticizing it.
- She is not likely to solve the problem.

Of course, in spite of its drawbacks, the first option is still the most widely preferred method in the world for solving problems.

The second option is to accept your partner just exactly the way he or she really is, to accept the behavior you don't like, the personality trait you would change if you had a magic wand. You recognize that when you fell in love with this person, you fell in love with a whole package, and you don't get to choose little parts of it to send back and exchange.

Accepting your partner has many advantages over trying to change him or her. When you work on accepting your partner:

- You will be focusing on your own spiritual growth, viewing the "problem" as an opportunity to develop your inner peace, your ability to love and tolerate.
- You will be creating peace within yourself; anger toward your spouse will cause *you* ongoing suffering.
- You will be supporting your partner by offering the most important gift anyone can give: the message, "You are accepted. You don't have to change to be a good person."
- You will be actively creating harmony in your relationship and avoiding upset.
- You will be "outgrowing" this problem by "developing a new level of consciousness," rather than assuming you can "solve" the problem through your own clever ways.
- *Perhaps most important, you will be creating an atmosphere in which true transformation is likely to occur (for example, in Todd's negativity).*

Notice, accepting something does not mean you like it. It doesn't mean you approve of it or that you respect it. It simply means that you stop fighting it. You stop wasting your precious energy railing against something you can't change by an act of

your own will. You graciously let go, and allow the universe to be
the way it is. Your partner is not likely to change deeply
entrenched characteristics. But if you accept them, gradually
over time the qualities you dislike will cease to be a problem.
Things will evolve. Your acceptance will make an impact.

Meredith and Sam had been married five years and were generally very happy together. But Meredith was distressed when she
came to see me. Whenever they got together with friends, she told
me, Sam would interrupt other people with what Meredith considered to be corny humor. She would talk with Sam about it, and
he would agree to cut back, but he never did. Meredith clearly
had the illusion that if she could only choose the right words, if
she could only find an effective way to convey to Sam how annoying his habit was, he would see her point and stop. She wanted me
to help her find a way to communicate with Sam.

Instead I said to her, "What if Sam never gets your point
about this? What if, forever, he always goes on interrupting
people with his corny humor? Maybe he is never going to
become the gracious social person you hope for."

The idea came as a shock to Meredith. We discussed it for a
while, and I could see that this was a genuinely new idea to her.
I could see a shift take place in her. She relaxed. She even
laughed at herself. "Gee," she said, "maybe that wouldn't be so
awful." What a concept!

When I spoke with her several weeks later, she told me that
a great weight had lifted from her shoulders. On several social
occasions, she noticed that other people apparently did not find
Sam so annoying. Or even if they did, so what? She realized it
was not her problem. "I'm having a lot more fun at these gather-
ings," she told me. "By superimposing this standard on Sam, I
was torturing myself. Now, all that is gone, and I just let Sam be

the way he is. I even laugh at his jokes myself sometimes, and he loves that. He even mentioned it. And he makes me laugh at home more. I was actually standing in the way of our having more fun! In a million years I would never have guessed that I was the problem here."

What most people do not realize is that *only when you accept what is will change ever occur.* What you resist will persist. When you accept something, only then do you set into motion the circumstances that will allow either you or it to change. Let us look in more detail at this little understood fact of life. Then we will talk more about exactly how you can "practice acceptance" within your relationship.

Acceptance Is the Starting Point for Change

Accepting the way a person is does *not* mean that that person will never change. Quite the contrary, as ironic as it may sound, *accepting that which is unchangeable is the starting point for deep and genuine change.*

To understand how acceptance is the starting point for change, let's begin by looking at the opposite.

When you try to persuade someone to change (instead of being totally accepting), the person will probably resist your efforts and is not likely to change. We discussed this earlier in the book, but we'll go into more detail here.

Let's return to the example in which Marcia kept trying to persuade Todd to be less negative. Todd is negative by nature. Negativity and pessimism is a "mask" or defense he adopted early in his life, to give himself a feeling of control. Negativity is his way of staying safe. At some deep, unconscious level, Todd believes that the negative worldview is necessary for his survival. To threaten his negativity is to threaten his very existence. This may not seem true to the rest of us, but it is true inside Todd.

Therefore, it makes perfect sense for Todd to fight to keep his negativity alive. When Marcia assaults his negativity, his reaction is to strengthen it all the more! He believes his very survival depends on it.

I had a personal experience of this early in my own spiritual growth. I must have been reinforced as a child for my big smile and cheerful demeanor. So I somehow got the message that smile equals survival. When in doubt, smile. When in trouble, smile. When feeling fragile, smile. When I became an adult, people told me they found my persistent smile to be inauthentic. I was stunned at the strength of my hurt and upset! I now see that trying to live without my smile terrified me. The level of fear was irrational. I felt as though I would disappear. I recall trying to give a presentation without smiling, as an experiment, and finding myself so panicked that I could not continue. *So I returned to smiling with even more conviction.*

My smiling was fighting with great passion for its own survival. At some level I believed that my smiling habit was the key to my survival, that without my ability to smile my way through fear, I would die.

This may sound melodramatic, but I assure you it is true.

Psychologist Harville Hendrix explains deep survival instincts physiologically. The brain, he says, in *Getting the Love You Want,* is divided into two basic parts, which he calls the "old brain" and the "new brain." The old brain links us with all other living things on the planet, because "all vertebrates from reptiles to mammals share this portion of the anatomy," and with the history of the development of life on the planet.

... you are unaware of most of the function of your old brain.... Scientists ... tell us that its main concern is self-preservation. Ever on the alert, the old brain constantly asks the primeval question: "Is it safe?" ... As it goes about its job of ensuring your safety, your old brain operates in a fundamentally different manner from your new brain. One of the crucial differences is that the old brain appears to have only a hazy awareness of the external world.

So here's what happened inside me: I felt vulnerable or attacked or unsure of myself. My old brain, not logically attached to events in the real world, said, "This is not safe! Go directly to old brain survival drill: smile!"

In the same way, Todd's survival instinct kicked in when Marcia criticized his negativity, and the negativity, in its "old brain" attempt to protect Todd, became all the stronger.

That's what happens when, instead of accepting the traits in your partner that you don't love, you criticize them.

Now let's look at what happens when you practice acceptance.

Todd makes one of his negative predictions. Before, Marcia would have said, "There you go, being so negative again. Think of the positive side. You are so doom and gloom." Or whatever.

But because she now accepts that negative comments are a part of the package that is Todd, she says something like, "Yeah, it probably won't turn out well." Or, "You may be right." And that's it. It's over. There's no upset, no bickering. Somewhere, Todd's subconscious picks up that he has been validated. As Todd feels increasingly validated, loved, and accepted by Marcia, maybe his "old brain" will feel less need for its protective negative behavior.

Todd will never transform into Pollyanna. But as he experiences unmitigated love and support within his marriage, his negativity may lose its urgency and may become less predominant. Marcia may never come to love this quality in Todd, but by accepting it she is eliminating one entire area of potential conflict.

Changing the "System"

Notice that when Marcia accepted Todd's negativity, she also changed her own response to it. This changed the dynamics between the two of them right away. And because Marcia changed, Todd may eventually change also. Here's why:

Every relationship is a "system," a unit. Every part within the system has an impact on every other part of the system. So if one of you makes a change, it will make an impact on the other.

This is why the spiritual approach to relationships requires less effort than the Old Model in which both partners had to "work." If you change the way you respond to your partner, you will be setting in motion a change in the system.

The "system theory" of family therapy was a revolutionary breakthrough when it became widespread in the 1950s and 1960s. Before that, the only strategy available to us was psychotherapy, in which pathology was assumed to be psychological. Treatment would consist of figuring out who in the family was the problem person, and "fixing" that person. Family therapy recognized that the pathology was not within one troublemaker, but was instead in the interaction among the family members. Maybe the son was angry and withdrawn not because he had a psychological problem, but because his mother was invasive and controlling. What family therapists discovered was

that one small change in the system would change the entire system and all of the people in it.

This theory explains why practicing acceptance will bring
about change in your relationship.

Let's say your problem is that your partner is critical of you.
I grant you, that is very hard to accept in a spirit of goodwill. But
if you can be the "big" person, practice restraint, and refrain
from making an issue out of the criticism, it will just become part
of the landscape. If your partner never derives any satisfaction
from criticizing you, he or she may eventually take this criticism
habit elsewhere and do less of it in your marriage. The system
won't keep operating if you don't react in your old habitual ways.

I saw this exact phenomenon happen recently with a friend
I'll call Chris. She and Warren had been living together for six
months and were compatible and happy together. There was a
problem, however. Warren was having trouble letting go of a previous relationship, with a woman named Marne who lived two
thousand miles away in Cleveland. Warren had the illusion that
if he talked enough about her, at the same time affirming Chris
and saying how much he loved her, he could make his obsession
go away. At first Chris tolerated these conversations. But she
quickly realized that she was a biased listener since she had a
stake in the outcome, and she felt it was inappropriate for her to
serve as Warren's therapist. So, acting on her own, being both
empathic and decisive, she nicely told him that she would not be
a part of any more Marne conversations.

This decision created some tension. Every time Marne's
name came up, Chris would begin to bristle. "I'd rather not hear
this," she would say. She resisted. But she also saw that this was
creating tension that had not been present before, and that what
she was resisting was persisting. So she changed tactics again.

I just tell him, "Go to Cleveland. Go see her. Work it out with her," not sarcastically, but sincerely. He gets clear he doesn't want to do that, and the whole thing goes away. I use the martial arts approach. I just continue in the direction he is already going. I don't resist it. I accept that that's where he is. I can't change it. It's just what is.

Chris's comments remind me again of this passage from Lao-tsu:

> As the soft yield of water cleaves obstinate stone,
> So to yield with life solves the insoluble.

What happened with me and my inappropriate smile was that I began to pay attention to it, rather than judge it or force it away by an act of will. One day I was talking in a small group about something unpleasant and I noticed that I was smiling! It felt weird. As I continued, I let myself *not* smile, and I could feel a big difference inside myself. I felt more relaxed, more connected to what I was saying, and more connected to the people in the group. After that experience, I paid attention more often, and gradually the inappropriate smiling disappeared—not because I forced it away by an act of will, but because I *accepted* it. When I allowed it to be there and began paying closer attention to it, I noticed how toxic inappropriate smiling felt to me, and the habit began to disappear all by itself. I was allowing myself to be more authentic.

Of course, most of us want certain changes in our partners. The way to create these changes is to begin with what is actually the case and to accept it. Change happens when you stop trying to control everything yourself. When you allow things to be the way they are and resist intervention, natural processes generally work toward what's best. Even competent therapeutic intervention starts with total acceptance of what is. That is where change has to start.

The English novelist G. K. Chesterton said, "Faith means believing the unbelievable, or it is no virtue at all." Having faith that acceptance will lead to change is just this sort of virtue. It means believing the unbelievable. Right now you cannot even imagine that some unpleasant quality in your partner will ever transform. But by now I hope you do understand that badgering him or her to change will never have the desired effect. So your alternative is to accept the unpleasant quality and find creative ways to live with it.

Genuine acceptance is a way of gaining a larger perspective and a new level of consciousness so you will be able to "outgrow" your problems.

Guidelines for Moving toward Acceptance

1. Decide Whether This Trait Is a "Deal-Breaker"

You may decide that some quality or behavior in your mate is something you do not choose to live with.

- Your partner is physically or verbally abusive or addicted to drugs or alcohol.
- Your partner is not loyal to you.
- You want a baby and your partner doesn't.
- Your partner can't control his or her temper.
- You see that staying with your partner will not contribute to his or her or your own spiritual growth.

Everyone draws the line at a different place, and you have a
right to draw it wherever you want. Especially if you are not yet
married to this person, keep your eyes wide open. Pay attention.
Accept the real person you are with, not a fantasy of who you
hope the person will become.

If the trait is something you choose not to live with, then you
need to make a decision. Do you want to leave the relationship?
Or do you want to practice acceptance within the relationship?
For example, if your partner is an alcoholic, if you accept this
and you decide you want to stay with him or her, then you will
join an Alanon group and adopt a clear strategy about what to do
when your partner upsets the family by drinking.

Spiritual writer Gary Zukav is very clear that spiritual growth
is a higher priority than any vows one once made:

> All of the vows that a human being can take cannot prevent the
> spiritual path from exploding through and breaking those vows
> if the spirit must move on. It is appropriate for Spiritual Part-
> ners to remain together only as long as they grow together.

Of course, the welfare of any children who will be affected
must also be considered.

If you are having trouble deciding whether a certain trait is a
deal-breaker for you, whether or not you are married, I devoted
a chapter to it in *How One of You Can Bring the Two of You
Together.* Also, you may want to try the guidelines below as a way
to help you discover whether you want to stay in your situation.

Most of the changes you wish you could create in your partner are not "deal-breakers" at all but fall within the vast realm
of little and big qualities that you wish were different but that
you can in the end accept.

2. LOOK FOR YOUR PARTNER'S NATURAL TENDENCIES

One of the great benefits of the personality systems that have now become popular, like the Enneagram or the Myers-Briggs Personality Inventory, is that all this information has helped us become more accepting of each other.

The Enneagram, for example, is an ancient system that divides everyone into nine basic personality types. Type 1 people have a tendency to be perfectionist; type 4, to be melancholy; or type 6, to worry and be anxious. This system says that such personality traits arise from deep in our psyches and are fundamentally unchangeable.

The effect on most people of studying the Enneagram is an almost instant greater acceptance of people in their lives. "Oh, now I totally understand my boss," one Enneagram workshop graduate told me. "It is deep in his very nature to worry, and to be anxious about everything. Now I see that all his checking up on me and advising me has nothing to do with me. He has a need to do this because of his own irrational fears. He's a 6. He is just behaving the way 6's behave."

Enneagram students also learn how to respond most effectively to the various personality types. "The way to get through to perfectionists is to validate them for their thoroughness," one Enneagram teacher told me. She went on:

> For example, a friend was helping me to get ready for a party, but because she was spending way too much time perfecting our minimal decorations, we were not going to be ready on time. At first I said to her, "Just let that go. Forget the balloons. Just scribble those little signs, they don't have to be so neat." That

was completely ineffective. Then I realized, she's a 1! Perfectionism runs very deep with her. So I validated her perfectionism. I climbed right in there with her. I said something like, "Those signs look beautiful. You've done a gorgeous job with them. Would you mind getting back to the rest of them later and helping me with the table right now?"

The Enneagram is a useful system, and becoming familiar with it can help you understand and accept difficult personality traits in other people (and in yourself).

However, you don't have to learn the Enneagram to take advantage of the lesson it or other personality systems teach. The lesson is this: People's fundamental personality characteristics will never truly change. So, both to support other people in a spirit of love and goodwill, and to get along better with them, we can (1) pay attention to what a person's basic traits are and (2) accept and adapt to these traits.

Take a moment now to think about this. List a few adjectives that describe your partner's basic personality.

Now think about a recent incident that upset you. Was your partner just being his or her natural self? Can you feel more accepting and tolerant knowing that your partner was expressing a deep innate quality?

After an Enneagram class, Jerry realized that his wife Sylvia has a natural, deep-seated tendency to be helpful and caring, to reach out and support others. She feels safe and happy only when she has some ways to express this intrinsic need. Jerry viewed her need to help as excessive. When the neighbor's mother died and Sylvia spent two days over there, managing phone calls, cooking, and generally running the crisis while his own household was neglected, he became irate. Looking back on the situation now, he sees that helping out in a crisis is who

Sylvia is. It would truly be going against her fundamental nature to come home and take care of her (or her family's) own needs when someone else was in a crisis.

Mayer and I are at opposite ends of the "be spontaneous/plan ahead" continuum. When I try to schedule something two weeks ahead, he becomes anxious. "I don't know whether I'll want to do that then," he'll say. On the other hand, if we don't plan way ahead, I become anxious because I'm afraid we will never do anything.

One time, we each took the same personality test. One of the charts we received after the test was scored measured this very quality. We couldn't have been further apart on the scale. We had a good laugh over it. Now that the quality has been labeled and measured in us, we have an easier time accepting it in each other. Our difference has been the source of a lot of humor, and we are clear that we have to find ways to accommodate each other's needs while not betraying our own.

Like the various personality charts, information about gender differences has also helped couples become more accepting of each other. Though the popular press has perhaps diminished the value of important studies by oversimplifying them, general ideas can nevertheless be useful: Women want affection and closeness; men want security. Men tend to withdraw under stress; women want to connect, to talk things through. Men use conversation to make decisions and solve problems; women use conversation to express feelings and establish connection.

Just being aware of these tendencies helps us accept them when we see them. Instead of trying in vain to change the opposite sex, we adapt. For example, if I am trying to talk something through, just to express my feelings and see if I can achieve greater clarity, but Mayer is busily trying to solve my problem, I can say to him, "Thanks for your ideas, but I just want to talk this through for now." He understands what I mean, and he is not offended. Accepting and labeling our differing propensities ahead of time help us to manage them.

In short, then, look for your partner's natural tendencies. This will help you accept that these are part of the package you love.

3. Pretend the Quality You Dislike Is a Scar

Suppose the person you love has an accident that results in an unfortunate scar on his or her face. You wouldn't like this, but you also wouldn't reject your mate for it. You would be supportive, and help him or her to accept the unacceptable. Imagine it was a physical disability or illness. Would you be critical and demand change?

Our deep personality characteristics are somewhat like scars. They are difficult and maybe even impossible to change. What is the "scar" in your partner that you can learn to accept, as you progress in your spiritual journey toward connection, love, and surrender?

4. "Act As If"

It may be hard to imagine accepting something that annoys you terribly about your partner. His libido is way too high. She interrupts all the time. He'll never go with you to your beloved horse shows. She's a workaholic and never around. He's an Internet junkie, married to his computer. She flies off the handle and becomes angry way too often. He always puts his own needs first.

You want change. It's hard to accept living with these qualities.

So begin by using our always helpful strategy: "act as if."

Behave as if you are accepting of your partner's annoying trait. In the end it is your behavior that is going to make a difference. If you act accepting, even when you don't feel accepting, you will get to see what this feels like. Your behavior may actually have an impact on your feelings; you may become more accepting. Plus, you will be changing the dynamic between you and your partner, so something different is likely to happen.

Jim was unhappy with his wife Diane for becoming active in her professional association, which met on Saturdays. He wanted so much to have the whole day with her so they could plan excursions or just relax together. Every Saturday he made an issue out of it, always trying to persuade her that this organization was part of her old life, not her current one, that she received little benefit from it, that their relationship was so much more important. He would go on and on, and Diane always left for her meetings feeling annoyed and hurt and angry. After I talked with Jim about the idea of acceptance, he shifted. Although he was not at all in the mood to accept Diane's behavior, he decided to behave as though he was. His first move was to plan a hike for himself, so, as Diane went to her meeting, he left for the woods. The next Saturday he did the same thing. Suddenly they stopped fighting. Jim still wished Diane would come with him, but he found that he was actually accepting that this probably wouldn't happen. By *acting as if* he accepted her decision, he found he *was* accepting it.

"I made an important discovery," Jim told me excitedly. "I was the one causing the problem, just because I wouldn't accept Diane for who she was."

Jim's discovery is so important, it is worth repeating: When there is a problem, it is caused, not by the one who won't change, but by the one who won't accept what is!

So start by acting as if you accept something that upsets you, and see what happens.

5. Say to Yourself, "This Is Not a Problem, It Is a Fact of Life"

When you view something as a problem, you assume there must be a solution. When you view something as a fact of life, you realize that your task is simply to begin to work with it, to adapt to it, in a word, to accept it.

This is exactly the shift that Jim made when he began to accept Diane's Saturday meetings. Jim told me:

> I realized I had been working really hard to solve this problem. In my fantasy, the solution was that Diane would see the light and let go of her whole organization thing. The more that didn't happen, the more out of control I felt. I kept imagining the perfect conversation with her in which, if I just said the right thing in the right way, she would be willing to compromise. When I realized that I had no problem to solve, the whole thing shifted for me. When I started thinking about adapting to this fact of life, I came up with different ideas. For one thing, I asked Diane more about the organization, why it was so important to her and what she liked most about it. I was surprised to learn, when I really listened to her, that the social contacts there were as important to her as the business aspects of it. And then, of course, I took initiative and started planning my own activities so I wouldn't feel I was wasting Saturdays.
>
> Diane told me that the hardest part of my unhappiness with her was not that I complained about the time on Saturdays, but that I was actually putting her down for something she loved. I was belittling her and her favorite pursuit. I now see that she has a right to an interest that doesn't interest me, and that part of loving someone is loving the parts you aren't so happy about.

When you try to solve a problem by persuading your partner to change, you will often carry around the belief, as Jim did, and as Meredith did when she was unhappy with Sam's joking, that if you can only state your request in the right way, somehow find the right words, you will succeed. You think the problem is that you have not communicated well enough with your partner. It may come as a great relief to learn that you can give up on this quest for the perfect words or the perfect timing. Maybe the answer is that you will never achieve the change in your partner that you so long for.

This may make you feel sad, and even resentful or deprived. That's okay. Those feelings are appropriate when you let go of a cherished dream and realize you may not ever get what you want. But you should also feel relief. You can give up trying to move this mountain, and get on with your life.

6. SAY TO YOURSELF, "THIS HAS NOTHING TO DO WITH ME"

The "mantra" we learned in Sacred Act #1, "This has nothing to do with me," is useful here again. Let's review it briefly.

It is difficult to be graciously accepting when your mate's annoying habit is aimed directly at you. For example, if your partner tries to control you, or often nags at you, criticizes you, advises you, ignores you, is impatient with you, or even yells at you, it may feel to you as though you are living with a fly buzzing around your head, and it may be very difficult to "accept."

This is a challenge. But remember, your partner would be this way with anyone. The behavior isn't aimed specifically at you; you just happen to be the one who is in the way when the behavior is happening.

> ❧ EXPERIMENT #15:
>   ACCEPTANCE
>
> If you had a magic wand, what would you change about your
> mate? Make a list in your journal.
>   Now, look at each quality you have written down and say to
> yourself, "What if this never changes? What if my partner will
> always be this way?"

When you say to yourself, "This has nothing to do with me,"
it will help you remember, "This unpleasant behavior on the part
of my partner is like a scar; I don't like it, but I can learn to live
with it, graciously and quietly, without reacting."

Self-Acceptance

The fourth Sacred Act of Spiritual Partnership is to practice
accepting your partner. But one of the best ways to learn acceptance is to begin with yourself.

And self-acceptance is the ultimate aphrodisiac. As we've
seen, when you know and love your authentic self and feel comfortable with all your best and worst qualities, you become more
approachable and easy to love.

Self-esteem can be said to be the ultimate goal of all spiritual
practice. In his book *A Path with Heart,* spiritual teacher and
writer Jack Kornfield writes, "Much of spiritual life is self-
acceptance, maybe all of it."

Though they talk about it in different languages, all the great
religious traditions teach self-acceptance. "Love your neighbor

as yourself," Jesus said. God loves you, just the way you are. Christ died for your sins—another way of saying that, no matter what your shortcomings are, you are okay. Buddhism teaches that we create our own suffering through attachment, anger, and hatred. Anger or hatred toward your partner will cause you limitless suffering. When you accept what is and let go of needing to be or to have something else, that is when you truly find inner peace.

You are fine exactly the way you are right now. Even if you don't exercise enough. Even if you don't have the possessions or status or job you wish you had. Even if you have doubts about your marriage. Even if you hurt or failed someone. You can't change reality, you can only either fight it or accept it. Accepting it, however unpleasant, is the only route to inner peace. When you refuse to accept any part of what is true for you, you are making life harder for yourself. What you refuse to accept will persist.

Accepting yourself is not about getting yourself into a perfect state so that it is easy to accept yourself. First you lose weight, win the lottery, establish your dream home, fall in love with a perfect person, rise to the top of your profession—and then you accept yourself. No, accepting yourself means that right now, exactly as things really are in this moment, you accept them. "This is my existence, this is my life." It's not about getting better; it's about accepting who you are right now. If you decide you have to be someone else in order to love yourself, you will never find self-love.

Does accepting yourself mean you can't have goals and dreams? Not at all. It means that you don't have to achieve those goals or dreams in order to be a good person. Having goals and dreams is part of what you accept about yourself. It's part of what is real for you right now. Maybe you are even experiencing envy right now, or anger, or failure. That's what is going on for you right now. It's okay. It doesn't need to be any other way.

The continuing search for improvement—in yourself, in your relationships—keeps you in a state of discontent. In spiritual work, the discontent is the problem. If at each moment you can accept that "this is what is happening right now; this is reality; this is my existence," that in itself will remove the discontent and move you closer to the objectives you desire.

You may be feeling upset, but you are not also putting yourself down for feeling upset. Even if what is happening right now is that you are depressed, or your partner is angry with you, or you are anxious or under stress, you will get through it faster and be calmer as you go through it if you can say, "This is what is happening right now. It isn't pleasant, but I accept it, and I know it will pass. This is not a problem, it is a fact of life."

When you feel you are doing the best you can, at any given moment, given your particular circumstances, that is all you can ask of yourself. Doing the best you can is total and complete success. You may be aware that you could do better in some ways. Good! You haven't arrived at perfection yet. Accept that too.

The opposite of self-acceptance is self-put-downs or self-hate. This is the part of you that rails against some aspect of who you are and what your life is right now. It is like trying to swim upstream. Self-judgment uses up lots of your good energy, in a way that does not serve you at all.

Once again, remember that accepting something does not mean you necessarily like it. In fact, self-acceptance is precisely about accepting those parts of yourself that you don't like. Accepting the parts of yourself that you like is no challenge.

Self-acceptance gives you inner power and strength. If you accept the whole imperfect package that is you, rather than fight against it, you are freed from ever having to prove to anyone that you're a good person. You know, deep within, that although in some ways you can always do better, you don't have to do better before you can totally love yourself. When you get this feeling, you will experience yourself as powerful in the world. And you will be able to give up struggling. Self-acceptance is freedom.

It is possible to "work on" becoming more self-accepting. Most of this work is about getting to know yourself better, because you can't love or accept parts of yourself that you don't even know about yet. That's why all spiritual work, all "waking up," leads to self-acceptance, as Jack Kornfield suggested.

For example, when I became aware of my inappropriate smiling, I had to look beneath the behavior to figure out why I was doing that. I asked experienced guides (therapists and spiritual teachers) to help me, and it took time. But I began to see that I smiled because I feared that the real me—that is, the little ember that glowed beneath the persistent smile—wouldn't be lovable, or even likable. I began to discover parts of myself that I didn't like at all and was eager to hide from the world. I had to become acquainted with those parts—painful regrets, insecurities, fears. Only when I found out what was in the dark snake pit of my psyche could I possibly begin to accept those parts of myself. Gradually I began to see that all those awful things weren't so awful after all. I could live with them. Denying that they were there took away too much energy, and made me feel like a half person. I began to see that I wasn't only the good parts of me, I was all of me. And all of me was perfectly okay.

So you can work toward self-acceptance.

However, it is also true that you cannot earn self-acceptance the way you work through school and earn a degree. Self-acceptance is a gift that comes at unexpected moments. It settles over you, in a gently ecstatic moment, unbeckoned, like grace.

When I worked as a hospital chaplain, I spent many hours in

conversations with David, an athletic young man who had broken his neck in a diving accident and was almost completely paralyzed. His rage and cynicism were boundless. He felt he should have known better than to dive where he did and blamed himself for the accident. He told me over and over that he wished the accident had killed him, and that he hated the stranger who had rescued him. He also talked a great deal about his grandfather, whom he adored, who had died just three months before the accident.

One day he couldn't wait to talk with me. He'd had a dream in which the stranger who saved him came back and offered to help him take his own life. They were just about to do it. But then his grandfather came into the room and just looked at him, so heartbroken and disappointed. So he stopped.

David could talk about nothing else but that dream. We started writing letters to his grandfather. One morning, he told me his grandfather visited him again during the night and told him to get involved with helping other patients in the hospital. So David started helping in the rehab room, talking people through their routines. One day, he met a man who was injured in a car accident on the way to his own wedding. The story touched David so much that when he came back to his room, he couldn't stop sobbing. He cried for about two weeks, every time I saw him.

Then his mood began to soften. He talked about his family. He even began to talk, ever so tentatively, about his plans for the future.

Another day, I entered his room and was actually startled by what I saw. David looked gorgeous. There was a new energy in his face, a relaxed quality I had never seen. I'll never forget his next words.

"I'm a quadriplegic," he said to me. "I have a new life."

His revelation came to him in a telephone conversation with

℘ EXPERIMENT #16:
    SELF-ACCEPTANCE

If you had a magic wand, what would you change about yourself? Make a list in your journal.

Now, look at each quality you have written down and say to yourself, "What if this never changes? What if I will always be this way?"

---

his mother. She was trying to arrange a way for him to be a part of the neighborhood football game when he came home for Thanksgiving. "My mother is still wishing this accident didn't happen. She doesn't accept it," David told me. "But I do."

He was experiencing the grace of self-acceptance. Never before or since have I seen such a clear example of it.

Just as all roads in early times led to Rome, all "spiritual work" leads to self-acceptance. Each of the Five Sacred Acts of Spiritual Partnership—such as practicing restraint, "acting as if," and acting on your own—will lead you to greater and greater self-acceptance. It is a lifelong journey. Sometimes we feel more self-accepting, sometimes less. But the more we engage in spiritual practice, the more we can accept ourselves—even when we are not being self-accepting!

NINE

Sacred Act #5:
Cultivate Compassion

If you want to be happy, be compassionate.
If you want others to be happy, be compassionate.

—THE DALAI LAMA

Compassion is the ability to imagine yourself in someone else's shoes and to behave accordingly. It means you deeply understand what someone else is going through *and* you are moved to help. The literal meaning from the Latin root is to suffer (passion) with (com), or to feel with. The Dalai Lama calls compassion "a mental attitude based on the wish for others to be free of their suffering, associated with a sense of commitment, responsibility, and respect towards the other."

So what does it mean to say that compassion is a Sacred Act in your relationship?

It means when your husband is yelling at you because you spent too much money on clothes, you take a deep breath and say to yourself, "The poor guy grew up in such a poor family and his father was so terrified about money all the time, it must be so hard for him to see all that money I spent. Underneath the anger, he's scared. I can respect his point of view. I need to find a way to meet my own needs and his too. I can do this."

Maybe you don't do that instantly, but as time passes that is the direction in which you move. Shift the focus from yourself to

your partner. Put yourself in your partner's shoes. Try to understand *why* your partner behaves in this way that bugs you.
Remember that your partner has a right to behave that way, and
has reasons for behaving that way, reasons that go way back in
history. It is not the case that you are right and he or she is
wrong; you see things differently. You both have a right to your
opinions.

That's compassion. That's providing spiritual leadership in
your relationship and being the "big" person.

Or when your wife is nagging at you for the millionth time
that you should be better organized, you say to yourself, "She
has a right to want me to be better organized. She's doing her
control thing again. She had to be controlling to survive in her
family. But she is making progress, and I can support that
progress by gently affirming her and then finding a way to be dis-
organized that won't upset her."

That may seem like a tall order, but that's what compassion
means. You see your partner upset, even if it is at you. This pains
you too, and you feel moved to help.

We'll return to these examples later in the chapter to see
exactly *what you can do* when you feel compassion in these situations. But first let's look at a simpler example.

It is easier to experience and express compassion when your
partner does not view you as the cause of the pain. For example,
she announces she did not receive the promotion she had so
hoped for. Or he learns that his mother has cancer. Now, you feel
sad, you can imagine how you would feel if you were in this situation, and you feel moved to do whatever you can to help. You
may hold your partner while he or she cries. You might offer to
fix dinner that night, or make flight arrangements, or take over
extra household chores. You truly wish you could take the pain
away. That's compassion.

The opposite of compassion is blame.

Many people go through life blaming their parents for their personal problems, blaming their partner for the difficulties in their relationship, blaming their boss for their unhappiness at work, and blaming the universe for being unfair in general.

"My parents favored my brother; they abandoned me. My partner is too controlling, too demanding, too self-oriented. My mate talks too much, talks too little, doesn't listen to me, works all the time, is inconsiderate. My boss is unreasonable."

You may be right about what your parents did wrong, how your spouse could improve, and how your boss could be more effective. But staying stuck at the level of blaming them will never move you forward. When you blame someone else for whatever is going on in your life, two things happen:

1. You have to carry around toxic, negative, angry thoughts and feelings.
2. You prevent yourself from looking at your own role in the problems, which is the only area you can do anything about.

Let's say your partner is being his usual thoughtless self. He fixed himself a sandwich and didn't even think to ask whether you might want one.

If you blame him, you will be carrying around the "blame poison" inside of you: Look at how thoughtless that was! It makes me so angry! I can't believe someone can be that self-absorbed and selfish! Meanwhile, your partner is enjoying his sandwich. He did something that triggered it, but you are creating your own upset.

If you take a compassionate approach instead, you might say

to yourself something like, "My poor, sweet husband. He grew up in such a selfish family, where they didn't do favors for each other. He still hasn't been able to overcome that. It probably never even occurred to him to make me a sandwich. Imagine!"

Now, you act on your own, make yourself a sandwich, and join him for a pleasant lunch. There is no toxic anger inside you, and you have found a way to fix the situation for yourself by using a Sacred Act. You know inside yourself that he will probably never completely change this self-involved aspect of his personality. So you don't even need to bring it up. You just be the "big" person by understanding that he is limited in this area by the childhood he had, and you let it go.

Compassion is not about who is right and who is wrong; it is about where you choose to put your energy. Can you forgive someone for making a mistake? For doing something that hurt you? For being less than what you hoped for?

Intuitive writer and teacher Caroline Myss says that not forgiving someone is like taking rat poison and hoping the other person will die. If you remain angry and self-righteous about your partner's forgetting to make you a sandwich, he will be enjoying his sandwich while you are poisoning yourself with anger. Anger, blame, and self-righteousness diminish the quality of *your own* life, and do nothing to change the situation that is causing your anger.

Gordon and His Parents

Gordon's father was abusive and unpleasant. His mother divorced him when Gordon was nine. For the next three years his mother paid a great deal of attention to Gordon; they were a pair and went everywhere together. Gordon felt loved and affirmed, at last. Then Gordon's mother fell in love and married again, to a man who liked Gordon and did all he could to establish a relationship with him. But Gordon would have none of it. He resented this stepfather for coming between him and his mother.

Now Gordon is thirty-two and has a son of his own. He is still cool toward his stepfather and angry with his mother. He feels his mother should have done more to protect him from his real father in the early years, and that she should not have "abandoned" him when she remarried. His parents do all they can to build bridges with Gordon, but he is not receptive. He wants them to see what they did to him and admit they were wrong. Now that he sees how much he loves his own son, he is incredulous that they could have treated him as they did when he was a small child. Why didn't they love and adore and protect him the way he now loves his own son?

Gordon is right. But he is drinking the rat poison and hoping his parents will die—or at least feel punished. It is Gordon who is unhappy and confused, angry and unforgiving. His parents now feel bad over what happened in the past, but realize they are helpless to change that. They watch Gordon suffer and struggle, but they are helpless to do anything about it.

The choice is Gordon's: He can continue to blame his parents for years to come, or he can have compassion for them, realize they did the best they could at the time, given who they were and what resources they had available to them, and let go of the hurt he is choosing to carry around.

Recall what we said above about blame: By blaming his parents, Gordon is (1) carrying around toxic, negative, angry thoughts and feelings, and (2) preventing himself from looking at his own role in the problems. Only Gordon can free himself from this toxic energy of blame and anger that he is still carrying around. His parents remain patient and are accepting of Gordon, just the way he is. They hope someday that he will experience compassion for them and forgive them, but apart from their ongoing acceptance of him, they can do nothing to help bring this about.

Moving from blame to compassion is not easy. When the pain is very deep, compassion doesn't happen overnight, and it won't happen just because you read about it. It takes work, and it takes time.

Doris and Fred

Doris had an affair, lasting about two months. She finally told her husband Fred about it, full of remorse and regret. She begged for forgiveness and assured Fred over and over that what she really wanted was him and their wonderful former relationship back. Fred told her that he wanted to forgive her, that he believed her remorse. But he was deeply hurt, and found that as much as he wanted to move toward her, he couldn't. His heart was closed. Doris had to be patient. She kept behaving in a loving way toward him, and she waited and waited. They talked. They both wanted to be in love again. Fred tried.

After almost a year, Doris thought up an unusual surprise for Fred. She arranged for a very favorite old high school buddy of his to make an unexpected visit. Fred was moved when he realized all Doris had to go through to arrange this, and something inside him shifted. His heart began opening again.

Both Fred and Doris had compassion for each other throughout their whole year of struggle, but the healing took time.

Compassion will ultimately lead to forgiveness. When you genuinely and wholeheartedly forgive someone, you will become a freer, happier person. Hanging onto hurt and failing to forgive keeps the rat poison inside you, not the person who hurt you. Forgiving is a difficult journey, but it will set you free. The reward is commensurate with the pain.

The journey to genuine forgiveness can begin with "acting as if" you forgive, which is essentially what Fred did. Intellectually he forgave Doris; he wanted to forgive her; he tried to behave as if he forgave her. But the deep wound took time to heal. Like the process of grief, forgiving someone goes through stages, especially if the hurt is profound.

While Fred was going through his healing, Doris had compassion for him. She understood that he needed time, and she was able to be patient and give it to him. The year was terribly painful for both of them. But their patience and compassion were rewarded.

Time alone is not sufficient to heal a wound and to bring about forgiveness. Both Doris and Fred wanted to be in love again. Their will was strong. So they didn't just wait. While they were letting time go by, they were both working to exhibit compassion for each other. They were envisioning their hearts being open to each other again. And, above all, they were paying attention.

Learning Compassion

You can begin to cultivate compassion by being alert for your own feelings of compassion toward others. For example, when you hear a tragic story in the news and your heart goes out to the people involved, pay attention to that. It is a good, healthy, spiritual feeling. Begin to practice feeling compassion for people in the news. Whether it is victims of a famine or the horrible atrocities of war, or a family who lost a child in a freak accident, let yourself feel the sadness along with the desire to help. You may feel you would do anything if you could take their pain away. That's compassion.

You don't have to act on all the compassion you feel. Unless you are Mother Teresa, you can't. But do act on your compassion when you can, when you are especially suited to help in some way, or if the situation falls right into your lap.

Melodie Chavis, author of the remarkable book *Altars in the Street,* lived in a violent, drug- and gang-infested neighborhood, and was committed to staying there to be a part of turning the neighborhood around against, as it turned out, staggering odds. One day, after several years of this, she read a story in the paper about a woman who had called the police to report drug activity right in front of her house. The very next day the woman's house was set on fire and burned to the ground. Melodie didn't hesitate a moment when she read this: She got in her car and drove right over to see this woman, to express her compassion and see what she could do to help.

Cultivate Compassion for Yourself

Developing compassion for yourself will help you feel it for others, and the opposite is also true. Sometimes you can feel it more easily for others than you can for yourself, but start paying attention to both. If you are filled with self-loathing, insecurities, low self-esteem; if you don't like yourself very much; then your first job is to "deeply understand what you are going through *and* be moved to help." It may be even easier to minister to someone else's pain when you are—or have been—in pain yourself.

Life is hard. Pain is inevitable. Envy, loss, low self-esteem, fear, betrayal, jealousy, heartbreak—it is all bound to arise within you at some time or another. The mistake is to run from the pain, to try to escape it, deny it, cover it up—because pain is a direct channel to your authentic self, your soul, and being in alignment with your soul is the source of joy. Accept the pain, and then do the work to heal it, and that starts with compassion.

If you can stay with your pain, even for a few minutes, you can learn from it and begin to heal it.

Rachel was a senior in college when she joined one of my support groups. She had been a star in high school. She earned all A's, had the lead in the class play, and was president of the French Club. But her high school was small and rural, and when she came to a big, tough university, she had to struggle the whole time. She was graduating somewhere in the middle of her class, and in spite of several earnest attempts, had never found a place to fit in during her whole four years. She tried to keep up a bright front, but we could sense despair lingering just beneath her pleasant demeanor.

We encouraged her to explore the despair. Little by little, over several weeks, she discussed it, until one week she began to sob, saying, "I feel so lost. I don't know who I am anymore. I feel I have nothing to offer in a relationship." When her strong emotions began to subside, she told us how good it felt to express this despair and to feel our compassion pour out to her.

Then we encouraged Rachel to *be* the friend she wished she had, and to talk to Rachel. We asked her to start by saying, "Rachel, I deeply understand what you are going through, and I am here to help."

Rachel was a paragon of compassion. She said something like this:

Poor thing. You have had such a rough time in school! You had so many rough breaks and near misses. It just feels like the universe is in a conspiracy against you, doesn't it? It's no wonder at all that you feel so alone, and that you don't feel good about yourself the way you used to in high school. You were a brave soul to come to this huge university and to stick it out here. I promise you, things are going to get better. You still are that same Rachel you were in high school, only now you are a lot wiser. You are going to be fine. Soon, you will get a lucky break. Putting yourself in this group was a wonderful thing for you to do. Just stay with yourself, keep believing in yourself. I'm here with you. I'm not going anywhere.

Rachel is a model for all of us.

It is hard to reach out with compassion to someone else if you have never experienced it for yourself.

Yet it is also true that experiencing genuine compassion for someone else will help you develop the capacity to feel it for yourself.

If you are feeling low, try the same experiment Rachel did. Be your best friend and write a letter to yourself.

The more compassion you experience for yourself, the more you can feel for others. You won't have to "imagine yourself in someone else's shoes," because you have actually been in those shoes yourself. Then you become a "wounded healer," by far the most effective kind.

The medical model of healing is that one person is the wounded or ill, and the other person is the all-knowing healer. In the "wounded healer" model of healing, both persons are wounded. The healer heals not by handing down superior knowledge, but by eliciting the "wounded" person's own internal healer. We are all in this boat together. We are all wounded and in pain. And it is that commonality that enables us all to heal each other. My role as "healer" is simply to remind you that you can heal yourself, and vice versa. The twelve-step programs are filled with healers who have deep compassion for others in the program because they learned how to have compassion for themselves. They know exactly what it feels like to be there. They are all wounded healers, filled with compassion for themselves and others who have experienced similar pain.

You can heal yourself with compassion. Compassion for yourself will enable you to experience it for others. And compassion for others will help you feel it for yourself. Both are critically important.

DEVELOPING COMPASSION FOR YOUR PARTNER

To convert resentment or blame into compassion you need to look beyond the immediate situation to the person behind it.

What is the source of your partner's behavior? What led up to this personality trait that you don't like? Maybe, given the circumstances, your partner is doing the best he or she can be expected to do. If, for example, your mate grew up in a family where everyone was cool and undemonstrative, where no one ever hugged or said, "I love you," that may be a big part of the reason your partner is not romantic with you.

Here are four experiments that will help you develop compassion toward your partner. If you can set aside some time to think through or, even better, write through these exercises, they will help you build your capacity for compassion in your day-to-day routines with your partner.

Compassion-Building Exercises

A. Look Behind the Person

Look at your partner's background and ask yourself how it might have contributed to who he or she is today.

In our workshops, we use the following questions as a guide. I suggest you take some time to either (a) write out your answers, (b) discuss these questions with a friend, or (c) use these as a guide for discussion in your support group, if you are in one. If you and your mate are building your spiritual lives and Spiritual Partnership together, by all means sit down and interview each other. Such a conversation might be very enjoyable for you, possibly moving, and certainly educational. But in phrasing the questions, I will assume you are doing the exercise by yourself.

FAMILY BACKGROUND

1. What was it like for your partner to grow up in his or her family?
2. How is your partner like his or her mother in attitudes, behavior, and beliefs?
3. How is your partner like his or her father in attitudes, behavior, and beliefs?
4. Is your partner heavily influenced by any siblings or by his or her relationship with any siblings?
5. How does your partner feel now about his or her family?

PREVIOUS EXPERIENCES

1. What do you know about your mate's previous experiences that might have had an impact on the situation or behavior that troubles you now?

2. How might these previous experiences be influencing him or her?

GENERAL PERSONALITY TYPE

1. What are the two or three most dominant qualities in your partner's personality?

2. Complete this sentence with as many different adjectives as seem appropriate: My partner has a strong tendency to be _____. (For example, your partner might tend to be perfectionistic, helpful, achievement-oriented, melancholy, overinvolved, optimistic, quick to anger, good-natured, well organized, left brain, right brain, etc.)

3. What is your partner's astrological sign? How does he or she match or fail to match the characteristics that are traditionally assigned to that sign?

4. In general, men have a tendency to invalidate or ignore feelings and move directly to solutions; to cope with stress by becoming silent and withdrawn; and to show their love by being good at what they do or by doing big, impressive favors. Women have a tendency to value and express feelings; to cope with stress by asking for support and talking things through; and to show their love with small favors and affectionate gestures. In what ways does your mate correspond or fail to correspond to these generalities?

What did you discover by asking these questions? Maybe your mate isn't being malicious, thoughtless, ungrateful, or deliberately neglectful of you. Maybe you are just seeing your partner being the very best at who he or she really is.

B. Look for Significant Stories

Think back over the stories you have heard about your mate's childhood. Is there a story that exactly characterizes him or her?

For example, one workshop participant, Matt, was upset with his wife Nicole because he felt she took gift-giving to a ridiculous extreme. She was always bringing little gifts to her friends, for even the slightest excuse. She gave lavish presents to her nieces and nephews on their birthdays, and Christmas shopping always started about February for her. When we came to this exercise, Matt told us this story that had been repeated many times about his wife:

> On my mother-in-law's sideboard sits a little porcelain sculpture of a small family around a table. The story is that when my wife was about nine, she had a job helping neighbors rake up their leaves in the fall. When her parents' anniversary arrived, she took all the money she had saved up for a couple of years, went to her favorite store all by herself, spent a long time picking out the perfect little sculpture (according to the store owner, who was a friend), and proudly presented it to her parents.

As Matt told us the story, several of us even felt a tear on our cheek, imagining this sweet nine-year-old selecting her gift and happily, proudly spending all her money on it. We helped Matt to realize that giving and generosity are part of Nicole's true essence, part of what makes her feel happy and fulfilled.

Many of the stories we hear are not so touching; they are painful. Stories of children being neglected, or beaten, or even abused. Stories of parents being too busy, missing important events, or forgetting to pick up a child at the right time.

Whatever story you pick that helps you understand your loved one, remember, that little child still lives inside your grown-up mate. When you see that behavior coming out, relate directly to the little child. Does it help put you in touch with your compassion?

C. The "Mantra"

Part of compassion is holding your partner up to his or her own standard, not some arbitrary standard or fantasy that you have in your head.

Memorize this "mantra": "She is doing the best she can," or "He is doing the best he can." And when you are having trouble feeling compassion for your partner, say it over and over to yourself.

People bring different resources to a marriage. For example, with regard to thoughtfulness, when you are giving 100 percent, you may be wrapping up clever gifts, leaving notes in funny places, doing the dishes for your partner, and bringing home a book or new jacket for your mate, just as a surprise. But when your partner is thoughtful 100 percent, maybe all that means is opening the garage door for you, as usual. Maybe thoughtfulness was not part of your partner's family growing up, and his or her experience with it is limited.

One woman told me she was so disappointed every year on Valentine's Day because her husband always brought home exactly the same box of candy, just a plain white box of the same old chocolates. Then, one year, he showed up with a gorgeous heart-shaped box of chocolates *and* flowers. She was thrilled, because she knew that was a big leap for him.

When you feel anger toward your partner and are unable to be in touch with any compassion, you will probably think this is because your partner's behavior is so unreasonable. *But in fact you are coming up against your own limitations, not your partner's.* Your spiritual challenge is to make a shift. Work hard, even for a moment, to put yourself in your partner's shoes and think about compassion. Say to yourself, "He's doing the best he can," or "She's doing the best she can." Whatever the wounds are that cause your mate to behave in certain ways, your compassionate attitude may begin to heal them. As we've said over and over, in order to heal, we all need compassion and love, not criticism and blame.

D. Cultivate Your Partner's Dreams

Make a deliberate effort to find out what your partner's dreams are. Then put yourself in his or her shoes and see if you feel moved to support these dreams. When you catch yourself focusing on what you consider your mate's deficits or drawbacks, consciously think instead about the person he or she is striving to become. When you look at your mate, don't be thinking, What can you do for me? but rather, How can I support you? What is the deep desire in you that I might nurture? What is the hurt in you that I might help to heal?

It's easy to love people when they are happy and doing well and are generous and loving back. But they most need your love when they aren't doing well, when they feel low and can't believe in themselves, when they are having setbacks in their lives.

Finally, remember that, like all spiritual ideals, the real benefit of compassion is to make you into a happier, more peaceful and fulfilled person. It sounds as if compassion is about helping the other person. But the more compassion you can find in your heart, the more loving kindness you can offer to those around you, the more joy you will experience for yourself.

Putting Compassion to Work
in Your Relationship

Let us return now to the example above in which your husband
is having a fit at the amount of money you spent on clothes. As
we see how a Spiritual Partner might play this out, we will also
review some of the other spiritual principles we have learned
so far.

You start proudly and excitedly showing your husband the
clothes you have just bought for a special occasion. He becomes
upset and anxious and tries to convince you to take the clothes
back. Of course the knee-jerk, unconscious response would be
to hurl back a defensive retort. "This was not a lot of money. You
have no idea what clothes cost. And *you* just spent all that
money on running shoes! That was okay. Stop and look at how
these look on me! You're so anxious about money, it's going to
shrivel you up with worry. Life is too short." Whatever.

But as a Spiritual Partner, instead of this return tirade, the
first thing you would do is employ several skills we have already
learned. You would "use restraint" by saying, perhaps, "I feel
defensive." That would give you time to breathe and think. Next,
you could be both empathic and decisive. You might say something like, "I know you feel that this is a lot to spend on clothes.
It is a lot of money. I don't disagree with that. And I'm so sorry
it upsets you when I spend money on clothes. Believe me, that is
not my intention." That's the empathic part, and it may be
enough for the time being. Let your partner talk, and continue to
be understanding.

Now, where does the compassion come in? Compassion
means you are truly unhappy that your partner feels so upset,
and you are moved to do whatever you can to help. Now you are
in a difficult place. Here is where you must draw on your own

commitment to *balance* taking care of yourself and taking care of your partner, Principle #4. To give yourself some time, you might say, "Honey, let me look this over. I did spend a lot today. Maybe there is something I can take back. Give me a little while to think about this."

Good! You have stopped trying to get anywhere through more communication. You have refrained from blaming your husband and making him wrong, and have asked yourself, "What can I do?" With your spirit of goodwill, by agreeing to review your purchases, you have created harmony in place of upset. You have not asked your partner to change. And you have taken both the burden and the power of maintaining the balance of giving and taking upon yourself.

No formula can tell you what to decide now. Only you know whether there is in fact something you could take back that would please your husband and not make you feel resentful. Or whether you believe the amount you spent is truly reasonable, and that you need to convey your opinion to him, decisively, but without making him wrong, as we learned to do back in Chapter Seven. Your job is not to persuade him to agree with you. Your job is to be understanding and affirming of his feelings and opinions, and at the same time clear that, this time, you are going to go ahead with what you believe is right for you.

The above example is very close to home. When I went shopping with an image consultant for my very first book tour, this was our scene. I was *not* a model of compassion and goodwill. In fact I became defensive, and Mayer and I had quite a fight. We both felt unsupported and betrayed. When we stopped fighting, no one felt good, and we just went off in our separate corners.

After a couple of hours I looked back over all the clothes and decided there was one very expensive suit I could return, and that I would actually feel better about that too. It was a lot of money. But before I could go downstairs to tell Mayer this, he came up and said, "Sweetheart, go ahead and keep everything. I want you to feel absolutely wonderful on this book tour. We can spend the money. It's not that big a deal."

We were both exhibiting a spirit of goodwill arising out of compassion. We were both very sad that the other person was upset, and we were motivated to do something about it.

If you think it is difficult, even unrealistic, to be feeling compassion for your partner when *you* are the one who is feeling wronged, deprived, or unsupported, think about the Dalai Lama. The Chinese invaded his spectacularly beautiful, deeply spiritual country that had not been at war for many centuries. They have tortured and brutalized peace-loving monks, destroyed monasteries, murdered thousands of innocent people, and driven the Dalai Lama himself from his beloved homeland. Yet listen to this story he relates in *The Art of Happiness:*

> . . . [A] senior chant master who is staying at Namgyal Monas-
> tery . . . was in Chinese prisons as a political prisoner and in
> labor camps for twenty years. Once I asked him what was the
> most difficult situation he faced when he was in prison. Sur-
> prisingly, he said that he felt the greatest danger was of losing
> compassion for the Chinese!

Truly, there are degrees of spiritual awakening! Most of us cannot even imagine being as enlightened as this monk. But perhaps you can imagine moving in that direction. That's all the spiritual journey is about.

Think of a model of compassion that works for you. While Jesus was in the act of being wrongfully murdered, he was able to say, "Forgive them, Father, for they know not what they do."

Their evil, Jesus knew, was a result only of their ignorance, their low level of consciousness. He felt compassion for them.

And I love what Vietnamese Buddhist monk Thich Nhat Hanh said about Buddha:

> When I was a novice, I could not understand why, if the world is filled with suffering, the Buddha has such a beautiful smile. Why isn't he disturbed by all the suffering? Later I discovered that the Buddha has enough understanding, calm, and strength; that is why the suffering does not overwhelm him. He is able to smile to suffering because he knows how to take care of it and to help transform it.

A World without Compassion

We live in a culture that laughs at the idea of compassion. While most spiritual teachers call it a fundamental component of spiritual life, we have virtually no familiarity with compassion in our public or private lives.

The model that permeates our lives is retribution. Someone is to blame, and someone must pay. Our prison system is the most blatant example of a complete and utter lack of compassion. Within the last several years even the term "correctional institution," which hinted at some attention to rehabilitation, has been officially dropped. Now, our prison system doesn't even pretend the least interest in helping or supporting inmates. They did something wrong; they pay the price. It's only fair. Each individual alone is to blame (as if he or she didn't emerge out of a dysfunctional subculture or family, created by overwhelming social and economic realities), and when you screw up, these are the consequences: an even worse, appallingly dysfunctional society (prison), fully supported by our tax dollars. "In God We Trust"? Not here. In our ability to be as cruel and vindictive as possible we trust.

The demand for retribution arises out of righteousness and hatred. "I'm right and you are wrong. I'm the good person, you are the bad person." And, implied, "I would never do anything that horrible. You must be punished." And in some cases even, "I'm so good, and you are so bad, I get to say that you must die!"

This sounds extreme, yet I have heard politicians say almost these very words, with a completely self-righteous tone in their voices. This is the model our country sets for us. It is most unspiritual.

This general attitude easily filters down to our personal lives. A therapist told me that during the third session with a couple she was seeing, the wife became very angry and shouted, "Why don't you tell him he's wrong!" The very idea that her husband might be doing the best he could, or that she herself might have some role in the problems they were having, or that she might even be able to exhibit some degree of compassion, was foreign to her. To fix the problem, punish the person who is wrong!

Is it any wonder Mother Teresa once commented that the United States was the most loveless country she ever visited? And of course, with the rapid advance of the global economy, we are now exporting our values all over the world. As spiritual people, we have a huge job to do, and we need to work fast.

But, you may ask, doesn't it make sense to be angry and self-righteous in the presence of obvious malice and ill will? How will we bring about change if we don't get up a good head of steam when we see destructive behavior? What about genocide? What about the destruction of the planet for short-term profit?

Anger is a natural human emotion (when it has not been softened through spiritual practice). But judgment and blame are the antithesis of compassion and are not "spiritual," that is, they do not "bring you into closer alignment with your highest self."

When someone does something mean-spirited or cruel, that person is experiencing a lack within him or herself. A nonspiritual person will see only the cruel or thoughtless act. But a compassionate person will feel the underlying pain of the mean-spirited person and want to reach out and help.

As we observed in Chapter Two, evil, thoughtlessness, and cruelty are simply ignorance. Evil people would not be evil if they were spiritually aware, if they were guided by their soul's longing for inner peace, if they were moved by love. They are evil because their spiritual consciousness has not been raised. They are not motivated by deep inner convictions, but are able only to respond to the world around them on a moment by moment basis. They live out of habit, with a limited view of the world. This is ignorance, deprivation. It is to be pitied, not judged.

If you respond to someone who is cruel with more hate, you will be compounding the darkness, moving both of you further from the light, further from consciousness. When you hate and feel self-righteous about evil, you do not diminish the evil; you increase it! Now, there are two people moving away from light and toward darkness!

Blaming and hating do nothing to reduce the problem at hand. All they do is diminish the one who is doing the hating and blaming. The spiritual response to anything negative is compassion.

Compassion does not preclude constructive action to limit the damage of the selfish, greedy, or mean-spirited aggressors. Gandhi was compassionate toward his British oppressors. But out of his compassion, he "acted on his own" to gain independence for his people. Compassion increases consciousness, love, and connection, in both the one who experiences the compassion and the object of the compassion. Anger, judgment, and blame decrease these spiritual qualities for everyone involved.

I had a personal experience recently that taught me this lesson. It was a mild incident to be sure, but it showed me the dramatic difference, within myself, between judgment and compassion.

I called a single friend of mine, very excited because I wanted to introduce her to a man I thought she would genuinely like. I had an intuition there might be a real match there. I left an animated message on her voice mail. The next day, I received a response on my voice mail that was unexpectedly negative. "I don't know," my friend said. "You and I have very different tastes in men. From your description, I'm pretty sure it wouldn't work. I mean, I'd meet him if you insisted, but I have my doubts."

I was stunned by this response, and as the moments passed I realized I was angry. I felt I had presented her with a beautiful package, all wrapped up with a big bow, and she had thrown it in the trash—without even opening it. I had the good sense not to call her back for a few days, since all that was running through my head were sarcastic and nasty retorts.

I thought she was being unappreciative and rude. But I was increasing the "darkness" by blaming and being angry with her. I was right, and she was wrong. I felt insulted, belittled. That was all I could see.

I mentioned the incident to another friend, who promptly said to me, "She must just be scared about meeting anybody who might really work for her." In an instant my anger softened. Suddenly, I felt sad for my friend. *My focus shifted from me to her.* Whatever was keeping her from meeting this lovely man was narrowing her life, limiting her options. Maybe it was fear, maybe it was her need to be in control. Or maybe her intuition

was more on target than mine! She has a right to be who she is,
I realized. I don't know what is going on inside her. I want to support her, not force my agenda on her.

When I shifted from focusing on how this incident affected
me to looking at what might be motivating her, I felt compassion,
and let go of my own hurt.

The Christian mystic Thomas Merton says:

> . . . true love and prayer are learned in the moment when prayer
> has become impossible and the heart has turned to stone.

When you are angry and full of blame, when your heart has
turned to stone, when compassion is difficult even to imagine,
then feeling compassion will be a challenge and will truly lead
to spiritual growth.

We do not live in a world overflowing with compassion; quite
the opposite. All the more reason that those of us who are on a
spiritual path, who are striving to become more in alignment
with our highest potential, need to cultivate compassion. Begin
with your partner.

The power of compassion is unlimited. All of the great models of spiritual leadership in history have had true compassion
for their enemies, people like Jesus, Gandhi, and Martin Luther
King.

And compassion starts with each of us, within ourselves and
toward all those around us. The more we each exhibit compassion at home and at work, the more it will spread, until, con-
ceivably, compassion could begin to have an impact on corporate
greed, world poverty and hunger, the destruction of our planet,
and even war. I will let Thich Nhat Hanh have the last word. As
you read this, think not only about our planet, but about your
own relationship:

One compassionate word, action, or thought can reduce another person's suffering and bring him joy. One word can give comfort and confidence, destroy doubt, help someone avoid a mistake, reconcile a conflict, or open the door to liberation. One action can save a person's life or help him take advantage of a rare opportunity. One thought can do the same, because thoughts always lead to words and actions. With compassion in our heart, every thought, word, and deed can bring about a miracle.

✍ EXPERIMENT # 17:
COMPASSION

1. In your journal, write answers to these questions:
   In what ways am I *not* being compassionate toward my partner?
   How would I behave if I were feeling compassion?
2. Gradually work on the questions in the "Developing Compassion for Your Partner" section in this chapter. As you have time, write out the answers in your journal, or discuss them with a friend.
3. In what ways are you "increasing the darkness" rather than "moving toward the light"? That is, what are you feeling angry or self-righteous, or even hateful, about? What would it be like for you to convert these feelings of anger into compassion, as I did with my friend, when I began focusing on her instead of on myself?

Part III

Deepening
Spiritual
Partnership

TEN

When to Break
the Rules for
Infinite Potential

Only when you have religiously followed the Five Principles of Spiritual Partnership and experimented with Sacred Actions for a period of eight weeks or so should you even consider breaking any of "the rules." You need to learn them thoroughly first by deliberately exaggerating them so they become a habit for you. You will always need to follow the principles, and to use the Sacred Actions most of the time. But once you have seen how they open up boundless possibilities in your relationship, you will develop a sense about when you should follow them, and when it is time to move beyond them to expand your love even more.

Before we look at the exceptions, let's review the five principles:

1. Use loving actions instead of communication. Keep your mouth out of it.
2. Never try to solve a problem by asking your partner to change.
3. Don't think about who is right. Instead, ask yourself,

"What can I do to make a difference here?" Think
"goodwill."

4. Strive to keep in balance the times you stand up for
   your partner's needs and the times you stand up for
   your own.

5. Don't discuss problems; don't try to solve problems.
   Instead, create a positive, harmonious atmosphere,
   right now.

Principles three, four, and five have no exceptions: It is never
helpful to insist that you are right and someone else is wrong; a
spirit of goodwill is always important. (Well, okay. You are
allowed an occasional lapse when you need to blow off steam
and indulge your "inner child" in a fit of immature ravings. No
harm done, if you come back later and behave as an adult. But
even that is happening in the atmosphere of goodwill that you
have established day after day.) Balancing the amount you give
and the amount you take in your relationship is always ongoing.
And finally, I have never seen a marital problem that did not
respond better to one or more of the Five Sacred Acts than to any
deliberate attempt to sit down and solve it by "discussing" it.
(You will definitely find yourselves discussing or arguing about
conflicts you have or decisions you have to make. But you will
virtually always find that the actual solution will be one or more
of the Five Sacred Acts, as we have seen repeatedly throughout
this book.)

The two big exceptions to the principles are these:

1. There is a role for communication in Spiritual Partnership.

2. You may ask your partner to change.

There Is a Role for Communication in Spiritual Partnership

As we have established throughout this book, communication is not the best tool for achieving a healthy relationship. To establish health, use Sacred Actions. If your relationship has been troubled, Sacred Acts will bring you to the center of the hourglass, to the "pinnacle of functionality." Using Sacred Acts, you will learn to enjoy each other. Most of your demons will be quieted, out of the way, stored in the garage where they can only occasionally make themselves heard. (Of course, Sacred Actions will also carry you far beyond a "healthy" relationship, and you will never discontinue them once you have discovered their magic. Also, establishing a functional relationship and moving beyond that to an intimate one do not occur in a tidy order as I am presenting them here. I make them sound chronological for the sake of discussion, but in fact they might both be going on all the time.)

It is after you have established a base of closeness and love by using Sacred Actions to manage your conflicts and incompatibilities that communication plays its appropriate role: deepening the connection between you. Communicate, not to move to a functional relationship, but to move from a functional relationship to soul connection and true intimacy.

To understand the proper role of communication in love, we must first review the meaning of "intimacy," a much misunderstood term. As we saw, intimacy is not romantic walks on the beach, sexy evenings in front of a warm fireplace, or elegant dinners. Intimacy is not sex. These activities might take place between two people who are intimate, but they are not themselves "intimate." In fact, when they take place between two people who are not genuinely intimate, they are what I call "pseudointimacy," or intimate-type behavior.

Intimacy is, quite simply, stripping away your outer, more public ways of being and sharing your inner life with another person. It is radically honest self-disclosure, trusting another person enough to share your deepest fears and your greatest vulnerabilities. Intimacy is all about discovering and telling your truth.

There are two steps involved in telling the truth. First, you have to discover what your truth is; and second, you have to trust another person enough to share it. Communication—that is, talking to another person—is a part of both of these steps.

DISCOVERING YOUR TRUTH

Jessica could feel herself becoming anxious. After eating well for months she suddenly found herself snacking on junk foods. She wasn't sleeping well. When a friend asked her how she was, she discovered that she felt uncomfortable saying, "Things are great," but she didn't know why. Everything she looked at in her life seemed to be going well. Her friend wisely took her out for a glass of wine one evening and asked her a few questions, like, "Tell me, how is your new job going?"

"Oh, I just love it," Jessica started out. "I feel so lucky. The people I work with are really good."

It took Jessica thirty or forty minutes of telling stories about work and describing the people there for her to discover, to her own surprise, that she was actually feeling undermined and unsupported at work, and that she was insecure about one aspect of her job. She realized she was quite angry—with herself mostly—for not standing up to two people who, she now saw, were sabotaging her own work.

Communication helped Jessica *discover* what her own truth was. Step one.

Jessica was grateful to her friend for picking up on her anxiety and offering to help her explore it. It frightened her to realize that without the opportunity to think out loud about what was going on at work, she might have gone for months without understanding the source of her anxiety, and without recognizing that she needed to stop being so "nice" at work and to become more assertive.

It is a sad fact of life in these times that, for many people, there are few opportunities to discover what is truly going on inside them. Such opportunities usually don't arise spontaneously; we have to create them, and we usually don't take the time to do it.

What is required is leisurely, open-ended time in which you deliberately talk with another person about your life, your feelings, your aspirations, your disappointments, your worries. The other person can be a friend or relative, an intimate group, a paid professional such as a therapist or counselor, or your intimate partner. Women's groups and men's groups often provide an excellent opportunity for self-discovery. You have to meet long enough to establish trust with one another. Then, typically, each person is allotted at least a half hour to talk about one worrisome issue. Alert group members can listen for clues about what might need to be explored in more depth. For example, at a recent meeting of my own women's group, one member, whom I'll call Brenda, said, "I think I'm feeling okay about my father's death. I seem not to have any more unfinished business about that." One woman, listening below the surface of these words, said,

"Tell us a little more about that." Brenda spent the next forty minutes talking about her father, including one awful regret she found terribly hard to tell us about. Her tears came from a very deep place.

Both Jessica and Brenda used communication to discover what was true for them. All of us need to do this. Truths that are difficult to talk about *want* to stay hidden. But when they stay undercover, they will certainly betray you. The parts of yourself that you don't know about have disproportionate power over you. They take control. Talking about your feelings is one of the few ways to discover more about them. Another way is to communicate with yourself by writing. Usually, you have to find some proactive way to dig around inside yourself in order to discover what is true for you right now.

Many people go through their whole lives without doing this work. People who have done little to discover their buried truths are often quite transparent to other people. Think about the boss who subtly belittles his employees all the time as a way to make himself feel better. To those around him, his insecurities are obvious, but he may never discover them himself. He may never create an opportunity for himself to examine his own behavior, to sort through his feelings, to say out loud to someone else the thing that makes him feel most vulnerable, most afraid. There is obviously a great deal about himself that he doesn't know, and unless he deliberately begins to explore his feelings, he will never find these things out.

Couples sometimes avoid talking about painful truths for years. They realize that they are feeling more distant and may crave a return to their former feelings of closeness and love. But because our culture is devoid of rituals to help couples talk with each other, because most people are not part of a community of friends or extended family who might offer support, couples can take many years to uncover painful topics or may never talk about them at all. What a tragic waste!

Mitch and Opal loved being together and had much in common. After the birth of their second child, Opal's interest in sex fell off dramatically. As their formerly pleasurable sex life became almost nonexistent, they were both afraid to talk about it. Each became resentful of the other. They longed for their old closeness, but the less they talked about the forbidden topic, the more frightening it became. They were both afraid that if they brought it up, they would destroy their relationship altogether.

After ten years of virtually no sex, Opal read an article in a magazine about women like herself. She felt the article must be talking about her, it was so accurate. Although she was afraid to do it, she found the courage to show the article to Mitch. They stayed up an entire night and into the next day (they both called in sick—well, they surely were healing), talking, talking, talking, crying, holding each other, talking some more, and finally making love. The problem didn't reverse itself dramatically, but the difference was that now it was a problem they would work to solve together, lovingly and patiently; they no longer blamed Opal for it. They sought professional help, and, largely because they restored their spiritual connection, they once again became sexually desirable to each other.

"If only we had had that conversation ten years ago," Opal told me. "I guess we didn't know enough. We weren't ready. But I am so grateful that we didn't wait another ten years."

In my women's group we have a saying: "If there is a charge on it, talk about it." We mean, if you feel any kind of energy surrounding a certain topic, and especially if you feel resistance to talking about it, *talk about it.* The harder it is to bring it up or to get going on it, the more important it is to discuss. We have an understanding that it is perfectly okay, in fact encouraged, to start your time for working by saying, "I don't know what I want to talk about today," or "I think I want to talk about my relationship, but I have nothing in particular to say." Often, these are the most productive sessions. While the person talking explores complicated feelings, we listen. We support her fully. We witness her giving birth to some new understanding about herself.

Note that "resistance" to talking about something often comes in the form of excuses like, "This isn't very important," or "I keep thinking I should talk about this, but I don't have anything to say about it." Consider using those statements to start a conversation with your partner or with a friend. You may have to preface your statement by saying something like, "Would you mind just listening for a while so I can try to figure out what is going on with me?"

I believe "If there is a charge on it, talk about it" is one of the most important guidelines in life. Sometimes it takes a while to realize that there is a "charge" (emotional energy) on a certain topic. But whenever you realize that there is something important you are not talking about, find someone, somewhere, with whom you can discuss it in an open-ended fashion. This is one of the most direct routes to your authentic self, to consciousness, and to connection—to your spiritual growth.

Having a "discovery" conversation with your intimate partner can be a beautiful experience and can build closeness between you. But, as we've seen, these conversations often take place in other contexts, with other people. What is essential for intimacy, however, is that you share with your intimate partner what you have discovered, even if you discovered it elsewhere. This is step two. When you share your truth with someone who receives it lovingly and without judgment, this is intimacy.

STRUCTURES FOR COMMUNICATION

One of the best structures for intimacy-building communication is no structure at all. But for most of us with our busy lives, we need to structure unstructured time!

I believe we all need "no agenda" time with a person or people we trust. When you are driving somewhere together, lingering over Sunday breakfast with nothing special to do later (but talking, not reading the paper), soaking in a hot tub before bed, taking a walk—these are times when topics that you had no intention of discussing but that need to be discussed have a way of surfacing.

Mayer and I feel grateful to our dogs for compelling us to take walks every evening. No matter how late it is, no matter how tired we are, we *have* to walk the dogs. We always enjoy it. Many evenings, we know we would never have spontaneously decided to go outside and take a walk. But every evening, there we are, enjoying the evening air, the quiet of our neighborhood, the bright sky; watching the progress of the moon and the planets; and talking. Often, we drive a mile to a spectacular park where we can see the Golden Gate Bridge and San Francisco glowing like a jewel box across the bay, the setting sun behind the gentle mountains of Marin County, and the twinkling lights of the East Bay hills. We can hear the bay waters gently lapping against the shoreline and take in vast amounts of the starry sky. We brainstorm together about each other's businesses. We talk about what is going on in our families. We speculate and dream about the future. We share feelings about movies or current events. I often think after something gets said that it probably never would have been spoken if we hadn't been engaging in idle conversation. Most of these things aren't life-changing. But there have been times when we generated ideas or shared feelings that did turn out to be important.

Soaking in a hot tub, lingering after dinner with friends, weekend outings, lazy Sunday afternoons, long drives in the country—you know how best to build these unstructured times in your own family to allow for spontaneous conversation, as well as relaxed times of sharing each other's company with no conversation at all. This kind of "communication" is critically important in Spiritual Partnership.

In addition to structuring unstructured times for conversation, superimposing structure on your conversation from time to time is also invaluable. Some feelings are so deeply buried, so frightening, and leave you so vulnerable that they will never rise to the surface during casual conversation. You must make an effort to elicit them deliberately.

Love Letters and Feelings Dialogues

The Marriage Encounter movement pioneered the idea of using a love letter and "dialogue" to help couples discover and reveal the depth of their connection. It is a powerful formula. Simply put, you are invited to write a love letter to your partner about your feelings, read it to your partner, and then "dialogue" about it. *A dialogue is a conversation in which the only goal is to express feelings and to understand each other's feelings fully. In a dialogue, there is to be no decision making and no problem solving of any kind.*

Usually, you will decide to dialogue about a particular topic. Even if you think at the outset that you have nothing to say about a certain subject, give yourself the opportunity to write about it anyway. The point of these love letters is precisely to help you dig below the surface to discover parts of yourself that you don't know about yet. The doorway to self-exploration is your feelings. Discovering and sharing deeply buried or even new feelings with your partner will build your closeness. Discovering and sharing feelings is really *all* that intimacy is about. If you never give yourselves a structured opportunity to explore feelings with each other, you are missing one of the most awesome opportunities that your relationship can provide for you. Love letters are a direct, easy way to mobilize your relationship in the service of your mutual spiritual growth, and to experience, express, and expand the intimacy you long to develop and sustain.

Feelings dialogues, whether you structure them the way I suggest below or find some other way to talk about your feelings with each other, can take you to the farthest reaches of Spiritual Partnership. If you never take advantage of this potential in your relationship, you will be stopping short of your potential for closeness and spiritual growth.

It is human nature to resist talking about difficult feelings. Excuses are no doubt running through your own brain right now:

- Some couples may need that, but we don't.
- I don't think we have any feelings we haven't talked about.
- Sounds like a nice idea, but we'll never really do it.
- I'm too ashamed of _____ ever to be able to talk about it.
- It feels way too scary to bring _____ up with my partner.

You may think that exposing your worst fears will make you seem weak in your partner's eyes, that your partner won't love you if he or she knows your awful secret. The opposite is actually the case: In an intimate relationship, digging for and revealing your true feelings is an indication that you are far along on your spiritual path, that you care about healing, that you trust your partner to treat your pain with gentle, loving care. Exploring and sharing your feelings is a sign of strength, not weakness. What is weak and cowardly is giving in to your excuses, being afraid to explore your feelings, keeping your secrets buried deep within you, and relying on your personality to get you through.

I promise you, no matter how busy you are, you can find time to write love letters and to dialogue. Once you get the idea of it, you can do the whole exercise in twenty minutes, ten for writing and ten for dialoguing. After conveying your feelings to each other with a clear understanding that *this* conversation is not about decision making or problem solving, you will find yourself having dialogues without even writing a letter. But the discipline of taking special time out to write and dialogue about a topic that might not otherwise have come up gives you a rich opportunity for spiritual growth and closeness that you will miss if you don't do it. If lovemaking is an expression of your physical intimacy, verbally exploring the depths of your feelings is an expression of your spiritual intimacy. And dialoguing can be every bit as pleasurable as lovemaking. You may be a witness to your loved one's deeply personal insight or emotional letting go that has been a lifetime in coming.

If you dialogue frequently, several times a week, you can do it in twenty minutes, ten for writing and ten for dialoguing. If you do it once a week, once a month, or several times a year, you may want to take more time.

Here are the simple, powerful guidelines for writing love letters and dialoguing about them:

1. Set aside a block of time. Make arrangements so your children won't interrupt you, and agree not to answer

your phone. For a real treat, go away for an entire
weekend and plan several dialoguing sessions.

2. Each of you go off by yourself and write a letter to the
   other. If you do this exercise fairly often, the letter
   can be short. If you make this a more special occasion
   and do it only once or twice a year, your letter may be
   longer. Or you may choose to write several shorter
   letters over the course of a day or weekend.
       Tell your partner *something you feel* that you think
   he or she may not fully understand. It may be a
   positive or negative feeling. Work hard to convey this
   feeling the best way you can. Try using metaphors
   ("I felt like a ripe peach about to burst"), or refer to a
   similar experience ("Remember the time at the beach
   when you were so annoyed at the people next to us?
   Well, that's how I felt when . . . ")
       If you have mixed feelings, write that. If you aren't
   sure what you feel, describe that.
       Be careful not to start writing a lot of thoughts,
   instead of feelings. If you can substitute the words
   "I am" for "I feel," then you are probably writing
   about feelings. For example, "I feel lonely when you
   come home so late" could be "I *am* lonely . . . " which
   is a feeling. On the other hand, for "I feel that it isn't
   fair when you come home late," you could substitute
   "I *think* it isn't fair . . ." and you are actually writing a
   thought, not a feeling.

3. When both of you have completed your writing, come
   together. Touch. You may hold hands, or maybe you
   will be cuddled up on the couch beside each other.

Be in physical contact, and look at each other while
you are having your conversation.

4. Read your letter out loud to your partner.

5. Your partner may respond by repeating back to you,
in his or her own words, what you have said in the
letter. This is the critical part of the exercise. Even
though your partner may feel that what you have said
is obvious, and that repeating it is contrived and silly,
do it. What makes this exercise special is that you get
to hear your partner say out loud to you something
you have been longing to hear.

   If your partner doesn't quite get the feeling you
have tried to express, talk more. Your partner may ask
for more examples. Also, your partner may have
feelings about what you have said. If that is true, then
he or she should absolutely write you a love letter
about those feelings, and share them with you. But for
this dialogue, the discussion is about your feelings.
Keep it simple. Do just one thing at a time. And
remember, do not even slightly get into the area of
problem solving or decision making. You might say,
"I just got an idea for a solution to this," and write
it down for later. But let this dialogue be about
feelings only.

6. When you both feel that this communication is
complete, savor the moment. Don't hurry. Take
pleasure in the close experience you have just shared.

7. Then switch roles. Let your partner read to you. You
listen carefully and repeat back what you have heard

until your partner is satisfied that you truly
understand the feeling in the letter.

Topics

You may already know what you want to dialogue about: a feeling you have about something that occurred this week, or your
feelings about some long-term, ongoing issue between the two of
you. It is also a good idea to have a special place to write down
dialogue ideas that come to you spontaneously. One time, the two
of you may want to brainstorm together a list of topics for future
dialogues.

It is also important to dialogue about random topics about
which neither of you has a "charge," so that you can use this
process to discover feelings that may be deeply hidden, and to
express feelings that you have all the time but that never get ver-
balized. For example, "I feel so lucky that you are such a good
cook, and every single evening I am filled with appreciation that
you do such a wonderful job of handling this part of our life
together."

At one time or another try dialoguing about *your feelings*
regarding each of these topics, in any order:

- Money
- Health
- Time
- Work
- Rest
- Sex
- Children
- Relatives
- Spirituality

- Atmosphere in the home
- My strengths and
  weaknesses
- Your strengths and
  weaknesses
- My purpose in life
- The purpose of our
  relationship
- What I feel insecure about

- My biggest fear
- What I love about our relationship
- What I don't like about our relationship
- Our ability to accept each other
- Our compassion for each other
- Our balance of giving and taking

- An area where I feel I need your help and support
- What I appreciate you for
- What I like about you
- What I don't like about you
- What I am withholding from you

Psychologist John Gray suggests a special love letter outline for times when you are feeling upset about something in particular. Because "upset" often consists of a stew of emotions, he suggests that you intentionally explore all of them in your letter. Some of your emotions may be defenses, part of your mask, or your knee-jerk reaction. Writing about all your emotions may help you discover the truer, deeper emotions under the superficial ones. For example, anger is often a mask for hurt or fear. So Gray suggests that when you are upset about something particular, you write about all of these feelings, in this order: anger, sadness, fear, regret, and love. Write about all of them in one letter, and then dialogue about all of those feelings with your partner.

Now we have a complete picture of the role of communication in Spiritual Partnership. When you are trying to live out your spiritual values in your relationship—trying to become more connected to the natural rhythms of the universe and the messages

ℬ EXPERIMENT #18:
DIALOGUE

1. Sit down with yourself and list topics about which you have feelings. Where in your life is your emotional energy right now? What feels unresolved to you? What areas are you avoiding?

2. Invite your partner to consider writing a love letter and having a dialogue with you in accord with the guidelines in this chapter. For your first dialogue, leave at least an hour. You may select the same topic as your partner, or you may each write about different ones.

If you have had a good experience dialoguing once, decide how often you both want to do this, and schedule more dialogues—in writing, on your calendar.

If your partner is not interested in trying this, remember, don't make him or her wrong and yourself right. Honor this choice. But consider going ahead and doing it yourself. Write on a certain topic, and then ask your partner to listen while you read, or talk about what you wrote in your own words. Then ask your partner for feelings or thoughts about what you wrote.

Taking the time to explore and express your own feelings is what will most contribute to your own spiritual growth. And your partner will benefit from this too. If he or she isn't ready to do this kind of exploration for any reason, it need not detract from your own experience.

from your own soul, more in alignment with your essential nature, more conscious, and more motivated by love—you will *not* use "communication skills" to try to change your partner to better meet your own needs or to persuade your partner that you are right and he or she is wrong. Rather than trying to solve problems by endlessly discussing and arguing about them, you will lovingly act to bring about change. You will use restraint, act in loving and generous ways even when you don't feel like it, take creative initiatives to find ways of working with incompatibilities and conflicts, and be as accepting and compassionate as you can be.

What you *will* use communication for is to further your own and your partner's spiritual growth. Since feelings are the avenue to expanded consciousness, you will use communication to discover and explore feelings that lie deep within you, feelings that may be difficult, surprising, loathsome. In the safe and loving bosom of your Spiritual Partnership, you will continue your journey of self-discovery and of bringing yourself into greater alignment with your highest self.

You May Ask Your Partner to Change

It is neither loving nor effective to ask your partner to become a different person, as we have established. Your partner won't and can't change in order to solve your problem.

However, once you have solidly established that principle in your own mind and heart, there is a whole range of changes in activities and behavior that it is appropriate to ask for—even when you are practicing Spiritual Partnership. What's important is how you do the asking.

Here are the guidelines for asking your partner for something in a spiritual way:

1. First, be sure that what you are asking for is something that your partner can actually give. "I'd really appreciate it if you would make a real effort not to be late all the time" is not a realistic request. Either your partner has been trying unsuccessfully for years to be more punctual, or she has some inner reason why being late works for her.

   On the other hand, "Would you be willing to pick up some whipping cream on your way home?" may be something your partner can actually do. If not, he or she will tell you so.

2. Be sure that you have been practicing restraint and refraining from making demands on a frequent basis.

3. Clarify exactly what you want, and be as specific as you can get. Rather than, "I would really like it if you made more of an effort to remember my birthday," say, "I'd love it if you would actually go shopping and surprise me with something on my birthday. You have such wonderful taste. Just one little gift, wrapped up, would really please me." Or, rather than, "I wish you seemed happier to see me when we get home in the evening," say, "I'd love it if, soon after we arrive home in the evening, after we have set down our stuff, we have a big, warm hug." Or again, "It is very, very important to me that we not be late for this event. Would you be willing to make a commitment to be

home by four-thirty so we can really leave on time?"
(Leave more time than you think is necessary, a form
of Sacred Act #4: accepting who your partner is and
adapting.)

4. Be fully prepared that your partner may say no, and
convey this when you make your request. Be clear in
your own mind that your partner has a right to say no.
Do not make your request sound like a non-negotiable
demand.

    Phrases that are almost guaranteed to
communicate your openness about this request are:
"Would you consider . . . " or "Would you be willing
to . . . " as in, "Would you consider taking the boys to
soccer on Saturday?" or "Would you be willing to fix
that door handle before next weekend when my folks
are coming?"

    For more major requests try, "How would you feel
about . . . " as in, "How would you feel about taking a
drive up north this weekend?" or "I think it's time for
us to buy a new computer. How do you feel about
that?" With these phrases, you aren't simply asking
for a yes or no answer; you are starting a
conversation, and you are definitely conveying that
you are open to a positive or negative response.

5. If your partner says yes, express appreciation. If you
get a no, graciously accept the decline. Remember
not to be too attached to any one particular outcome
that you may have hoped for. Maybe the universe has
some other, ultimately better-for-you outcome in store.
Be open.

Then give yourself time to regroup and decide
what to do next. Maybe your next alternative for
addressing this issue will be a Sacred Act.

Asking your partner for favors, or to do something your way,
is a natural part of Spiritual Partnership, as long as you are practicing acceptance and compassion and not asking for something
your partner cannot realistically give you, and as long as you ask
with the clear understanding that your partner has a right to
say no.

Rob kept asking his partner, David, to call him if he was
going to be late for dinner. Over and over, David would come
home late, full of apologies. Finally, Rob realized that what
seemed to him like a simple request wasn't at all simple for
David, because David became so immersed in his work, he literally wasn't aware of the passage of time, and calling Rob was
the furthest thing from his mind. So Rob dropped his request. He
realized that David's devotion to his work was an admirable
quality, and appreciated the extent to which he was able to let go
of it when he finally did arrive home.

When, as an experiment, you have followed the Five Principles by not asking your partner to change for a period of at least
eight weeks, you will develop a sense of when it is appropriate
to break this "rule." But break it only judiciously, carefully, and
with great respect. Every time you think about asking your partner to change in some way, ask yourself whether you could actually get along just fine if you didn't ask for this thing. Save your
requests for ones that really matter to you.

Spiritual Partners do ask each other for favors, but always in
a spirit of goodwill.

So now we have seen the appropriate role of communication
in Spiritual Partnership: not to solve problems or to try to change

your partner, but rather, to create intimacy and expand your own spirituality through honest exploration and sharing of feelings. And we have seen an effective and loving way to ask for what you need from your partner. Now let's look at another aspect of "advanced" Spiritual Partnership: making mature spiritual judgments.

ℬ EXPERIMENT #19

Make two lists of requests you would like to make of your partner: One list should be "Big Things" and the other "Little Things." Keep them handy so you can add items to the lists as you think of them.

List the items in each list again in the order of their importance to you.

With your number one item on the "Little Things" list, follow the guidelines in this chapter.

In your journal, record how this experiment worked out. What did you learn from it?

After you have mastered the art with several of your "Little Things," try one of your "Big Things."

Wait as long as you can between your requests, at least a week, and practice restraint the rest of the time.

ELEVEN

Making Mature
Spiritual Judgments

Principles, Sacred Acts, rules, and even rules for breaking the rules will always eventually reach their limit. They are useful learning tools, but of course, the world doesn't conform to the tidy categories we establish for the sake of pedagogical simplicity.

As we gain spiritual maturity we will confront situations in which the Five Principles and the Sacred Actions are insufficient guidelines.

Marianne and Bert had been married for forty-one years when Bert had a stroke that left him severely impaired, both mentally and physically. He lived in a nursing home, and Marianne visited him every day for the first year he was there, but he didn't know her and didn't seem to respond to her presence. Gradually, Marianne visited less frequently, but always two or three times a week. She loved Bert, and knew that at some level her visits were important to him.

Then she met a man whose company she enjoyed. His wife had died five years before. The two of them provided wonderful companionship for each other. They wanted to live together. Would this be dishonest at some level? Would it be an act of betrayal against Bert? Would it be "adulterous" and therefore a "sin"?

Although some religions would superimpose inflexible rules upon this situation, the "spiritual" approach, as we defined it in Chapter Two, is to ask, What course of action is the most authentic for each of us? What would lead toward connection and away from separation? What does love require? Where does our consciousness lead us? How can we surrender to the natural flow of the universe?

The answers to these questions will be different for different individuals. No preestablished principles or Sacred Acts cover this situation. We have now moved into the vast realm where spirituality doesn't prescribe a course of action, but instead prescribes a set of questions. Now, as a spiritual seeker, you have to rely on the effort you have put into your spiritual practice and on the answers you receive when you go deep within to your most authentic self.

What does love require? What course of action will cause the least harm and hurt? What will bring about the most love and happiness? Whatever we decide, will our action be kind? Will it be consistent with our compassion? Will it bring about good?

Marsha was twenty-five and about to enter law school when she learned she was pregnant. She was stunned, for she had been careful to use contraception. Though she was fond of the boyfriend who was the father of this child, she knew he was not the person she wanted to marry. She now wished she had not rushed into being sexual with this man, and felt she had learned a spiritual lesson, that she needed to make decisions like that with her deeper, more authentic self, rather than her eager-to-be-liked "public" self.

Marsha's clear feeling, coming from her most authentic self, was that she did not want to continue her pregnancy. She did not

want her child to have only one parent. She did not want to interrupt her plans for her life, where she felt she could make her
best contribution, nor did she want to parent an infant while trying to do well in law school.

Yet she was deeply affected by knowing that she had created
a new life within her.

"What does love require?" she asked herself. What course of
action will cause the least harm and hurt? What will bring about
the most love and happiness? Whatever I decide, will my action
be kind? Will it be consistent with compassion? Will it bring
about good? What action will bring me into closer alignment
with my higher self?

Though Marianne, Bert, and Marsha represent real situations, I'm not going to tell you what they each decided. Because
what matters here is, if you were in these situations, how would
you decide?

Maybe your decision is completely obvious to you; maybe it
would be a terrible struggle for you. But what will make your
decision "spiritual" is not what you decide, but how you decide.

Spirituality is not the easy route; it is the "road less traveled."

Let's look at the sometimes ambiguous area of telling the
truth.

Common wisdom is that when you are close with someone,
you will be fully honest with that person at all times. When you
are angry, withholding your anger will eat away at your insides
and show up indirectly somewhere else. When you feel cheated,
you are responsible to speak up and ask for what you want.
When you have done something you regret, you must confess
it right away. Withholding is unhealthy for yourself and your
relationship.

In some situations these statements will be true.

But the spiritual approach is not always so clean and

straightforward. The pressure to be fully honest at all times robs you of the right to make discriminating judgments in different situations. Sometimes the wiser and more spiritually enlightened choice is to withhold painful information, or to manage your feelings on your own and not inflict them on your partner. Judgments like these must always be made in consultation with your higher self after asking not only what is truthful, but also what is useful and loving.

Your spiritual task is to be fully honest *with yourself* at all times. This is a major undertaking. Then, with your partner, use judgment about what you say and when you say it.

I have a friend who sometimes splits the cost of a purchase between her credit card and her checkbook. "My husband sees the credit card bill," she explained to me, "but my checkbook is my own business. He doesn't understand what clothes cost, but I feel clear that we can afford what I buy. I'm not going to negotiate every purchase with him, or justify my purchases to him. So why not spare him the pain?"

Is my friend being deceptive? For some people, such a practice might be dishonest. If, for example, you had promised your husband that you would not exceed a certain dollar amount, or that you would not buy a certain item, and you did so anyway, concealing the purchase by paying cash for it, that would clearly be deceptive. In my friend's case, however, I believe she was being loving. She was being fully honest with herself and felt no ambiguity about her own actions. By "acting on her own," she was reducing the conflict in her relationship and taking care of herself.

What did love require in this situation? What course of action caused the least harm and hurt? What brought about the most love and happiness? Was my friend's action consistent with compassion? Did it bring her into closer alignment with her higher self?

You decide.

The tricky part of withholding something from your partner to "spare him or her pain" is to figure out whether you are deceiving yourself for your own convenience. Are you denying the true impact of your actions on the two of you?

A woman in one of my groups used the same thinking to justify an affair she once had. She and her husband had an excellent relationship with no major problems and were very involved with each other's lives. They both felt secure and knew that nothing and no one could destroy what they had together. Barbara, I'll call her, was 2,500 miles from home at a convention. She ended up going to the convention dance with Roy, a friend and colleague, and by the end of the evening, one thing led to another.

> This was someone I knew well and trusted thoroughly. I knew our secret would be safe. And I just couldn't see how anyone would be harmed by my letting myself go into this pleasurable experience. I will say, though, that I never wanted to do it again. I didn't feel it would be the same if it were premeditated. And now I don't like having this deep dark secret that I will never tell my husband. But I still definitely feel that it was the right thing to do at the time. For what reason should I have denied myself this deeply pleasurable moment? Who would have been served?

I have told Barbara's story in many of my groups, and never seen consensus. Some feel that Barbara's deception clearly does hurt her husband and tarnishes forever the closeness between them. Some feel that spirituality calls upon her to tell him the whole, unvarnished truth. Others disagree, saying that truth-telling in this situation would cause unnecessary pain and would be "self-indulgent" of Barbara.

What do you think?

Spirituality calls upon you to ask the right questions. But it doesn't dictate what the right answers will be—for you. What will help you make mature spiritual decisions is your spiritual practice. The more you commit yourself to the Five Principles of Spiritual Partnership and the Sacred Acts, the more you will experience the power of love, compassion, and acceptance. And the better equipped you will be to make difficult decisions based on spiritual principles. When you are aligned with your soul and at peace with yourself, you will trust the messages that flow from your authentic self. This state is the ultimate goal of any spiritual practice, including Spiritual Partnership.

TWELVE

Spiritual Partnership in Your Life and Beyond

When I had been married to my first husband for just a short while, friends of my parents announced they were going to divorce. My mother was dismayed. What she said to me has remained with me all these years, and was probably the seed for this book: "Marge should have worried a lot less about 'getting her needs met' and a lot more about going over and giving her husband a shoulder rub at the end of the day."

My mother knew all about what I have been trying to express in this book. Her statement is not simplistic or Pollyannaish; it is profound and absolutely true. The hitch is, it takes a strong person to do what my mother was suggesting, exactly the strong person you will become by practicing Spiritual Partnership. As you practice, you will feel good about yourself, and you won't be dependent upon your spouse to give you a rich life. You will know how to get your own needs met, and be fulfilled enough yourself that you will receive genuine pleasure from giving to the one you love, even if he or she isn't perfect. You will become engaged with your higher self; aligned with your true essential nature; not isolated, but connected with your soul. You will view

your spouse not as someone who completes you, but as someone
with whom you can share your completeness.

You and your partner, practicing Spiritual Partnership
together, will elicit and support your strong, spiritually developed higher selves in each other.

When Your Cup Overflows

When you practice Spiritual Partnership, you will find that it
spills over into every aspect of your life. Through spiritual practice within your partnership, as you become increasingly aligned
with your higher self, you and your partner will not be content to
experience your passion only with each other; you will be compelled to share it with those around you. You will spend time not
only face-to-face with each other, but side by side looking out at
the world together to see where your passion, born of your spiritual practice together, can best be used.

A spiritual relationship is like a reservoir. It is fed by the
streams and rivers of love, mutual support, goodwill, and compassion. When it becomes full, it overflows, offering its abundance to others who need it. If love were focused only on itself,
it would soon shrivel up. The nature of Spiritual Partnership is
that it expands, grows, spills over, and rushes out like a teeming
river into the world around it, enlivening all it comes in contact
with. The peace and happiness Spiritual Partners find with each
other is not something they ever keep to themselves.

All the Relationships in Your Life

As you practice Spiritual Partnership with your mate, it will become obvious to you that the Five Principles and the Sacred Acts will transform every relationship in your life.

David loved his job as a furniture salesman in an elegant store—until the store manager changed. The new manager raised everyone's wages but stopped paying commissions. He wouldn't allow salespeople to exchange shifts without first checking with him. And he would interfere with sales. Once, David was in the middle of a negotiation that was going well, and the manager came over and horned in, with the result that the couple decided against the purchase. And worst of all, the manager blamed David for losing the sale!

The whole thing was terribly upsetting to him, especially because David had been so happy before. First, all the salespeople got together and wrote a letter, asking to have commissions reinstated. The manager pulled them all together and discussed their ideas, essentially agreeing with their reasoning, and then turned down their request with no explanation. When that happened, a lightbulb went on for David, who had been learning Spiritual Partnership principles for several months. He remembered: You can't solve a problem by trying to persuade the other person to change. So David switched his strategy.

First, he worked on accepting his situation: It had been wonderful; now it was awful. Definitely a lousy break, but that's the way it *is*. Next, he made an effort to turn his self-righteous anger into compassion: This poor guy! He's so inept, he must have many demons inside that he has to overcome. I truly want him to be happier and to succeed. Then David made a commitment to himself to "act as if" he enjoyed his job. He wouldn't allow himself to participate in negative conversations with his fellow employees. "Keep your mouth out of it," he told himself. This was difficult, but he could see that all their complaining was just making them all feel worse.

Dave knew that to some degree he was "faking" all of this. Inside, he still felt terrible pangs over the loss of his old job and anger at such unreasonable abuse of power. But he also knew that railing against it would accomplish nothing—except contribute to his own internal upset. He breathed and did little minimeditations all day, and remained calm.

Before long he acted on his own by finding a different job. Later, he told me:

> Spiritual Partnership made a difference in the way I handled that situation. Before, I would have spent a lot of time ranting and raving at the injustice, *and* trying to change it. When I shifted, almost immediately, I saw the quiet power of accepting what is and moving forward. There were always two levels of me operating: I still had vengeful fantasies against this guy and feelings of loss and betrayal. But I didn't act on those; instead, I used spiritual discipline in my actions. I opened up new possibilities for myself much sooner and maintained my sense of calm and inner power.

It's not difficult to transfer the Five Principles and the Sacred Actions to all other areas of your life besides just your intimate partner: friends, family, colleagues, associates, your supervisor and those you supervise, and even acquaintances. Spiritual Partnership is the *spiritual* way to conduct all of your relationships. Don't allow your knee-jerk response to determine what happens in your relationships; instead, provide spiritual leadership.

The Larger Impact of Your Own Spiritual Journey

Rarer by far than originality in science or art is originality in political action. And rarer still is original political action that enlarges, rather than blights or destroys, human possibilities.

—JONATHAN SCHELL

Spiritual Partnership *is* political action, the rare kind of political action that "enlarges, rather than blights or destroys, human possibilities." It is political action because (1) our private behaviors make an impact, not only on us and our families and friends, but on our greater political and social community, and (2) Spiritual Partnership is a model for the kind of political action that "enlarges, rather than blights or destroys, human possibilities." When you behave in accord with spiritual values in your personal life, you are contributing to the eventual shift of our self-destructing world to one that is filled with love and light. It may not be *enough* for us all to behave spiritually in our daily lives, but it is impossible to imagine widespread spiritual transformation if we don't each model love, authenticity, connection, consciousness, and surrender in our daily lives. The healing of our troubled world begins with each of us in our daily spiritual practice.

Women who joined "consciousness raising groups" at the beginning of the contemporary women's movement learned firsthand that the personal is political. Every woman who stood up against discrimination in her family or at work was part of a movement that eventually made a substantial impact on our society. If you hold that vision in mind, you will know that every time you "act on your own" or "act as if" or experience compas-

sion toward your mate, you will be contributing to the shift
toward a more spiritual, more loving planet.

As Spirit Spreads

It is stunning to imagine what our world could be like if business
and government were influenced by spiritual values. If everyone
always acted out of love, there would be no poverty or hunger, no
environmental ravaging, no inadequate education, no limited
access to health care, no drug pushers, no discrimination against
"minorities," no predatory capitalism, no wars. And in the world
of work, there would be no unreasonable, arbitrary bosses and
incompetent supervisors; no inhumane, antifamily work policies;
no unfair wages; no discrimination in employment.

All of these problems are a result of someone, somewhere,
operating from some principle other than love. Fear, greed, and
the insatiable thirst for profit are the most common substitutes
for love in our culture. Government and business leaders who
make decisions that affect our lives are, for the most part, not
spiritual, as we have used the term in this book. Some of them
may be religious, but if they were spiritual, they wouldn't be able
to make decisions that flout human needs in favor of short-term
financial gain. They are not in alignment with their authentic
selves, not conscious, not motivated by their connection with the
universe and everyone and everything in it. Their decisions
move us toward separation, not connection.

The Western scientific vision of a mechanical universe has cre-
ated an . . . alienation from our own inherent spiritual nature.
This has been reinforced in our daily lives by the increasing
alignment of our institutions with the monetary values of the
marketplace. The more dominant money has become in our lives,

the less place there has been for any sense of the spiritual bond that is the foundation of community and a balanced relationship with nature. The pursuit of spiritual fulfillment has been increasingly displaced by an all-consuming and increasingly self-destructive obsession with the pursuit of money—a useful but wholly substanceless and intrinsically valueless human artifact.

—DAVID KORTEN,
WHEN CORPORATIONS RULE THE WORLD

Imagine the heads of giant corporations, which now have more control over our lives than our governments, agreeing to consult all their stakeholders before making a decision; that is, not only their stockholders, but also their employees, their customers, their suppliers, and the residents of the towns in which they are located. Why would they ever do such an outrageous thing? Only if they were motivated by love instead of greed, only if they cared about the quality of the lives they affect with their business.

Imagine heads of state sitting at a table trying to negotiate peace after decades of conflict between their nations. Imagine them saying among themselves, "What does love require? What would be loving to us and at the same time loving to them? How can we love and honor ourselves and at the same time have compassion for and honor the needs of the other side?" The questions wouldn't always present obvious answers, but they would be the right questions to ask. What negotiators usually ask themselves is something more like, "How can we get the most for ourselves, salvage the most pride, and be the most vindictive toward these enemies whom we hate?"

We live in difficult political times, and feel the frustration of having little impact on the corporations and political institutions that wield undue influence in our lives. Yet, as spiritual people, we sense that a turnaround is possible. The tide of spiritual values is rising, spilling over into more and more aspects of our lives. Spiritual values can be applied to social and political issues—Gandhi's peaceful resistance of British rule, and Martin Luther King's loving persistence in gaining rights for African Americans, come quickly to mind—and we all live with hope and vision that increasingly they will be.

> *Today, many things indicate that we are going through a transitional period, when it seems that something is on the way out and something else is painfully being born. It is as if something were crumbling, decaying and exhausting itself, while something else, still indistinct, were arising from the rubble.*
>
> —VACLAV HAVEL,
> PRESIDENT OF THE CZECH REPUBLIC

So, as you experiment with the Principles of Spiritual Partnership and the Sacred Actions in your own family and with your friends and at work, envision each loving act you do as one tiny part of a vast movement that is ever so gradually and certainly shifting us all to a time when love will prevail, in our homes and on our planet.

My best wishes to you and your Spiritual Partner. May we all blend our authentic, loving, conscious souls to help move everyone on the planet toward connection and away from separation.

Postscript

How to Refer to Your Spiritual Partner

For married Spiritual Partners, language is usually not a problem. But for several decades now, intimates who are not married have been searching for a way to introduce and talk about their partners. "I'd like you to meet my—er, ah . . . "

Life partner? Mate? Roommate? Partner? Companion? Or that quaint, homophobic term the census bureau invented, posslq (person of the opposite sex sharing living quarters)?

It turns out there is a perfectly good word already in the dictionary that means precisely "companion, comrade, friend, or spouse." It's an Old English word, marked "archaic." But I rather like it and feel it would serve us well if brought back into general parlance. The word is "fere."

"I'd like you to meet my fere, Richard."

"I have to call my fere at four-thirty to make plans for tonight."

"How are you and your fere doing?"

But I can't seem to get much support for "fere" among my friends and workshop participants. Instead, what always catches on much more quickly and readily is simply "SP."

"I'd like you to meet my SP, Sarah."

"I'll have to check with my SP first, then I'll get back to you."

"My SP and I are going out of town this weekend."

It rolls nicely off the tongue and brings with it all the connotations of the enlightened, conscious, deliberate spiritual commitment we have explored in this book.

Of course, in order for "SP" to be really useful, the idea of Spiritual Partnership would have to be more generally understood and accepted. But maybe it will work for you in your circle. My workshop participants and I offer it up as a possibility.

Bibliography

Blanton, Brad, Ph.D. *Radical Honesty.* New York: DTP, 1994.

Boorstein, Sylvia. *It's Easier Than You Think.* San Francisco: HarperSanFrancisco, 1995.

Campbell, Susan M., Ph.D. *The Couple's Journey.* San Luis Obispo, California: Impact Publishers, 1980.

Chopra, Deepak. *The Path to Love.* New York: Harmony Books, 1997.

Christensen, Andres, and Neil S. Jacobson. *Reconcilable Differences.* New York and London: The Guilford Press, 2000.

Creedon, Jeremiah. "God with a Million Faces," *Utne Reader.* July–August, 1998.

Dali Lama, His Holiness, and Howard C. Cutler, M.D. *The Art of Happiness.* New York: Riverhead Books, 1998.

Dossey, Larry, M.D. *Healing Words.* San Francisco: HarperSanFrancisco, 1993.

Gottman, John M., Ph.D., and Nan Silver. *The Seven Principles for Making Marriage Work.* New York: Crown Publishers, Inc., 1999.

Hanh, Thich Nhat. *Teachings on Love.* Berkeley, California: Parallax Press, 1997.

Hendrix, Harville, Ph.D. *Getting the Love You Want.* New York: Henry Holt and Company, Inc., 1988.

Kasl, Charlotte, Ph.D. *If the Buddha Dated.* New York: Penguin/Arkana, 1999.

Keen, Sam. *The Passionate Life: Stages of Loving.* San Francisco: Harper
& Row, Publishers, 1983.

Kornfield, Jack. *A Path with Heart.* New York: Bantam Books, 1993.

Lamott, Anne. *Traveling Mercies.* New York: Pantheon Books, 1999.

Levine, Stephen and Ondrea. *Embracing the Beloved.* New York: Double-
day, 1995.

Lew, Alan, with Sherril Jaffe. *One God Clapping.* New York: Kodansha
International, 1999.

McGraw, Phillip, Ph.D. *Relationship Rescue.* New York: Hyperion, 2000.

Moore, Thomas. *The Re-Enchantment of Everyday Life.* New York: Harper-
Collins Publishers, Inc., 1996.

———. *Soul Mates.* New York: HarperCollins Publishers, Inc., 1994.

Peck, Scott. *The Road Less Traveled.* New York: Touchstone, 1978.

Psaris, Jett, Ph.D., and Marlena S. Lyons, Ph.D. *Undefended Love.* Oak-
land, California: New Harbinger Publications, Inc., 2000.

Quick, Barbara. *Still Friends.* Berkeley, California: Wildcat Canyon Press,
1999.

Somé, Sobonfu. *The Spirit of Intimacy.* New York: Quill William Morrow,
1999.

Walsch, Neale Donald. *Conversations with God, Book 1.* New York: G. P.
Putnam's Sons, 1996.

Welwood, John, Ph.D. *Journey of the Heart.* New York: HarperCollins Publishers, 1990.

———. *Love and Awakening.* New York: HarperCollins Publishers, 1996.

Williamson, Marianne. *Enchanted Love.* New York: Simon & Schuster,
1999.

Zukav, Gary. *The Seat of the Soul.* New York: Fireside, 1989.

———. *Soul Stories.* New York: Simon & Schuster, 2000.

Acknowledgments

My first debt of gratitude is to the many couples whose stories I tell in these pages, who were willing to experiment with something different and stay with it until it made a difference. Thank you for so generously staying in touch, for sharing your success with others, and for all those follow-up interviews. Your joy and excitement is what compelled me to write this book.

My agent, Sandra Dijkstra, has been my business and literary partner for fifteen years; a more wise, skilled, supportive, and tenacious advocate I cannot imagine. Her role in bringing this book to light was significant. Thank you again, Sandy.

They say editors aren't editing books anymore, but it's not true of mine! Linda Loewenthal's heart is in this book too. Her excellent suggestions greatly improved the manuscript. Both she and her warm and capable assistant, Cara Warner, have been a pleasure to work with.

Alan Alberts, Diane Ohlsson, and Susan Schwartz all contributed special, much needed support at critical times. Diane, Joan, Mara, Melinda, and Robin, with whom I have been meeting for more than twenty years, are my mental health maintenance and have provided love and support in many forms through all the stages of this project.

I couldn't manage without the inestimable help of my capable and efficient assistant, Alice Vdovin. Her support and friendship are a gift I cherish.

I am extremely grateful to spiritual teacher and writer Fran May, who edited the complete manuscript and made several important contributions to my spiritual education; and to Patricia Ellsberg, Kathleen McCleary, Victoria Nerenberg, Amanita Rosenbush, Harriet Sage, Dorothy Wall, and Ellen Weis for reading portions of the manuscript and providing valuable comments. And big thank-yous to Susan Christie, Golda Clendenin, Juan Espinoza, Robert Fish, Bonnie Davis, David Garfinkel, Anita Goldstein, Susan Goldstein, Helen Hammock, Paul and Jan Hammock, Melinda Henning, Azriela Jaffe, Richard Morrison, Roseanne Packard, Phyllis Shacter, Paul Schneider, Neil Tetkowski, Gordon Whiting, Patrice Wynne, and my beloved "Brain Exchange" group, all of whom contributed ideas that ended up in the book.

My spiritual partner, Mayer, supports me and my writing in more ways than I can enumerate here. Let's just say I love him madly!

Susan Page and Associates offer

Personal Coaching for Individuals and Couples

By Telephone from Anywhere in the World

Think of your coach as a personal trainer for your relationship. A regular, structured relationship with a professional coach will move you quickly beyond the stuck places in your relationship, guide you in creating warmth and closeness between you and your partner, offer you the general support of a loving and dedicated friend, and keep you focused on your own spiritual growth. Coaching will shorten your learning curve and move you more quickly to the spiritual partnership you seek with the person you love.

Susan Page and her colleagues all have at least fifteen years of experience working with couples and are trained and seasoned in working with the principles described in this book. They are long-time spiritual seekers themselves and bring empathy, compassion, and skill to their work.

For a free introductory consultation, call
510-843-2111

For information on Susan Page's schedule of workshops and personal appearances, visit her website at
www.susanpage.com

About the Author

SUSAN PAGE began her career as a campus minister and is the former director of women's programs at the University of California at Berkeley. She is the author of five books, including *If I'm So Wonderful, Why Am I Still Single?*, which has been translated into fourteen languages, and has appeared on *The Oprah Show* and *Good Morning America*. A native of Ohio, she lives in Berkeley, California, with her husband of twenty years.